Ex lib. 24⁹⁵

W9-BNU-051

INDIANAPOLIS MARION CO.

PUBLIC LIBRARY

FALSE ALARM

THE TRUTH ABOUT
THE EPIDEMIC OF FEAR

MARC SIEGEL, M.D.

John Wiley & Sons, Inc.

Copyright © 2005 by Marc Siegel. All rights reserved

Published by John Wiley & Sons, Inc., Hoboken, New Jersey

Published simultaneously in Canada

No part of this publication may be reproduced, stored in a retrieval system, or transmitted in any form or by any means, electronic, mechanical, photocopying, recording, scanning, or otherwise, except as permitted under Section 107 or 108 of the 1976 United States Copyright Act, without either the prior written permission of the Publisher, or authorization through payment of the appropriate per-copy fee to the Copyright Clearance Center, 222 Rosewood Drive, Danvers, MA 01923, (978) 750-8400, fax (978) 646-8600, or on the web at www.copyright.com. Requests to the Publisher for permission should be addressed to the Permissions Department, John Wiley & Sons, Inc., 111 River Street, Hoboken, NJ 07030, (201) 748-6011, fax (201) 748-6008, or online at http://www.wiley.com/go/permissions.

Limit of Liability/Disclaimer of Warranty: While the publisher and the author have used their best efforts in preparing this book, they make no representations or warranties with respect to the accuracy or complete-ness of the contents of this book and specifically disclaim any implied warranties of merchantability or fitness for a particular purpose. No warranty may be created or extended by sales representatives or written sales materials. The advice and strategies contained herein may not be suitable for your situation. You should consult with a professional where appropriate. Neither the publisher nor the author shall be liable for any loss of profit or any other commercial damages, including but not limited to special, incidental, consequential, or other damages.

For general information about our other products and services, please contact our Customer Care Department within the United States at (800) 762-2974, outside the United States at (317) 572-3993 or fax (317) 572-4002.

Wiley also publishes its books in a variety of electronic formats. Some content that appears in print may not be available in electronic books. For more information about Wiley products, visit our web site at www.wiley.com.

Library of Congress Cataloging-in-Publication Data

Siegel, Marc.
 False alarm : the truth about the epidemic of fear / Marc Siegel.
    p.   cm.
 Includes index.
 ISBN-13 978-0-471-67869-4 (cloth)
 ISBN-10 0-471-67869-4 (cloth)
 1. Fear—Social aspects.   2. Epidemics—Social aspects.   3. Security (Psychology)   4. Social control.   I. Title.
         HM1033.S525   2005
   302′.17—dc22   2004022952

Printed in the United States of America

10 9 8 7 6 5 4 3 2 1

To my son Joshua,
whose love has brought me courage

CONTENTS

CONTENTS

Part III
HEALING FEAR

PREFACE

This book was conceived unexpectedly during a south-bound trip on the FDR Drive in New York City on the morning of September 11, 2001. It was a bright, hot morning when I began to notice the multicolored ambulances from all over the city—Columbia Presbyterian, Metropolitan, St. Vincent's—traveling alongside and passing me, all exiting at Bellevue Hospital.

I volunteered my services to the transforming emergency center at Bellevue that morning, absorbing the rush of human emotion—at once committed to the task and yet frightened. The fact that ultimately there weren't the survivors to fill our beds did little to stem the fright. People worked to keep their minds off the unfolding disaster, and this, I discovered, was a necessary coping strategy.

As I volunteered my services to the Red Cross and to my patients in the succeeding months, I discovered a newfound vulnerability. I entered the media world and found that each health care topic I discussed in an article or on TV seemed blown out of proportion to the real danger. I seized the chance to learn about each succeeding "bug du jour" and to try to offer perspective and a salve of reassurance whenever I could.

We all personalized 9/11, and it made us all feel more at risk, whether we were really at risk or not. We grew afraid more easily than before, misinformed by our leaders and provoked by the news media.

Anthrax was the first manifestation in concrete terms of this personalized susceptibility. I was honored to participate in a U.S. Senate investigation into the handling of the anthrax crisis, directed by Senator Chuck Grassley of Iowa. I discovered amidst the CDC and U.S. Postal Service papers and letters to and from the senator a sense of fumbling. Fear out of proportion to the real risks was made worse by a lack of preparedness. Even if you didn't have a reason to be afraid before, you could see how poorly you would be protected if there really were a reason to fear.

During the health care scares of the next few years, my patients shared their fears with me every day. I have changed their names here in order to protect their privacy, but I would never have been able to conceive of fear in real terms if it weren't for their willingness to share their concerns and experiences.

I witnessed their fear of SARS, despite the fact that I never saw any evidence that SARS was close to becoming widespread. My office phone rang with anxieties over influenza as it went from being a ho-hum underappreciated killer to the latest rage.

In addition to my patients, I have a great appreciation for my family. Not only did they bear with the many investigations and revisions that constitute this book, but they also served as my subjects. I'll never forget the time that I came home from a conference on bioterror, where I had discouraged people from gearing up for worst-case scenarios all the time, only to find my wife Luda's medicine drawer emptied of cold remedies and replaced with Cipro as a precaution against an anthrax attack.

I understood from the outset that our fear mechanism had gone awry, but I didn't know exactly how. I could study the process by which dangers were manufactured and provoked, but as a medical doctor I also had to study the original fight-or-flight mechanism that was intended to protect us. The place to start was with animals. My patient and friend Sylvain Cappell, a top-flight mathematician at New York University and well connected to the scientific community, was very committed to the notion that my book be as scientifically based and accurate as possible. He helped me arrange interviews with some of the people who helped me articulate the core principles of fear physiology. I am indebted to his friends and colleagues Rachel Yehuda, Joe Ledoux, Chris Jolly, Esther Sabban, and John Mann.

Eric Nelson, senior editor at Wiley and a vegetarian, first heard about this book over eggplant parmigiana at a midtown Italian restaurant. He immediately committed himself to the project with great excitement and has never looked back. I am very grateful for his generative ideas and great forbearance. Nancy Rothschild, P. J. Campbell, Anna Christensen, and Devra K. Nelson at Wiley have brought passion and skill to the project.

Likewise, Joëlle Delbourgo, agent for the book, has been devoted to it throughout the long process of its birth. She was faithful to my fear concept from the moment she first heard it.

Jennifer E. Berman and Jennifer Choi and the NYU School of Medicine public relations team, along with Nadine Woloshin of Rubenstein Associates all offered crucial support.

I am also grateful and privileged in terms of early readers of the manuscript. The views of the great novelist E. L. Doctorow were indispensable, as were those of the consummate sportswriter Ira Berkow. No one read this book more tirelessly and devotedly than my friend Kenneth Blaker. My sister Fran and the film producer Donald Laventhal also offered important suggestions throughout the editorial process. The final stages were aided by the insights of David Goldston, Hugh Gilmore, and Hesh Kestin.

In the end, though, I have the print and television media to thank the most. By allowing me to participate, as a spy as much as a contributor, the news media permitted this book, for the most part, to write itself.

Introduction

THE FEAR EPIDEMIC

There is—was the feeling, oh, gee, we didn't do
enough on 9/11, so let's make sure we warn everyone.

—Bob Woodward on CNN's *Larry King Live*,
April 23, 2004

Fear invades our homes like never before, affecting
more and more people. Newspaper headlines are
apocalyptic warnings. Media obsessions fuel our cycles of worry,
which burn out only to be replaced by more alarming cycles.

The passions and routines of everyday life are our primary
defenses against this contagious fear. These defenses, however, are
being eroded, bombarded by the ongoing doom-and-gloom of the
daily news. Twenty-four hours of cable news infiltrates our sleep
and may be as damaging to our health as cigarette smoke is to our
defenses against cancer.

How did it get to be this way? Fear is looming larger in our lives.
Yet no one has tried to integrate what scientists have learned about
the physiology of fear with the increased reliance on fear on the
part of both the media and the politicians. Of course some fears
have their origin in real events, most prominently the attacks of

1

September 11, 2001, but the overall climate of fear is inflated well out of proportion to the reality and is its own core danger to society.

My investigations of fear have shown that it is designed to be protective, that animals use it to sense genuine threats to their survival. At the same time, we humans have the ability to exaggerate fear until it threatens our health.

Under the stress of unremitting fear, we become more susceptible to disease, including heart disease, stroke, and cancer. Once we become sick, our fear grows. In my medical practice I deal with many patients who are so alarmed by their illness that even offering an effective treatment isn't enough to reassure them. In treating this fear in my patients, and in analyzing health care scares in my newspaper writing and on television, I have tried to uncover the moment of lost perspective when dangers are first distorted.

My investigation of fear started with the discovery that animals respond by instinct and conditioning, while we, with the same essential fear apparatus as they have, feed our fears through verbal communication. A zebra is wise to be afraid of a roaring lion, yet we are not so wise to fear a metaphorical lion that is a thousand miles away from us. As soon as we hear about a danger, however remote, we tend to see it as a personal threat, especially if the danger is exaggerated to begin with.

 This pattern of distortion led me directly to the media. How many of us listen to somber-toned newscasters and expect that what we are hearing is valid information? Many of us grew up believing we could find truth in the news. When did the crew-cut, thick-glasses, thin-tie anchorman become today's harbinger of doom?

For me, realization of the fundamental change in the media occurred at the beginning of May 2004, when I received a phone call from the WNBC-TV doctor, David Marks. He was looking for a sound bite about the new Medicare discount cards, the latest in false comfort.

Marks was a well-dressed young internist with news-anchor features and a kindly face. He had a private practice in Connecticut,

2

and he came to New York two days a week to tape health spots for the TV station.

As we were being powdered and prepped for the interview, I mentioned that I was investigating the epidemic spread of fear.

"What role do you think the media play?" I asked him.

"We're so guilty of spreading it," he said. "I don't like reporting the overhyped stories that unnecessarily scare people. But these are my assignments. I try to put things in perspective, to do my best to tone things down, but sometimes I wish we weren't covering these stories at all."

I was looking for just this kind of direct admission from a card-carrying member of the media.

Media people I've met are serious and sincere, which doesn't mean they always see risk in a proper context. Newspapers issue daily corrections but do not routinely acknowledge when threats that are reported don't materialize.

In studying fear, I have come to believe that it has a tendency to reignite itself. Once a fear fire is extinguished, another one takes its place. There are fear seekers in our society, and these groups are always expanding in number and infecting new members. People are especially susceptible on the coasts, where fear of terrorism is greatest, but there are plenty of worriers in between.

When it comes to the fear epidemic, are we Americans unique? In parts of the world where wars and acts of terrorism have been more commonplace, America has the reputation of being a country with a soft underbelly. In Israel most people manage to live relatively normal lives despite frequent suicide bombings and constant military conflict. This is because statistically, a walk to the supermarket in Israel is still far more likely to be uneventful than unsafe, and the public has come to understand and accept the small level of individual risk. As a result, in Israel and in other societies whose citizens live with similar uncertainties, people become desensitized to the chance of terrorism over time; the threat gradually becomes less immediate, and thus more in keeping with the statistical probability of terrorism actually taking place.

Still, even in Israel the threat of terrorism has had a cumulative effect on health. Desensitization, as I will show throughout this book, is not a cure, and people in Israel live stressful lives. Suicide bombings that occurred there in 2001 have been shown to have an impact on the perceived sense of safety in 2002.

A study that appeared in the journal *Psychosomatic Medicine* in July 2004 showed that Israeli women who expressed fear of terrorism had twice as high a level of an enzyme that correlates with heart disease, compared with their less fearful compatriots.

It is not necessary to have a psychiatric disorder in order to be made ill by fear. This is the essential distinction between the well-described diagnoses of anxiety and phobia and the new fear disease that can victimize anyone. And superimposing fears on a population that is already riddled with phobias and anxieties can induce paralysis.

Imagine how someone who is afraid of flying felt after being saturated by the media images of September 11. Or someone who loathes insects, when she reads about mosquitoes and West Nile. Or a healthy person, trying to control his cholesterol by diet alone, who is compelled to view ad after ad of smiling athletes who supposedly stay healthy only by taking a certain cholesterol drug.

The symptoms of fear, the maladaptive kind, include an exaggerated sense of vulnerability, fear of a danger that doesn't exist, or fear out of proportion to the risk. Like any illness, the illness of fear interferes with function. Fear victims are revved up in fight-or-flight mode. Their bodies ask them, how is a person to be protected from an ever-growing threat without being on the alert? Stress hormones—adrenaline, catecholamines, and cortisol—are secreted in excess amounts. These counterregulatory hormones cause the liver to make more sugar and create more and more energy, which builds up without outlet. To this, nervous sedentary people add more stimulants such as coffee, which revs them up further. People don't eat well, sleep well, or experience sufficient pleasure because they are always on the alert.

Why such an easy path to hysteria? For months I pored through books and articles trying to figure this out. The tiny pecan-shaped organ deep in the center of all animal brains—the amygdala—serves as the central station for processing fear. Once it has been triggered, the amygdala is difficult to deprogram. The higher centers that help you to unlearn fear are weak compared to the hard-wiring of the central amygdala.

Beyond our animal instincts, for many of us our Judeo-Christian background makes fear a familiar concept that can easily motivate us. A disapproving God, we learn, is ready to punish us. Postmodern panic may have its origins in the collective memory of biblical scourges.

With fear infecting and reinfecting us, our pill-happy culture looks for treatments rather than cures. Whether this pill is propranolol, Valium, Prozac, or another new brew, we are told that without it, we will be compelled to live in terror. Rather than examine why we are unnecessarily afraid, rather than ripping out this weed of fear by its roots, we attempt to neutralize it with postmodern concoctions.

In addition to pills, we seek the ultimate vaccine. In a study from Israel in May 2004, Jonathan Kipnis gave a chemical cocktail to panicked mice and found that by bolstering their beleaguered neurons, the mice were once again able to perform their usual tasks. The implication of these results—if they prove applicable to humans—is that immunologically engineered "vaccines" may help to make people impervious to panic. But it is one thing to employ sophisticated technologies to bolster an overworked nerve fiber in a troubled brain, it is another to bottle the latest preventative and market it widely to treat all fear. Instead of learning how to assess risk realistically, we will try to treat fear with the latest in immunology.

Traditional vaccines already provide us with an apparent shield against our fear of illness. In the fall of 2004, many of the people who trampled over each other in line to get a flu shot at a time of sudden shortage were more at risk of exhaustion than of flu. But as with the faraway roar of the lion, the widely held belief that people are at great risk of the flu is a media creation. So too is the perception that a simple inoculation removes that risk.

The public pendulum swings from dependency on a supposed panacea to panic when a vaccine is found to be flawed or is no longer available. The government makes fear a central part of its agenda, trying to weigh in as our protector. In the process of being so "protected," we learn about dangers we didn't know existed. The real danger of being manipulated in this way is to our health.

I learned firsthand of the devastating reach of governmental fear mongering when, at the request of Senator Chuck Grassley, I examined the response to the 2001 anthrax mailings. The Centers for Disease Control (CDC) attached itself to the media megaphone and made us all feel afraid to open our mail. This response was a way of covering up the miscommunication and mishandling of the evidence by all the federal agencies involved.

The anthrax scare established a precedent for public health hysteria that has been racheted up with each new bug du jour, to the point where the public feels threatened by every possible source of contagion. Smallpox extended the hype to a bug that is no longer infecting anyone. SARS was the first panic to involve the worldwide health community and petrify Asia and Canada along with the United States. The flu scare turned an overlooked disease into a sensation overnight.

The government was sometimes a greater danger than the supposed threat. In its haste to protect us from chemical and biological weapons, for example, the government built expensive high-security laboratories to study these potential weapons. But a study published in February 2001 found that of twenty-one known germ attacks, most were conducted not by terrorists but by government researchers-turned-terrorists who had gained access to human pathogens.

And until it becomes an election issue, our leaders practically ignore the risk of nuclear terrorism, where a terrorist smuggling a suitcase onto a plane or boat can get past the porous safety net and cause great harm. As Harvard scholar Graham Allison wrote in his book *Nuclear Terrorism*, this is one worst-case scenario that we aren't doing enough to prevent.

As I interviewed people for this book, I found many who were wistful for the "good old days." Perhaps our greatest immunity against panic has always come from go-to people in charge of our safety: the policemen, firefighters, and emergency medical technicians. But these comforting presences are being forced to compete with the all-purpose information glut. Tiny bites of data are always within reach via the Internet, the television, and the radio. Many of my patients complain that they don't know where to go to find answers that don't frighten them. Our personal narratives are gradually giving way more and more to the discourse of risk and danger.

We believe that strangers are a threat to us, but as Barry Glassner, the author of *The Culture of Fear*, has pointed out, most crimes involve people known to the victim.

The narratives of this book are drawn from the many patients I know who live in fear and who struggle to cope in the face of growing misinformation. Their stories are juxtaposed here with the true science that eludes them and the societal trends that heighten their anxiety.

Despite the growing fear, there are those who develop hard reflexes to cope with real dangers. Emergency workers are trained to put their own risks in perspective. Firefighters cannot function if they are afraid of being burned or overcome by smoke, and doctors have to put aside their fear of catching a patient's illness in order to do their jobs. This training requires a concentrated effort.

A social plan for stabilizing public hysteria involves countering false beliefs regarding danger. But fear researchers have determined that seeing fear in practical terms isn't easy.

In examining fear, I have attempted to find a new social model to explain today's post-9/11 outbreak. Using my tools as an internist, I have discovered that the disease model for infection and epidemic fits fear the best. Fear is physiological, but today's fear has become pathological. It spreads via distorted hype to those who may not have been worried in the first place.

We build up a partial immunity to each cycle of fear with the simple passage of time. We become desensitized, and we learn that the threat we have been coached to fear is not likely to occur. But fear is not easily unlearned. Our deep emotions can override our reason at any time.

Groundbreaking animal studies by Dr. Esther Sabban show that once frightened, an animal is more susceptible to the next threat that comes along. Fear memory, like all the powerful emotions deep in our brains, is hard for us to overcome, or outreason.

Fear has become pervasive. In order to eradicate it, we must first understand it from the microscopic level all the way to the larger issues of national defense and public safety. In examining fear, I have attempted to use my understanding of health and disease as a lens to spot the epidemic as it is spreading and infecting more and more people. I begin with the biology, move on to the personal, and then widen my lens to the systemic.

To understand why our society's hysteria has grown, I've found it is important to look at the individual. I've tried to determine why a person's physiology can turn so quickly to pathology.

Part I examines how our fear biology can wear us down rather than protect us. Fear deeply affects individual patients, from physical illness all the way to imagined terrorism. The government, media, and private businesses contribute to the perpetual pressure to be afraid.

Part II takes a look at the phenomena of publicly reported infections and how these scares contribute to a growing climate of panic.

Part III explores the border between religion and superstition, as well as the relationship between hypochondria, anxiety, and common fear. I examine the question of whether unnecessary fear can be eliminated.

 In my life, in treating my patients, and in studying fear, I have found that one effective treatment for fear is to replace it with another deep emotion, like caring. If a person develops a passion that takes him beyond a self-absorbing cycle of worry, this passion can be used to breed the antithesis of fear, also known as courage.

My three-year-old daughter, Rebecca, fractured her thigh bone in a fall. For several days after the cast was removed and an X-ray had shown that the bone had healed, she remained afraid to walk on it. Finally, during an exciting time at the beach she stood on the sand and watched the waves come in. By the time fear memory got ready to extend its shadowy tentacles, it was too late—she was already placing weight on the healed leg. Once Rebecca experienced the reward of renewed mobility, she was able to neutralize her fear.

Those with courage or passion may be able to experience the relative safety of our society by standing up to fear arising from exaggerated dangers. If enough people develop courage, this immunized group can slow the spread of fear through their community in the same way that those who have been vaccinated slow the spread of any contagion.

Part I

FIGHT OR FLIGHT

1

WHY ARE WE
SO AFRAID?

We cannot wait while dangers gather.

—Condoleezza Rice, then national security adviser,
addressing the 9/11 Commission on April 8, 2004

Fear has been with humankind from the beginning and is part of our psychological makeup from birth. Our earliest fears are tied to Mommy disappearing even for an instant, taking away our only comfort and protection. Children are afraid of the unknown. It is only as they develop that they learn to distinguish a sense of global uncertainty from a specific danger.

As we become adults, our fears are tied to specific threats, an association that distinguishes fear from anxiety. Anxiety can be self-perpetuating, as it often originates in neurosis or self-doubt. Anxious people worry when they don't need to. Fear, on the other hand, is meant to be an essential tool. We have inherited the fear apparatus, practically unchanged, from our animal forebears, but we often allow it to generate self-defeating hysteria.

When fear is unremitting, especially when it is constantly provoked but no protective action can be taken, anxiety and hysteria often result.

"You're absolutely fine," I say to my patient who can't catch her breath.

"No, I'm not," she insists, coughing and wheezing.

It is only when she tells me that her wedding is the following weekend that I see her fear turning to anxiety, and decide to forgo an extensive lung workup.

The Biology of Fear

Fear is more than a state of mind; it's chemical. It is present in the circuitry of our brains, in the neurochemical exchanges between nerves. Fear is a physical reaction to a perceived threat. As long as the danger is direct and real, fear is normal and helps to protect us.

When an individual feels threatened, fear revs up the metabolism in anticipation of an imminent need to defend oneself or flee. "Fight or flight," or the "acute stress response," was first described by Walter Cannon, an American physiologist, in the 1920s. Cannon observed that animals, including humans, react to threats with a hormonal discharge of the nervous system. There is an outpouring of vessel-constricting, heart-thumping hormones, including noradrenaline (norepinephrine) and adrenaline (epinephrine), followed by the steroid cortisol. The heart speeds up and pumps harder, the nerves fire more quickly, the skin cools and gets goose bumps, the eyes dilate to see better, and the brain receives a message that it is time to do something.

We need to know when another animal is threatening to attack us in order to kill us and eat us. The fact that this particular threat doesn't exist anymore outside of the darkest jungles doesn't mean that fear can no longer be useful, as it is when we stand too close to the edge of a building or turn the wrong way down a one-way street. Triggers of fear involve sudden or dramatic changes in our environment, including dark, light, cold, heat, noise, isolation, or irritation. We react by getting ready, either to attack the source of our fear or to move away from it.

But not all danger is palpable or immediate. Many of the things that scare us aren't sudden, surprising, or matters of life or death. Fear has many guises. For every change of life there is a new set of concerns. For every milestone there is a transition, and fear and foreboding are normal aspects of making these transitions. They are the body's way of cautioning us that the change may or may not be for the better.

People enter puberty, graduate from high school, leave home to attend college, have sex for the first time, get married, give birth to a child, lose a parent, face serious illness, have surgery, lose a spouse, and finally, face their own death. In each case, fearfulness may accompany the life adjustment as a physiological warning to go slow. The fear reaction is normal and even protective, provided that it wears off after a while. The body needs time to adjust to new circumstances, after which it should return to a state of normal function.

Fear is a natural reaction to the unknown and is part of our built-in defense against a potentially hostile environment. We are afraid of suffering and pain, and we seek to avoid it at all costs.

WHAT HAS GONE AWRY?

In recent years the climate of fear has changed.

Statistically, the industrialized world has never been safer. Many of us are living longer and more uneventfully. Nevertheless, we live in fear of worst-case scenarios. Over the past century, armed with scientific and technological breakthroughs, we Americans have dramatically reduced our risk in virtually every area of life, resulting in life spans 60 percent longer in 2000 than in 1900. Antibiotics have reduced the likelihood of dying from infections. It used to be that a person could die from a scratch. Now we gobble down antibiotics at the first sign of trouble. Public health measures dictate standards for drinkable water and breathable air. Our garbage is removed quickly. We live temperature-controlled, disease-controlled lives.

15

And yet, we worry more than ever before. The natural dangers are no longer there, but the response mechanisms are still in place, and now they are turned on much of the time. We implode, turning our adaptive fear mechanism into a maladaptive panicked response.

We are bombarded with information. We live by TV sound bite and by Internet hyperbite. Medical information has become agenda-driven, exaggerated by the media and disseminated on the Internet. The expectation of perfect health is perpetuated by these sources. Illness is no longer accepted as part of the natural order of things, and as consumers, we have become terrified of all disease, even though most of the time, doctors can diagnose an illness and offer either a cure or an effective treatment. Still, we continue to worry.

Our brains are not being infiltrated or provoked to panic by accident. Since 9/11 especially, the government has exploited its role as our official protector, from Homeland Security to the CDC. Airport screeners and the FBI are supposedly the last line of defense between Osama bin Laden and the citizens of western Ohio.

Every warning about a scary new disease, every report of terrorist chatter, and every ultra-frail senior citizen becomes a justification for some government worker's job, from a research scientist all the way to President Bush himself. Government officials and politicians employ the media megaphone to promote the idea that they are keeping the populace safe. Unfortunately, there is no evidence that ongoing terror alerts correlate with the actual risk of a potential attack. After a while the public becomes desensitized and can't tell a real alert from the latest hype. For example, promoting worst-case scenarios with biological or chemical weapons that may easily be blown away by the wind or destroyed by heat is a form of propaganda that makes people afraid and ready to comply with the government's agenda. It is misleading to call nerve gas or anthrax weapons of mass destruction when these are more likely tools that terrorists would use on a smaller scale. It would be extremely difficult to deploy chemical or biological agents to large numbers of potential victims at once. Drone planes seeding the air would likely be shot down before they could complete their tasks.

Of course, government officials can't grab the media mega-phone if the media themselves don't make it available. The mass media tend to magnify the latest health concern and broadcast it to millions of people at once. This has the effect of elevating an issue to a grand scale and provoking panic way out of proportion to the risks. I call this phenomenon the "bug du jour." The craze of the moment appears to be a threat to our personal safety until it runs its course through the media spotlight. And when a new threat hits, private companies take their cues from media outlets and begin to line up for profit.

The authorities we used to look to in the community have been replaced by unfeeling conglomerates that thrive in a climate of uncertainty. The old leather-handed pharmacist, who suggested what type of condoms or deodorant to buy, has been replaced by the impersonality of a twenty-four-hour, neon-beaming chain store. Our old librarian, once more interested in children even than books, has given way to software; how much reassurance can be found in an Internet search engine?

We turn to quick and easy prescriptions instead of reliable information. As I will examine in Chapter 7, pharmaceutical com-panies aren't just treating preexisting fears with the old standbys Prozac or Valium, they're also busy popularizing disorders to cre-ate demand for their new products.

WHY HAVE WE BECOME SO DEFENSELESS?

When Lyme disease, a troublesome bacteria transmitted to hu-mans by the bite of a deer tick, was being hyped ten years ago, one of my most rational patients, a mathematics professor, was certain he had it every time he got a rash, even when he was living in Los Angeles, a city with zero deer.

"The chances of your having it are almost nonexistent," I assured him.

"Forget probabilities, I can just feel it," he said on more than one occasion.

Ten years later, with Lyme very much on the increase but out of the media spotlight, this patient—who by this time had moved to deer-ridden Connecticut—no longer had concerns about the now prevalent Lyme disease, but worried instead about bioterrorism. As well as he understood probabilities and equations, when he turned on the news at night or read his newspaper in the morning, he often personalized the latest risk and became worried that he might die.

Like my professor patient, we absorb the sense of urgency and believe we are in danger. So busy are we with fake threats that we ignore real threats.

With over 8 million cases of tuberculosis every year in the world, 5 million new cases of AIDS, over 300 million cases of malaria, and over a million deaths due to each, Americans rarely worry about these diseases. In the United States approximately 40,000 people die of influenza every year, a statistic that went unnoticed until 2003, when it was the flu's turn on the wheel of hype. In 2000, 63,000 Americans died of pneumonia, and 15,000 people of AIDS. This information stayed out of the news. In comparison to our real killer bugs, only 284 people died here of West Nile virus in 2002, when it was publicized by the media and perceived as a great threat.

In 2003, when Severe Acute Respiratory Syndrome (SARS) arrived and became almost synonymous with the word *virus*, there were only 7,000 cases in the world, and fewer than 100 in the United States. No one here died of SARS, but a lot of people worried unnecessarily. Many patients called me in the spring of 2003 convinced that the slightest cough was SARS. People were afraid to sit next to an Asian person or to eat in a Chinese restaurant.

Our public health system, specifically the World Health Organization and the Centers for Disease Control here in the United States, drove the media response to help contain SARS, quarantining Canada and most of Asia, and ultimately taking credit when

SARS died down. Actually, there was no direct evidence that the massive travel alerts really squashed SARS as much as historically proven factors like isolating those who had the disease, as well as the arrival of summer, traditionally a difficult time for respiratory viruses to thrive. Still, the public perception was that SARS had gone overnight from being a worldwide threat in the spring of 2003 to no threat at all by June. We braced ourselves for the next bug du jour and forgot all about SARS. In the summer of 2003, we experienced a temporary reprieve—West Nile did not reappear on our media screens that summer, and hardly anyone was afraid that his next mosquito bite would be his last.

Many of the bugs du jour are cause for concern only among a narrow segment of the population. Only a small portion of those who believe they are at risk really are, and few who become infected actually die. But a strange disease that kills only a few people still makes for good headlines if the story is strategically hyped. Many news teasers use the line "Are you and your family at risk?" The answer is usually no, but that tagline generates concern in every viewer, and this is what keeps people tuned in. If we didn't fundamentally misunderstand the risk, we probably wouldn't watch.

Each terror alert is like another bug du jour. We talk of sarin, which killed only twelve people in a Japanese subway in 1995 but panicked thousands, and can panic us here without so much as a single case. Anthrax infected twenty-two people through the U.S. mail in the fall of 2001, killing five unfortunate people, yet had thirty thousand more taking the antibiotic Cipro, many indiscriminately and without a doctor's prescription. It's hard to believe that there hasn't been a case of smallpox here since the 1940s for all the attention it has received. If it is ever again introduced into the population, it is likely to spread slowly, by respiratory droplet. Meanwhile, in 2002, the *fear* of smallpox spread far more virulently through the public, transmitted by word of mouth.

In the fall of 2004, the sudden shortage of flu vaccine in the United States led to a stampede of people seeking the coveted elixir. During this vaccine shortage multitudes of healthy people became convinced that they could be overcome with the flu and die at any time. In fact, the first flu-related death that year came not from the disease, but from an elderly woman who fell while waiting for the vaccine amidst a thronging crowd. I wrote an op-ed piece in the *New York Post* pointing out that the CDC had determined that the vaccine hadn't helped much the year before, was only 40–60 percent effective, and was intended mostly for high-risk groups. My message: flu vaccine is not the health panacea that you think it is, you are not in great danger without it, and the sudden attention it is receiving has caused people to feel a sense of urgency out of proportion to the real danger.

I thought I'd accomplished something until I began to receive phone calls from patients who had read my piece. Almost as an afterthought I'd mentioned that I had five vials, or fifty doses, to give to my sickest patients.

"I saw your article," one call began.

"Are you reassured?" I asked.

The patient ignored me. "I understand you have some vaccine. Can I have a shot?"

Rather than worrying less after learning the facts, each patient wanted to be one of the lucky fifty and was calling me to beg for a dose.

Reeducating the public when it came to panic was going to take far more than a corrective article that unintentionally became part of the hype.

The year before, the deaths of a few children from flu in Colorado had led instantly to a nationwide panic before dropping from the news radar. Yet both years, despite all the concern, would turn out to be nonepidemic flu years.

When the media or the government focuses on the bug du jour, we all feel it, as though it's a palpable danger. When media attention is diverted elsewhere, the manifested fear fades but remains below the surface, waiting to attach itself to the next hyped target.

At a time in history when there are no true scourges, the population is controlled through fear. Rather than enjoy the safety that our technological advances have provided us, instead we feel uncertain. Respiratory masks and other paraphernalia meant to shield us actually spread panic more effectively than any terrorist agent by sending the message that something is in the offing. Our personal fear alerts are turned on all the time. Fear is not intrinsically pathological, it is a reaction to the pathology of our times.

We feel the stress and have become more prone to irritability, disagreement, worry, insomnia, anxiety, and depression. We are more likely to experience chest pain, shortness of breath, dizziness, and headache.

After weeks go by without our being shot by a sniper, bitten by a West Nile mosquito, gassed with sarin, or infected with SARS, people become desensitized. Each new phase of hysteria is followed by a brief period when our guard comes down.

But who can a frightened person count on for reliable information and reassurance?

Teachers absorb the same information fragments that students do, reinforcing the students' sense of fear. Patients fear becoming ill, they fear the onset of suffering, and yet, doctors specialize in, and are trained to treat, specific diseases rather than the patient as a whole.

Patients hover nervously around the medical secretary's desk as their diagnoses roll in via faxed reports. The pills are better, the surgeries are better, and the rehab techniques are better, but these positive developments are not enough to offset the fear of test results.

Managing Fear Like a Disease

Why are some people infected with hysteria out of proportion to the risks, while others seem impervious? Some of my patients worry over every symptom, while others never seem afraid of disease or death.

I recall a stoic ninety-three-year-old patient who had been a professional tap dancer for many years. She continued to dance in recitals despite her advancing age, until her back gave out. She went to several surgeons, all of whom advised against surgery, citing discouraging statistics. But she wasn't afraid. She had faith in her body and its ability to survive the surgery. Her passion for dancing outweighed any conceivable risk.

"Can the surgery help me dance again?" she asked me.

"It's possible."

"Then I'll take my chances," she said.

She sailed through the surgery and was dancing again a month later. For this patient, no matter how many times I warned her about potential risk, she replied that she believed she would be fine, and the cycle of worry never started.

Ultimately, we must develop prescriptions for the range of fears that patients experience. These prescriptions must be practical and designed to break the cycle of worry. Those in society who inform us and who care for us—whether in government, the media, or health care—must be committed to maintaining a perspective based on realistic assessments of risk, rather than an agenda based on politics or profit.

2

IT WORKS FOR ANIMALS
BUT NOT FOR US

Take a rat and put it in a cage with a plexiglass divider. It sees the cat on the other side. It's afraid it's going to be attacked. The associated fear is very difficult to extinguish, even with the plexiglass there.

—Esther Sabban, professor and graduate program
director, Department of Biochemistry and Molecular
Biology, New York Medical College

When a patient is restrained inside a magnetic resonance imaging (MRI) machine during a scan of the brain, his head is strapped down and his body is enclosed in a coffinlike chamber. A loud metallic banging sound is heard, and the patient, like a restrained animal, may feel like he is never going to be released. The claustrophobia combines with the loud banging to cause an escalating fear.

Even worse is the terror some women feel when undergoing a mammogram. One of my patients described what it's like to wait while her breast has been painfully flattened to a pancake by the pressure of the equipment. "I have the awful fantasy," she said,

23

"that the technician will die of a sudden heart attack or there will be a power outage, and my breast won't be released."

A patient's instinct is to fight her confinement, even when she knows it is for her own good. This is the same instinct an animal experiences. In fact, accepting ourselves as animals is crucial to understanding how human fear is designed to work. The fear center of the human brain, the amygdala, is identical to the primitive fear center of the animal brain.

Dr. Joseph Ledoux, a prominent neuroscientist and the author of *The Emotional Brain*, has studied fear extensively. He told me: "When a rat is afraid and when a human is afraid, very similar things occur in the body." But Ledoux also believes that triggers of fear vary dramatically from species to species. He said, "When a monkey is attacked, it will give off calls to other monkeys that something has happened. If a rat is under attack by a cat, it will give off an ultrasonic frequency in the range of rats, not cats. The frequency will be too high for a cat to hear."

Ledoux described the amygdala as "the hub in the brain's wheel of fear." When the amygdala is stimulated, there is an outpouring of stress hormones, causing a state of hypervigilance. The amygdala processes the primitive emotions of fear, hate, love, bravery, and anger—all neighbors in the deep limbic brain that we inherit from animals. When the amygdala malfunctions, a mood disorder, or state of uncontrollable apprehension, results.

The amygdala works together only with other brain centers that feed it and respond to it. This fear hub senses via the thalamus (the brain's receiver), thinks through the cortex (the brain's seat of reasoning), and remembers via the hippocampus (the brain's file cabinet).

This cycle can become self-perpetuating. Here's an example of how it works: my young son was terrified by a sudden barking when we were hiking on a mountain trail at sunset.

I said, "The dog is gone," but he said, "No it's not. It keeps coming back."

Now each time a dog barks, it engages the same mechanism. My son's thalamus triggers his amygdala, which retrieves the fearful memory for him from the hippocampus, and his body goes into hyperdrive.

When the amygdala detects a threatening situation, out pour the stress hormones. The hippocampus alerts the amygdala's circuitry to a danger associated with a scary memory. At the same time, the hippocampus is also the center for caution. Under stress, the amygdala signals release while the hippocampus cautions slow down.

If the stress persists, the thinking brain falters, routine memories and behaviors shut down, and fear predominates. Previous trauma biases the brain toward fear pathways, which continue to fire again and again during flashbacks. This explains why even when we may not consciously remember a traumatic event, we retain a powerful emotional memory that we cannot reason ourselves away from. When the amygdala fires, it transmits fear signals too rapidly and powerfully for any of the brain's regular brakes to stop it.

Once a person has learned to fear something, he may always feel fear associated with that experience. But unlike mice, we humans can fear events we have only read or heard about, and so we worry about disasters we may never experience.

If we are unable to respond for lack of an appropriate target, the fear accumulates, and we become anxious.

FEAR CONDITIONING

Fear is user-ready at birth. As we grow, we are conditioned to respond to certain triggers. The fear response becomes automatic, though the dangers may not always be visible. If you put a rat in a box and shock it in the presence of a tone, it will become conditioned to respond to the shock, the tone, and the box. This contextual response helps an animal protect itself. The ability to recognize the box increases the likelihood of surviving the danger within by reacting quickly.

We are not rats, but we react similarly in terms of our primitive conditioning. Once a fear response is triggered, it may not diminish over time. Sometimes fears incubate, become indelible, and even increase in potency. They are often brought back to life by stressful events. This is both good and bad. It is useful for us to be able to remember situations associated with past dangers. But these memories may find their way into our daily lives, intruding on situations where the fears have no use, causing panic, phobias, or posttraumatic stress. We may feel compelled to avoid anything associated with a seminal fear event, including something that is neutral or even positive. If a barking dog bites a child, it may even lead to a self-defeating fear of all loud noises (including concert music), not just an adaptive fear of dogs.

The dangers that provoke the fear response in humans can be real or imagined, concrete or abstract. We may witness them firsthand or hear about them from others. We have a far greater capacity to imagine dangers than a rat does, and the potential for misperception is one of the major concerns of this book.

Drs. Robert and Caroline Blanchard have studied how humans evaluate situations for risk using our most highly evolved brain functions. Despite our advanced evolution, we often fail to assess the level of risk accurately. We humans tend to overpersonalize risk and to experience an unrealistic sense of danger whenever we hear or read of a bad event occurring to someone else. Many of my patients going for a routine CT scan will worry that they have a serious illness as soon as they see the sicker patients in the waiting room. My parents, healthy but in their late seventies, respond with a "We'll be next" attitude whenever an ambulance is called to the retirement complex in Florida where they live.

A PRIMAL RESPONSE

Humans transmit danger signals in a way different from that used by animals. Ledoux said, "Social communication is greater for humans than for any other species. But it is difficult for humans to communicate fear accurately. The evolution of the human brain allows us to have ideas that don't match reality that well. This mismatch is a source of human anxiety."

All fear systems are intended to increase the likelihood of surviving a dangerous situation. Ledoux has shown that this response fires so rapidly and so powerfully that it overrides conscious thought.

A balding man in his fifties with intensely focused eyes and a resonant voice, Ledoux gave a careful reasoned talk on the neuroscience of fear at New School University on February 6, 2004, as part of a multidisciplinary conference there.

"Fear is a natural part of life," Ledoux said. "A snake on a path in the woods is threatening. So is an angry human. We respond with bodily upheaval. Fight or flight. Muscles tighten in response to a threat or in anticipation of one. We come into the world knowing how to be afraid. We learn what to be afraid of."

All animals with a backbone also have an amygdala. It takes only twelve milliseconds, according to Ledoux, for the thalamus to process sensory imput and signal the amygdala. He called this emotional brain the "low road." The high road, or the thinking brain, takes thirty to forty milliseconds to process what is happening. The hippocampal memory center provides the context. "People have fear they don't understand or can't control because it is processed by the low road," Ledoux said.

The emotional brain also has its own intrinsic fear memory. Cells remember the fear and don't need to be reactivated, or reminded. Rats automatically respond to dangers they've seen previously.

During stress, reasoned memory is impaired, and emotional memory predominates, since the amygdala sends more signals to the thinking brain than the other way around. Humans are at the mercy of fear impulses that override reason. The upper brain tries to regulate fear, but its brakes are often ineffective at slowing the powerful emotions of the system. Valium and Prozac block the amygdala by different mechanisms, creating an artificial shield against fear.

Take away the amygdala and you take away fear. In 1999 researchers at the University of Southern California and the Université de Bordeaux published a study in *Nature* in which they demonstrated the role of the amygdala in emotional memory. They implanted electrodes in the brains of laboratory mice and measured the strong response to a tone and a subsequent electric shock. When the amygdala was surgically removed, both the animals' panicked immobility and the frenetic brain wave pattern disappeared.

Similar results have been found in humans who have suffered trauma and damage to the amygdala. They become unable to feel afraid even when they are presented with clear danger signals.

At the fear conference, Ledoux spoke about the nature of the fear response across the entire animal kingdom. "Fear is learned instantly. Fear is remembered forever. Fear is self-sustaining. Fear motivates other kinds of behavior that are designed to affect its impact."

But inevitably, an appropriate fear response depends on access to accurate information. As Ledoux said at New School University, "Will fear be based on an honest assessment of the threat, or will it be trumped up?"

Characteristics of Fear

Back in the mid-1980s, Isaac Marks, a prominent fear theorist, described the basic fear responses of withdrawal, immobility, fighting back, or submission. When these responses are not effective or when they become internalized over a period of time, anxiety may well result.

What distinguishes fear reactions between humans and other animals is not the physiology of fear but the triggers that activate it. For humans, our added brainpower allows defensive reactions to more and more triggers. Hence, we are more prone to social anxiety.

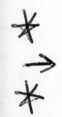
Fear also has a genetic component. A rat will rev up in response to the odor of a fox even if that rat has spent its whole life in the

laboratory. Humans are automatically fearful of situations that threatened our ancestors.

FEAR PATHOLOGY

Arne Ohman, a leader in the field of human fear and anxiety, has argued that panic, phobia, and posttraumatic stress all emanate from unremitting fears.

In *The Emotional Brain*, Ledoux showed how pathological anxiety evolves from the basic mechanisms of fear. Anxiety manifests itself in different ways: Phobias are avoidance fears that can't be suppressed, panic attacks are circumscribed periods of intense anxiety, and free-floating anxiety is worry that goes on and on. Obsessive-compulsive disorder involves rituals that are intended to neutralize anxiety but end up enhancing it by being so excessive. With posttraumatic stress disorder (PTSD), the fear response fails to diminish with the passage of time.

Psychotherapy is an attempt to retrain the higher centers of the brain to exert control over the lower centers, including the amygdala. This approach is similar to trying to rein in an untamed stallion. The amygdala may rear up at any time.

POSTTRAUMATIC STRESS

Dr. Rachel Yehuda, a professor of psychiatry at Mount Sinai School of Medicine, is a passionate researcher and a pioneer in understanding posttraumatic stress disorder. Her findings suggest that it is cortisol that helps the body adapt to heavy trauma over time. Without this crucial steroid to aid in coping, a trauma victim can fall into a pattern of unremitting fear.

In Dr. Yehuda's experience, many people exposed to extreme trauma do not develop PTSD precisely because cortisol protects them. She described PTSD as "a failure to control the adaptive mechanism of the fear response." The key to a perpetual state of terror, according to Yehuda, is an inability to suppress the amygdala. "The usual limbic brake on the amygdala isn't working. Cortisol is supposed to initiate this. Without it, the stress response isn't contained."

The popularizing of PTSD in the media has led many who aren't truly terrorized to use it as an excuse for their hysteria. Overstatement dilutes the language of terror and renders it less useful. "The mention of posttraumatic stress occurs when there is a shortage of terms for laypeople to use for their vulnerabilities when confronted by trauma," said Yehuda.

People who are afraid to get on a bus because they have seen a suicide bombing on the news are overpersonalizing a danger. This isn't really PTSD. It is an inflated perception of risk. Yehuda said, "In America, we worry about whether something that hasn't happened could happen. In Israel, when something does happen, we worry about it occurring again."

How Humans Learn to Fear

We humans take for granted that language helps us to negotiate our world, but it is also true that we often misuse and misinterpret words. The fear response works best based on nonverbal cues. When we humans try to use abstract language to communicate threats, we too easily overload and provoke the fear response.

Dr. Elizabeth Phelps, a psychologist and neuroscientist at New York University, has examined how our brains respond to threats we only envision. Although people learn about dangerous events through hard experience—a dog is deemed dangerous because it once bit you—we also learn about dangers by watching—you observe a dog bite someone else.

Using highly sensitive MRI scans, Phelps discovered that the amygdala can be activated in response to dangers a person merely observes. Phelps concluded that fear activation based on watching is just as powerful as direct experience, but easily prone to misinterpretation. She said, "When you are watching it and you are told that it is going to happen to you, it causes the same robust response by the amygdala as if you experienced it yourself."

TURNING OFF FEAR

In November 2002 researchers working for the National Institute of Mental Health published a study in *Nature* that described a way to turn off fear. Stimulating the front part of a rat's brain with an electrode caused it to automatically emit a "safety signal" that signaled the amygdala to slow down. When a tone was repeatedly presented to rats without the loud "danger" tone that at first accompanied it, over time the safety signal caused them to become less and less afraid.

In December 2002 researchers at Columbia University discovered the gene that turns off fear in mice. The results were reported in the journal *Cell*.

In September 2004 Dr. Phelps used specialized MRI to study the human brain, and she discovered fear extinction circuits in humans that correspond to those previously identified in rats. Phelps recognized the limitations of the animal model but concluded that our cognitive mechanisms are "interacting with the same circuitry as animals have."

Like rats, humans can temporarily turn off fear, though in both cases the wiring heavily favors the on switch. Unlike rats, we humans are forever trying to turn off something that should never have been turned on in the first place. "Extinction is not erasing a fear but trying to control it," Phelps said.

OUR CONSTANT STATE OF ALERT

Dr. Esther Sabban has studied fear by restraining animals. She believes the animals react to the loss of control and "not knowing if it's ever going to end." Dr. Sabban's work shows that animals that have been exposed to one danger have an exaggerated response to a new danger. When she exposed an animal to the cold, the animal could become used to it and learn not to react. But the same animal was then hypersensitive to being restrained. The fear neurochemicals shot up higher and stayed that way for many days after the animal was untied. In other words, certain primitive fears can't be extinguished even when there is no danger.

Once fear has been activated, it can lead to overreactions in all directions. This is how we feel when we are told that we could be attacked again by an unseen force like al-Qaeda. The fear response may well be suppressed over time, but it can resurface—stronger than before—and even extend to all aspects of our lives. A person who thinks he has gotten used to the orange terror alert message on the TV screen may nevertheless experience a hyper-alert response seeing someone with a gun in an airport, even if that person is a security guard. This new state of hyperalertness originates in neurochemical fear memory that develops over time. The capacity for desensitization is limited because the amygdala is stronger. It takes a lot of psychotherapy to override the fear message, and the fear center wakes up again with each new stimulus that comes along.

It is worrisome to consider what this state of free-floating communicated fear does to our bodies. We gain or lose weight, our immune systems become overloaded, and we become susceptible to diseases that we might otherwise have been able to resist.

WHAT WE GET FROM APES

Apes, like humans, have highly developed brain centers, with sophisticated memory and some ability to reason. But unlike humans, other primates appear to have a dependable society that determines what alarms them. I spoke with Dr. Chris Jolly, a good-natured British anthropologist at New York University, who maintains that apes have honest fear responses. Jolly has investigated aggressive behavior among baboons.

"Are threats among primates always real?" I asked him.

"Usually," he said, "primates don't use referential communication. Warning signals concern things that are directly dangerous. They don't use fear talk to distract."

I considered danger as perceived by the animal world. Has our technology made us too smart for our own good? Even if the animal world is more dangerous than ours, it is more honest: the threat of attack—when it occurs—is real.

"All animals that live in societies have a pecking order," Jolly said, "including chickens, where the expression comes from. Part of organizing into an animal society is to decide who is more powerful than you—animals convey a submissive posture to others who are dominant to them. In more intelligent mammals, like wolves, for example, fear is based on a memory of what the enemy has done in the past. There is a structure of tensions, flux in the hierarchy, young animals coming up to replace the older ones going down. The adherence to the structure provides comfort."

"We humans have created environments that don't comfort us," I said, and Dr. Jolly laughed.

"Can the same thing happen to other primates?" I asked. "Can they lose touch with real threats and create pseudothreats like humans do?"

Jolly paused, thinking carefully about this before he spoke.

"Rhesus monkeys have been studied in captivity. When they're crammed into smaller spaces like the animal equivalent of cities, they become more aggressive and more fearful. They also experience more stress and fear in ambiguous situations and in situations of change."

"This is true for humans as well."

Jolly agreed that in certain crowded baboon and chimpanzee societies we begin to see the fear-provoking abstractions that are so prevalent among us humans.

Dr. Robert Sapolsky, a researcher at Stanford, has examined baboon behavior under stress. By measuring stress hormones found in their stool, Sapolsky was able to determine that baboons, like humans, live in high-stress societies, with order maintained by intimidation. Sapolsky also showed that living in fear damages a baboon's health and, as with humans, that sustained production of stress hormones can damage the hippocampus, affecting learning and memory.

Chimps are probably the only nonhuman primate with a sense of self. "They can put themselves in the position of other chimps," Jolly said. "Chimps fool each other. They use deceptive behavior to get gain."

"This deception causes other chimps to be afraid of them?"

"The same as with humans," Jolly said.

Dr. Jane Goodall has studied chimpanzees extensively. Pertaining to fear, she observed that a band of young male chimps tenses up when it approaches the border of their group's domain, psyching themselves up for the possibility of battle with neighboring chimp groups, a form of danger recognition. When the chimps menace each other purely for the sake of control or domination, they are exhibiting traits recognizable in their self-defeating human counterparts.

What We Get from Each Other

Dr. Paul Ekman, a professor of psychology at the University of California, San Francisco, Medical School, has studied danger recognition in humans. In his 2003 book *Emotions Revealed*, he wrote that we can learn to be afraid of anything. Ekman focused on the facial expressions we use to communicate worry to each other. Worry about an impending threat causes muscular tension. Ekman observed that raised upper eyelids are fundamental in communicating fear. Unfortunately, these expressions can't easily communicate the degree of the threat, which is why expressions of fear are infectious and may alarm others unnecessarily.

Like rats, we have defined pathways for invoking fear and for attempting to suppress or extinguish it. Like rats, when we are caught in a maze of fear, we may learn to navigate for a time, but the price is a state of hyperalert vigilance that burns up our metabolism and renders us more susceptible to illness.

In addition to the fight-or-flight conditioned fear that we inherit from animals, there are the elaborate communicated and learned fear and worry that we humans alone possess and that we inflict on each other. The anticipation of danger based on risk involves the brain's highest centers, which then connect to the amygdala and cause the reverberating states of panic and worry.

This human fear is not reasonable but is driven by fragmented information, hype, miscommunication, and uncertainty. If we are unable to convert our uncertainty into a reasoned assessment of risk, we grow more and more afraid, caught up in a cycle of worry. Feeling safe means coming to realize that the probability of harm occurring to us is very small.

Feeling safe also means returning fear to its proper place as an animal instinct. Reason and abstract thinking are human trademarks. Our language is ill suited to communicating primitive emotions. Perhaps we can learn from animals a more limited but appropriate use of fear.

3

OUR CULTURE
OF WORRY

What an appalling affront to share the intense desire
for continued existence with all living things but be
smart enough to recognize the ultimate futility of this
most basic biological imperative. We think that clash
creates the potential for terror.

—Tom Pyszczynski, professor of psychology at
the University of Colorado and cofounder of
terror management theory

Animals may fear death as much as we do, but
whereas animals freeze in the face of immediate
danger, we experience an ongoing existential fear, connected to our
unique self-awareness. Our central fear of death reaches beyond
our animal instincts and may threaten to overwhelm us. But like
all our fears, our fear of death is overblown when we are wrongly
convinced that death is in the offing. Our fear of death is so pervasive it is too easily provoked.

At the New School University fear conference, Dr. Tom

Pyszczynski, a rumple-jacketed professor with flowing white hair, was a striking contrast to the balding, impeccably dressed Ledoux. Pyszczynski was one of the originators of terror management theory, and he described how all fear emanates from a primary fear of death. "Fear is supposed to function to keep us alive and help us stave off death. As an unpleasant emotion, it creates a barrier we're not supposed to cross."

Dr. John Mann is the director of neuroscience at the New York State Psychiatric Institute and an expert on suicide. In an interview, he said that even in the most extreme cases, fear of death is designed to have a protective aspect. "Take away this fear inhibition, and the person is no longer indecisive, and suicide may ensue."

But even if fear can be protective, it can also be destructive. As the only species that is aware of the inevitability of death, we have a great need for our culture to give us a sense of meaning and purpose. The growing unease in our society is testament to the fact that our culture is no longer capable of doing the job. Pyszczynski theorized that fear out of control erodes our perceived wellness. This fear of death, while essential, is self-defeating if it paralyzes people.

In order to buffer our dread, humans try to construct a shield—a value-laden belief system that bolsters our self-esteem and allows us to sublimate our greatest fears. We attempt to manage terror through a complex psychological defense mechanism. Our primary instinct to circumvent death becomes our drive to make art, pursue science, and construct civilizations that are intended to last beyond our years. The drive to have children is a biological, as well as a cultural, answer to the fear of death. Overall, we feel safer when we participate in this culture.

Unfortunately, this instinct toward culture may easily be transformed into a negative culture of worry. Multiple studies in the psychiatric literature over the past fifteen years have corroborated the link between fear of death and thinking negatively about others. The culture of fear is one that breeds prejudice and distrust.

The growing epidemic of fear also encourages the expectation of illness and death. Many of us are overly afraid of illnesses we don't have. We may personalize the risk of death while lacking any disease that could cause death. And once we have an illness, many fear an outcome much more ominous than the one indicated by reliable medical data.

Cancer serves as a graphic illustration of this phenomenon. While the public advocacy campaign for cancer prevention has shone a necessary light on the evils of cigarette smoking and carcinogens, it has also made people more fearful. Cancer is described in value-laden terminology like "end stage" or "pervasive." Most cancers are treatable, yet the disease is still assumed to be a death sentence. Thanks to technology, diagnoses are made quickly. One day you think you are healthy, the next you have a life-threatening illness. Therapies are misperceived as primitive rather than evolving. This perception is wrong.

In the late 1990s, AIDS fell out of the U.S. health care news cycle and stopped scaring us, while it continued to kill millions overseas and was misperceived as under control here. Meanwhile cancer continues to scare us, in part because we can't seem to control when and if we get it. Most patients are even frightened of the screening tests such as mammograms and colonoscopies that make it possible to treat cancer before it can kill them. Once cancer is found, and even if it is cured, fear is the uninvited guest that whispers of its possible recurrence. As threatening as a cancer is, fear of death from cancer's insidious tentacles is even worse.

As Dr. Pyszczynski might predict, there is a culture of cancer care that does its best to alleviate these fears. Chemotherapy involves multiple social workers and self-help support groups. The radiation suite at our hospital is a calm therapeutic milieu, including an aquarium with an extensive collection of multicolored tropical fish.

Unfortunately, the growing culture of hyped fears offsets these attempts at support and insight. Fueled by fragments of bad news

38

from media and Internet sources, patients fear the worst-case scenario—a painful imminent death.

ONE PATIENT'S FEAR OF DEATH

My waiting room was filled with patients, but one in particular was telling the nurse that he couldn't bear to wait another moment. He was peering at her through tiny spectacles, better suited for a much older patient, which had slid to the end of his nose.

He was a forty-four-year-old international businessman, and I could hear his nervous accented speech through the waiting room window glass.

I'd ordered a CT scan on "Ephraim Azziz" because he was a smoker. I reassure smokers that the test is routine, that I am being compulsive, that a CT scan is more sophisticated than an X-ray in analyzing a smoker's lungs. But almost all smokers fear cancer, and it takes a negative result to truly reassure them. Knowing that a CT scan or other state-of-the-art test can foretell their future puts many patients in a state of worry as soon as they are told to have the scan.

Azziz went for the scan a few weeks after seeing me. The report came to me a few days later, indicating a three-centimeter nodule at the top of the right lung, consistent with cancer. Upon seeing the report, I told the office nurse that I needed to see Ephraim Azziz right away.

By the time I saw him in the examination room, he was as nervous as I ever remember seeing a patient. He appeared ultrathin, gray around his temples, with piercing eyes.

"The report says there's a nodule there," I said. "We have to biopsy it. But it's small. And there are no swollen lymph nodes. It may well not be cancer. If it is, worst-case scenario, we should be able to operate on it and cure you."

"I want to know as soon as possible," he said, squeezing his ears and scratching the sides of his face, a gesture that conveyed extreme nervousness. He squirmed on the examination table. I performed a limited examination, as I'd just seen him a few weeks before. I invited him into my corner consultation room, a sanctum with walls of white brick and many windows. Mr. Azziz seemed to relax somewhat as he sank into the soft blue leather of my couch, as if the news couldn't get any worse in here.

I decided to show the CT scan to my office mate, "Dr. Madison." A prominent pulmonologist, he didn't accept Mr. Azziz's managed care insurance, but he was always willing to give me his opinion on an X-ray or CT scan.

He crisply snapped the scan up onto his view box. This type of doctorly precision and familiarity with potential cancers could frighten a patient if he saw it. The report already had the words "SUSPICIOUS FOR A BRONCHOGENIC NEOPLASM" written on it. The radiologist had pronounced sentence on a man he'd never met. Such an anonymous practice helps provoke patient panic.

A great diagnostician and a feeling physician, my office partner always looked for nuances. He analyzed all the possibilities, reluctant to jump to a conclusion at this stage. "It could be cancer," Madison said. "But it might just be scar. Needs a biopsy, but it could well be negative."

I brought this happy news right back to Azziz, and I could see a visible change. He stopped moving his hands back and forth in a purposeless pattern, and now he wiped his sweaty forehead with the back of his sleeve. Madison had introduced a tangible hope. We could envision a scenario that didn't involve cancer or require surgery. Cancer gave mortality a name and a timetable, but a negative result would return mortality to the abstract.

Still, as he rose to go, I could almost feel the animal fear welling up like an unstoppable current that would not ebb.

We both pressed to know the answer as soon as we could. Pushing hard past impassive clerks and loaded appointment schedules and the antagonistic world of managed care medicine, I gave this man all the priority and VIP status I could muster, internally with my staff and externally with other staffs. I could sense his helplessness, his guilt over his years of smoking, putting his three children at risk of a fatherless future.

He was overwhelmed by the mushrooming fear of his illness. He was under the control of this fear, and he could only hope to defeat it with the knowledge that the cancer wasn't there, couldn't be there, because the tissue itself said it wasn't true.

The degree of his worry was tied to imagining what he might feel if the cancer was there. Even if the surgery cured it and he faced only the specter of the cancer's returning, the fear would recur first. In Azziz's case, fear would be much more difficult to control than cancer. If there was a positive aspect to this fear, it was that Azziz would be too frightened to ever smoke again.

Azziz was lucky in one respect—medical testing would lead to a definite answer. Many times the patient is kept in limbo; for example, an MRI of the brain might show some signal abnormalities that could indicate multiple sclerosis. What is a doctor supposed to tell a patient who goes for an MRI because of a headache and comes back with a result that *could* mean she has this stigmatizing, disabling disease? Sometimes the technology increases the uncertainty. Some patients have to live under the shroud of worry that comes with a *possible* diagnosis.

For Azziz, at least, a definitive answer would be forthcoming, though now that his illusion of health had been disrupted, his worry was bound to persist.

Two weeks later, when he returned to my office, I was amazed to discover that he still hadn't had the biopsy. He'd found a pulmonologist who accepted his insurance, and this doctor had suggested a PET scan first to sense activity in the nodule before doing the biopsy. He'd also done a skin test for tuberculosis that turned out to be positive. Apparently the lung doctor, "Dr. Laby," had said the nodule could be a scar from tuberculosis rather than cancer. This was potentially good news, but Azziz seemed too worried to consider it. Azziz was picking up stray comments from his growing ensemble of doctors, and he was trying to put them together in some kind of order that would predict his future.

41

Instead of being reassured, he was more confused and frightened. He stuck out his arm and pointed to the cherry-red spot in the center, which was the positive skin test for TB. "Do I have TB too?" he asked. "Should I be treated for it? Wear a mask?"

We bypassed the examination room—I decided he had had enough examinations for the time being—and sat in my consultation room. He leaned forward on the couch across from me. Each new piece of information made him question how all the pieces fit together. In order to gain that elusive perspective as he obsessed over the potentially devastating illness, he had to hear the facts in a certain order, like the combination to a vault.

Dr. Laby, by being thorough and careful, had unintentionally alarmed Azziz further. Each new sophisticated test created another reason to worry, and delay only allowed the patient's fear to grow.

"You do not have active tuberculosis," I said.

Azziz smiled, glad there was something he didn't have.

A week later, my assistant placed the PET scan report on my desk with a message to call Azziz. I hesitated, not wanting to convey results via the telephone. Personal contact between doctor and patient helps a patient to put news in perspective instead of panicking. The more impersonal the communication, the more fear is transmitted along with the message.

But sometimes if I request a face-to-face discussion, the patient immediately assumes the worst. This approach had already backfired with Azziz. Some patients prefer to communicate by e-mail, but e-mail is not the place for serious results. I decided to try the telephone this time.

"Mr. Azziz, I have the results of your PET scan. The area of the nodule is a hot area."

"What does this mean?"

"It means it's not a scar. Something's going on there."

"What could it be?"

"It could be a tumor. But it's very small. It can be removed," I said.
Silence.

Without the help of facial expressions and a calm demeanor, it was difficult for me to convey the concept of "curable" and have it outweigh the concept of "tumor." I found I couldn't alleviate his nervousness over the phone as well as I could in person.

"I can't sleep," he said.

"Would you like a sleeping pill?"

"Okay," he said, sighing. "I'm going for the needle biopsy Thursday." There were no tests left to delay the biopsy, no more doctors to see.

The next time I heard from him was when he called from the waiting room before his biopsy.

"I've waited three hours already, and the doctor isn't here, but his partner showed up and wanted to do the biopsy. I sent him away. What should I do? Should I go home?"

I urged Azziz to let the second doctor do the procedure. His ambivalence about who performed it seemed another manifestation of his worry. He was trying to control his fear by creating more choices for himself.

He later described the radiologist as unsmiling behind a paper mask and gown. Mr. Azziz said he felt at the time that the doctor's unsympathetic posture was another indication that a cancer diagnosis was in the offing.

Rather than allowing the patient to succumb to premonitions or speculations that stoke the amygdala, it is important for a physician to have a strategy for dealing with the specter of cancer. This strategy must be based on a reasoned assessment of the facts, since most patients become more frightened if they think you are deceiving them.

"Dr. Yang," the cytologist (an expert in cells), called me with the results two days after the biopsy was taken. It was two hours before the start of Yom Kippur, the Jewish day of atonement. "It's squamous cell carcinoma of the lung," he said.

Squamous cancer meant skin cells in the lung gone berserk.

There was no good way to deliver bad news. I wondered if

Azziz, who was religious, might have preferred to know his fate as he prayed for forgiveness on Yom Kippur. Still, I decided to wait to tell him until after the holiday so that I could have a plan in place when I spoke with him.

On Tuesday, when Azziz leaned across from me in my consultation room, he seemed strangely detached, rather than expectant.

"I have the results," I began. "You do have a small cancer, but it's contained, it hasn't spread, it's curable by surgery."

"I know," he replied. "Dr. Laby called me with the results this morning."

"Laby?"

"Said he recommended surgery. Said he was happy that the tumor hadn't spread. Said I should go for chemotherapy afterwards just as an insurance policy."

Laby had charged to center stage before I could get there. He was the head of our hospital's end-of-life team, and he was used to facing cancer. He was a bullish doctor, but he was also highly skilled and responsible.

"Knowing made me feel better," Azziz said. "Imagining was far worse than knowing."

The knowledge that your future lies in a computerized scan or a tissue result can cause a welling up of uncontrollable panic. But when the definitive answer comes, the mystery is gone, which is for some the worst part. Unfortunately, fear of death remains a primary focus even in cancer that can be cured by surgery.

Azziz had come to this office visit with multiple printouts, charts, and information from various lung cancer Web sites. He knew the exact survival statistics and the worst-case scenario for his particular pathology. He was fully plugged in to our contemporary culture of worry.

"How do I know it won't come back?" he said, already seeing past the surgery to his future worry.

"This is squamous cell. A skin type that's also found in the lung. It tends to stay local and not spread."

I drew a picture of the lungs and showed his lesion perched atop the right lung, which had three lobes, whereas the left had only two. I told him that after the right upper lobe was removed, the remaining two lobes would expand over several months, and he would get almost all of his lung capacity back. I felt like a dry textbook, but he nodded slowly, contemplating, seeming partly reassured by the factoids and by the picture.

"Will I always need monitoring?"

"We'll continue to scan you, every six months at first, and then every year."

Azziz told me he'd rather not go to New York University for his surgery, because of his miserable three-hour wait for the needle biopsy. I was unable to convince him that the inconvenience and confusion could happen anywhere, in any hospital. The most important things about the biopsy were that they'd gotten a good sample, the pathology had come back quickly, and the scans had shown limited disease.

"But it was chaos there," he said. "Some people were hanging out while others were mourning. People in wheelchairs and stretchers were in the hallways, and around them staff were laughing and joking. I didn't feel confident they would really send you my results and not mix them up with someone else's."

But Azziz was not reasoning out the role the hospital had actually played in sussing out his cancer. Disarray and disorganization make patients more fearful. He was attributing to New York University a greater threat potential than I believed it had. This was all tied in with his emotional response to the news. His fear was deep and primitive, already verging on fight or flight. He couldn't reason through the actual risks presented by his cancer. He was consumed by the fear of death that cancer brings to many patients.

What stayed in Azziz's mind even after the good news of no spread was the threat of danger rather than the hope for cure. He remained on the alert. His fear wouldn't shut off. Instead of focusing on how to get better, he continued to collect information about how he might get worse, drawn from an interwoven network of alarming facts disseminated by the media.

I accepted his choice to leave NYU. Just as allowing a trapped animal to choose a possible path of escape may diminish its terror, so with humans regaining control in life-or-death situations is a way to channel primitive fear.

Azziz was going to go uptown to the Memorial Sloan-Kettering Cancer Center. He would have his surgery and his chemotherapy there. Reputation didn't ensure outcome, but it made Azziz feel slightly more comfortable.

We would keep in touch by phone, and he would return to see me two weeks after the surgery. We shook hands and hugged before he left.

A Healthy Patient's Worry

As soon as Azziz left the office, I encountered another worried patient. "Nelly Foster" had been my patient for eight years, and I rarely treated her for anything beyond the muscle soreness that came from running the New York City marathon.

Occasionally, she would call me for bronchitis, and I would prescribe an antibiotic. Like many American doctors, I sometimes tend to overprescribe antibiotics because of a placebo effect. There could be bacteria behind the coughing, but antibiotics also have a calming influence. Many patients are relieved by the doctor's taking action on their behalf.

Nelly was a patient who could not effectively use reason to diminish her fears. Nor did her extensive physical exercise routine help alleviate her concerns as it did for so many other patients. For Nelly, her worries required frequent attention and were out of proportion to the real risk of physical disease. She usually responded to large doses of my reassurance in addition to the occasional antibiotic.

This time, Nelly Foster was in a panic. She had been in to see me once weekly for the past three weeks. On the first visit she said she was so overcome with coughing and heavy breathing at night that she was petrified she might stop breathing altogether.

I'd diagnosed seasonal allergy plus a sinus infection, but antihistamines, antibiotics, steam, and a humidifier hadn't done the trick. On the second visit I prescribed a decongestant and a steroid nasal spray and arranged for her to see an allergist. Now she was back again, still overcome with worry, shouting at me in the examination room that the allergist had done nothing and that the only thing that helped her was the Robitussin the pharmacist had wisely offered.

But there was a greater agenda for Nelly Foster. She was getting married the following week, at the age of forty-seven, for the first time, to a man named Earl. Over the years that I'd taken care of her, she'd shared with me her desire to become pregnant even as her menstrual cycle waned. By the time she met Earl it was almost too late, and he, a veteran of one childless marriage already, said he didn't think he wanted children.

I mark my life by the milestones in my patients' lives, and now Nelly was coming to see me, not with child news, but with marriage news. A small ceremony was set for the following week, and I suddenly realized that Nelly's upcoming wedding had evoked feelings of grief over being childless. This marriage meant leaving behind for good her dream of having children.

When she acknowledged her commitment to Earl, she added that she was starting to feel better physically. She no longer felt like she would stop breathing in the middle of the night.

As much as treating her congestion, I realized I was performing a ritual of medical clearance for the next phase in her life. Each milestone is a marker on the road to a patient's death. For Nelly, these fears between milestones manifested themselves as nervous complaints.

No matter what a doctor does to counter the primary fear of illness and death, unmitigated fear can still take root. Uncertainty over illness is directly connected to a patient's fear of death. We humans have an instinctive fear of death, to which we add an awareness of death that easily overwhelms our ability to assess risk. Because of the power of this awareness, it is helpful if we can learn not to be afraid of diseases that don't directly threaten us.

FEAR BECOMES THE RISK

My nurse informed me that there was a new patient in my examination room. His name was "Donald Tribune," and he said he was the owner of a taxi company.

He had a raspy voice from many years of smoking three packs a day. He had been avoiding doctors for the past five years since an internist handed him a CT scan report of his lungs that mentioned the possibility of cancer but also read, "No discernible mass." Instead of repeating the scan in a few months the way the doctor had suggested, Tribune ran away, keeping the report in a back pocket and worrying that he was going to die at any time.

Tribune also kept a list of medications he was supposed to take but never did. As opposed to Nelly Foster, who was comforted by pills, for Tribune, medicines were reminders that good health was just an illusion.

Tribune sat in my consultation room right where Azziz had sat and began to weep when I told him that he might not have cancer. For five years he had lived with the fear while continuing to smoke at the same time. The X-ray taken in my office, like the previous CT scan, showed the scars of the smoke but no discernible mass.

We developed a rapport, and he decided to go for a new CT scan. The results came back a week later and confirmed no cancer.

DEATH BY FEAR

The end of this story is not a happy one. When fear becomes its own malignant disease, it can be as difficult to contain as any aggressive virus or tissue-transforming tumor.

Mr. Tribune remained so nervous despite his good news that his blood pressure rose. The original CT scan had primed his fear pump and kept him feeling chronically on the verge of catastrophe. He was anxious most of the time but wouldn't take medicine for anxiety, and he wouldn't see a psychotherapist. Finally, on one of his most anxious days, his blood pressure rose out of control—and with no one there to help him, he experienced a sudden bleed into his head and died.

4

PLAYING POLITICS
WITH FEAR

Bush, it's now clear, intends to run a campaign based
on fear. And for me, at least, it's working: Thinking
about what these people will do if they solidify their
grip on power makes me very, very afraid.

—Paul Krugman, *New York Times*,
September 3, 2004

Nervous anticipation is making emotional and physical wrecks of some of us who live in the big cities
or obsessively watch the ever-alert cable TV news shows. Politicians on all sides are broadcasting their danger/safety messages via
the media's hype apparatus. This tapping into today's fears for
political purposes is perhaps even more dangerous than the terrorist acts themselves.

Our post-9/11 fears have become a free-floating anxiety that
lacks a specific target. We lack information as to where, when, or
how, or even whether, the threat is greater today than it was yes-
terday. We no longer know who to blame or who to follow to
safety.

The collateral damage of these fears appears to be many Americans' health. We are on perpetual alert status, which stokes safety concerns. This process wears us down and interferes with our ability to function.

MEET THE PRESS

On February 7, 2004, George W. Bush sat in the Oval Office and was interviewed by Tim Russert for NBC's *Meet the Press*. A major topic of discussion, amidst flagging public sentiment that the war in Iraq was necessary in order to somehow defend our national security, was President Bush's continuing assertion that Saddam Hussein had possessed weapons of mass destruction along with the ability to use them against us. During the interview, the president said, "Saddam Hussein was dangerous with weapons. He was a dangerous man in the dangerous part of the world."

There was certainly a worldwide consensus that Hussein was heinous. There was little argument with the fact that he'd authorized torture and brutal killing of multitudes in his region. But was he a direct threat to America?

Bush's rhetoric was intended to instill the notion that Hussein was the embodiment of the evil our country faced, and that Bush, our president, our protector, was the strong leader who had rid the world of the threat before its capacity to destroy us was realized. Bush said, "These are people who kill in a moment's notice. . . . When we see a threat we deal with a threat because they become imminent. . . . Saddam Hussein was a danger to America. . . . As president of the United States, my most solemn responsibility is to keep this country safe."

How many people tried to envision what was actually being suggested here—Saddam supplying the terrorists with a large stash of chemical or biological weapons that would be smuggled here undetected, culminating in a drone plane flying from offshore to deliver its payload unobserved, with the wind blowing in just the right direction?

But in reality chemical and biological weapons are effective WMDs only in an extreme worst-case scenario. Under most circumstances they would actually be WSDs, weapons of *some* destruction, still hardly comforting, but a more accurate term.

Nevertheless, the rhetoric of protection continued. As Bush said on *Meet the Press*, "The war against terrorists is a war against individuals who hide in caves in remote parts of the world, individuals who have these kind of shadowy networks, individuals who deal with rogue nations."

Notice how the terrorist description merged with the description of Saddam and his henchmen. If the public believed there was a single danger, embodied in Iraq and its tentacles, then the president would have been justified in sending our troops over there to protect us. In taking this strong stand, he was echoing the position taken by prior presidents, specifically Abraham Lincoln and Franklin Roosevelt, who were reelected based on a promise to protect us from dangers.

To continue selling the war, the Bush administration, like both Democrats and Republicans before it, kept generating fear.

The same kind of fearmongering was used in the overall fight against terror. As the years elapsed since September 11, 2001, bin Laden and his al-Qaeda network remained a primary justification for an elaborate world war on terror.

The ultimate argument was put forth by Harvard professor Michael Ignatieff in his book *The Lesser Evil*. Unless we extinguish these terrorists now, the argument went, they could mushroom into nuclear-weapon-wielding menaces who could blow up our cities. Isn't it a small price to give up some liberties now rather than face an ineradicable danger later on?

The answer to this is no, if one believes that we can't allow fear to control us. Despite terrorism, the risk to the individual remains quite low.

Since it is difficult to actually quantify the real risk of disaster, it is easy for politicians to manipulate the public based on fear of the unknown or these worst-case scenarios. Time after time, the far-reaching fear and an increased sense of vulnerability tied to the World Trade Center attack were used by the Bush administration in its public cry to protect us. Time after time, coached by our leaders, we personalized risks that were remote.

OUR PROTECTORS FROM WHAT?

While drawing our attention to these unlikely dangers, at the same time the government revealed a porous safety net, which automatically spread more fear. As Robert Reich wrote in the *American Prospect* in August 2004, "America's intelligence system failed to see terrorist threats coming from al-Qaeda prior to September 11 that should have been evident, and then, after 9/11, saw terrorist threats coming from Iraq that didn't exist. A system that doesn't warn of real threats and does warn of unreal ones is broken."

The Bush administration refused to properly police and regulate certain potential targets such as chemical plants (among other big-money special interests). A 2002 Brookings Institution study, as well as a Government Accountability Office report, identified security at chemical plants as being underaddressed. The Brookings report held that chemical plants were not "adequately protected against terrorist attack." The GAO warned in March 2003 that "no one has comprehensively assessed the security of chemical facilities." Meanwhile, administration lawyers blocked efforts by the EPA to beef up security at chemical plants.

Bush and his team directed us away from these potential dangers involving private interest groups and toward those that were said to apply to our sense of personal safety, suggesting that our way of life, our "freedom," was under attack. The Bush wars and the associated rhetoric were supposedly a defense of that freedom.

THE FEAR CAMPAIGN

Fear became a major theme of the 2004 presidential campaign. As Frank Rich wrote in the *New York Times* on July 25, 2004, "In the fear game, the Democrats are the visiting team, playing at a serious disadvantage. Out of power, they can't suit up officials at will to go on camera to scare us." They did the next best thing by nominating a war hero, playing this credential for all it was worth, while the Republicans seemed to be counting on the historically proven paradox that the less safe we felt, the more likely we would be to stick with a familiar face come Election Day. And even for those who claimed they wanted someone different, judging from Kerry's endorsement of the war on terror and Iraq, there was no indication that fearmongering would have been less prevalent in a Kerry administration.

"The leitmotif of the 2004 election is fear," John Harwood wrote in the *Wall Street Journal* on September 1, 2004. While Republicans were promoting Bush as the securer of safety and denigrating Kerry as "unfit for command," Democrats in turn were warning of the danger of another four years with Bush, especially with regard to civil liberties. The *American Prospect*, a leading reflector of liberal Democratic sentiment, was running covers depicting an elephant's trunk around the neck of the Statue of Liberty, and labeling Bush "the Most Dangerous President Ever."

The overall effect of this back-and-forth fearmongering was to make the public feel even more unsafe.

The perpetual promulgation of worst-case scenarios causes unnecessary panic. In the political context it is clear that this panic can be used both to control and to rally support. In Bush's famous speech to the nation on March 17, 2003, giving Hussein forty-eight hours to get out of town, Bush said, "The danger is clear: using chemical, biological, or, one day, nuclear weapons, obtained with the help of Iraq, the terrorists could . . . kill thousands or hundreds of thousands of innocent people in our country."

How the Government Benefits from Fear

A year later, in February 2004, days before Bush's *Meet the Press* interview with Tim Russert, Al Gore, casting himself as a non-alarmist among Democrats, gave the keynote speech at the three-day conference on fear at New School University. While Bush was getting ready to project his protector image to millions via Russert, Gore spoke to mere hundreds about how fear was used as rhetoric to help politicians like Bush stay in office.

Gore began by stating that the goal of terrorists was to cause a wave of fear out of proportion to the true danger. "Terrorism, after all, is the ultimate misuse of fear for political ends. Indeed, its specific goal is to distort the political reality of a nation by creating fear in the general population that is hugely disproportionate to the actual danger the terrorists are capable of posing."

Gore continued with an indictment of how Bush's rush to war was itself a form of terrorism. "President Bush and his administration have been force-feeding the American people a grossly exaggerated fear of Iraq that was hugely disproportionate to the actual danger posed by Iraq."

His former woodenness gone, Gore weighed his words carefully and hammered them out to the rapt audience that filled the auditorium or watched him from video screens in nearby rooms. He provided historical perspective, showing how fear of terrorists rather than from terrorists had been used throughout American history to justify restrictions of our liberties. Examples included the Alien and Sedition Acts of 1798, the internment of Japanese Americans in World War II, and the McCarthy abuses of the Cold War.

As former vice president Gore's talk drew to a conclusion, he provided a vision of hope that might free us from the sense of capitulation that fear politics demanded from us. He said, "There are only the politics of fear and the politics of trust. One says: 'You are encircled by monstrous dangers. Give us power over your freedom so we may protect you.' The other says: 'The world is a baffling and hazardous place, but it can be shaped to the will of men.'"

When Fear Grabs the Headlines

The following morning, the fear conference reconvened in the same auditorium. This time there was a panel that included Joseph Ledoux, Barry Glassner, a professor of sociology at the University of Southern California and the author of *The Culture of Fear*, and Tom Pyszczynski.

Barry Glassner was the speaker just before Dr. Pyszczynski, and whereas Pyszczynski described the essential importance of culture to house and sublimate our fears, Glassner went to extensive lengths to show that ours was a culture of deception, in which we were misdirected to the wrong dangers. If culture was crucial to reassure us, the culture of deception could make us more afraid.

Glassner, appearing youthful with a full head of black curls and thick black retro glasses, said that we live in the safest times in human history and that we are being manipulated by fear unnecessarily. Said Glassner, "Crime rates plunge, while surveys show Americans think crime rates are rising. At a time when people are living longer and healthier, people are worried about iffy illnesses." The media focus on particular aspects of a problem, inflating and distorting it until the audience has internalized the experience and considers the reported danger an accepted fact.

Glassner's book focused on the 1990s, and though his conclusions were applicable to the post-9/11 period, there has been an important change since then. American society *feels* more vulnerable, not so much because of 9/11 itself as because of the extensive media coverage of it. The mushrooming of cable news coverage since 9/11 has added an important amplifier to the problem.

Amplification has been used repeatedly to hype potential contagions in the post-9/11 world, beginning with anthrax, in which the free-floating anxiety of 9/11 was transferred to a hysterical fear of our mail.

The fear apparatus was less pervasive before 9/11, though it was growing in that period. Said Glassner, "Between 1990 and 1998, the murder rate decreased by 20 percent, while murder stories on media newscasts increased by 600 percent (not even counting O. J. Simpson). Isolated incidents are treated as trends. Fearmongering focused on youth violence. In the 1980s and '90s, politicians and journalists acted as if just about every young American was a potential mass murderer, despite the actual decrease in murders. In 1996 and '97, fear was tied to school violence—William Bennett called it the violence of 'super predators.' Yet urban crime continued to drop, so the media was finally compelled to change its jargon to talk about isolated murders in suburban and rural areas. But three times more kids were killed by lightning than violence. The Columbine murders were unprecedented, but for twelve months before there was nothing. Less than 1 percent of homicides occur in or around schools."

Media obsession not only misinforms but also diverts attention from the real dangers. As Glassner pointed out, though the murder rate was decreasing in the 1990s, at the same time guns were responsible for an increasing percentage of murders. Guns were more readily available, and more and more people had them. Of course, the National Rifle Association tried to block widespread awareness of this fact, and the media enabled this misdirection because bald statistics aren't as sexy as the narrative of an individual attack.

Misdirection means ignoring the fact that millions don't have health insurance and millions are malnourished. Glassner said, "Mad cow is only a tiny risk. Only 150 deaths compared to other food borne illnesses. The media misdirects us away from 500,000 cases of salmonella food poisoning. They use an isolated incident to wrongly profess a trend."

Leaders create fear around their central issues, making them seem more urgent than the things they're less interested in. Republicans create fear by saying Social Security will go bankrupt if they aren't allowed to fix it, and Democrats create fear by saying the Republican plan will just end Social Security altogether. Democrats create fear of guns, and Republicans tap into a fear that the government will take guns away from law-abiding citizens. Democrats persuade people that Republicans will take away civil liberties, and then the Republicans enforce the Patriot Act to protect us, but make people feel afraid to show dissent.

Bureaucrats use fear by playing Chicken Little. They can claim at every turn that a disaster may be coming, thereby keeping their budgets high and avoiding blame should disaster really strike. Department of Homeland Security warnings may be driven more by the need for higher congressional appropriations and self-justification in case of an attack, rather than actually preventing or minimizing an attack.

OUR PROTECTOR

On December 21, 2003, four days before Christmas, Tom Ridge, who served as homeland security secretary during Bush's first term, had raised the terror alert status back to orange, which meant a high risk of a terrorist attack over the remainder of the holiday season in the United States. There were several reasons given for this announcement: the increased buzz and threats circulating among al-Qaeda members, the fact that this terrorist group tended to strike on an every-other-year basis, plus the logic that we were more vulnerable as a country with increased travel taking place during the holiday season.

Along with this announcement came the usual disclaimer—the MSNBC headline anchor said it was intended not to spread fear but to encourage preparation. Somehow we would be sending a message back to al-Qaeda that we were ready for them.

But no one out on the streets really knew how to conceptualize this. Was al-Qaeda coming? When and where? The alert had been raised many times, but many of us didn't know how to respond. We had gotten used to the warnings, but the possibility of an attack could still cause some nervousness.

Since 9/11, many of us have become more apprehensive. Like Dr. Sabban's rats, once alerted, we are more easily frightened a second time, or a third. Of course, worrywarts in places like Idaho and Montana don't have New York and Washington's sense of vulnerability to begin with, no matter how much cable news they watch.

Many in the United States had a false sense of security before 9/11. With the exception of the War of 1812, our continent had never been invaded while the American flag flew over it. The 9/11 attacks happened suddenly and opened us up to feelings of vulnerability that countries like Russia and Israel were more accustomed to. Over time, even if we gain a better perspective and learn to redefine our personal risk as low, still, the worldwide interconnection of our media outlets via satellite and Internet practically assures that the bug du jour, or the scare of the moment, will instantly escalate into worldwide concern via the media megaphone.

The sense of fear in the United States today seems greater than at the height of the Cold War, when the Soviet Union was a more tangible threat, with an enormous arsenal of nuclear weapons aimed at us.

Why? The greatest reason for the change is the growing fracturing and parceling of information into hyped media sound bites. No matter how safe we are, all we need to hear is the word *danger* or *threat,* and the cycle of worry starts. When one cycle is extinguished, another one takes its place.

In the post-9/11 world, the only cable station that doesn't scare us is the cartoon channel, which lacks headlines or news updates of any kind. However, in January 2004, I even noted on the cartoon channel a shift in the wrong direction, when "Grandpa" on *Hey, Arnold!* told the other characters that they'd better "watch out for weapons of mass destruction."

SAFETY SPEAK

The New York Police Department sent a memo to New York University Medical Center on December 23, 2003. It was filled with the kinds of warnings quickly becoming ubiquitous in New York

City. It was the new safety speak. It included sage advice on how to be on the lookout for a terrorist. The criteria for a suspected terrorist included someone who wore baggy clothing or who exhibited nervousness or extreme concentration, tunnel vision or singular determination, and perspiration. At NYU Medical Center, this description might fit a typical medical student.

Hyperattention to security and danger profiling spreads more worry than comfort, and there is no evidence that it increases actual safety one iota.

New Year's Eve 2003

With the holiday season approaching, terrorism fears were once again hyped. Homeland Security Secretary Ridge announced that he had good information that an attack was imminent, and we were back on orange alert nationwide. Here in New York City, we had never left orange, and we had long been used to seeing police with sniffing dogs and even National Guardsmen in combat fatigues at the entrances to our tunnels and bridges.

On Christmas Day 2003, Eric Lichtblau and Craig Smith of the *New York Times* reported that officials were tightening airport security from Paris to Los Angeles. CNN advised its viewers to go about their usual holiday plans while at the same time reporting that terrorists might once again attack a prominent U.S. target by hijacking an airplane.

In France, Air France canceled six flights between Paris and Los Angeles at the urging of United States officials, who said they suspected that up to a half-dozen passengers on the flights had "links to terrorism." In Chicago, officials imposed flight restrictions over downtown at the request of the mayor's office, blocking small aircraft below three thousand feet for fear the Sears Tower might be hit. Officials at Los Angeles International Airport banned passengers from being picked up or dropped off at the terminal curb. The intelligence agencies were reportedly most concerned about flights originating in France and Mexico based on terrorism intelligence, or chatter, gleaned from electronic spying as well as informants.

Jet fighters patrolled our skies and others were on alert, but rather than make us feel safer, it caused many of us to worry.

On December 31, Flight 490 from Mexico to the United States was canceled because American officials felt it might be the target of an attack, and then on New Year's Day, British Airways Flight 223, which was scheduled to embark for Dulles Airport in Washington, D.C., was canceled after British government officials warned the airline of security concerns, according to the *New York Times*. This same flight had been the subject of concern a day earlier, when it was accompanied to Dulles by F-16s, and the passengers were questioned upon landing. Again on Friday, January 2, 2004, Flight 223 was canceled and kept on the ground in London.

On New Year's Eve, I was in Fort Lauderdale with my wife and two young children. We were supposed to depart for New York's LaGuardia airport at 8:30 P.M., but the plane was held in Boston for "security reasons." We were assigned another plane but had to wait for the pilots to arrive from Boston to fly us to New York. The Boston plane finally arrived at 11:15 P.M., but even after we boarded the new plane, it was held until after midnight before departing. We were told that we were still waiting for the pilots, though I had seen them come off the Boston plane. It was clear to me—as well as to several other passengers—that we were being held on the ground until after midnight while New York was being watched.

This type of precaution, without being told the reasons behind it or the information that the government was acting on, caused a hum of nervousness to pervade airports everywhere on New Year's Eve. Unease and uncertainty caused us to be afraid.

Our government wanted its citizens to know that it was protecting us. But the way the information was being parceled out by the government followed by the jarring media announcements made us worry automatically. And the more we worried, the more our leaders maintained that we needed them to protect us from unseen dangers.

No matter what the reason for the alerts, they made us worry far more than we needed to in order to protect ourselves. We could ignore them, but we could never stop worrying entirely once the first fight-or-flight response had been triggered.

PREPARATIONS

In early 2004, I discussed our readiness for terrorism with my neighbor Dr. Leon Pachter, the head of the trauma service at New York University and Bellevue. He had stood outside Bellevue with me on September 11, 2001, waiting for the potential survivors who never came, and he had since volunteered his time to help organize an emergency response system in New York City.

"Forget it," he said. "Since September 11, there's been no real preparation. Doctors and so-called first responders are no more organized now than they were back then."

I shook my head. First the government and the media exaggerate a potential threat; then they try to show that they are protecting us from it; then we discover that the protection is faulty, and we become even more afraid.

It was a good thing that Dr. Pachter's comments weren't publicized. If the news media got hold of quotes like his, it might cause yet another unnecessary panic.

Instead, the *New York Times* headlined the opposite news on February 15, 2004, claiming that "New York Police Take Broad Steps in Facing Terror." I was more inclined to believe Pachter, especially since the *Times* was using mostly unnamed sources. This article attempted to show how extensive preparations were being made by the police in conjunction with "city health officials" and "federal authorities."

Training reportedly involved potential plans to board cruise ships, and there was a plan in the works to test the city's air for biological agents, and to provide antibiotics and vaccines if necessary. Another drill prepared the coroner's office for dealing with corpses contaminated from chemical weapons.

New sophisticated detection devices included a system that would detect the presence of more than a hundred different viruses or bacteria within forty-five minutes. Since poor New York didn't yet have this latest technology, it was forced to rely in the meantime on Biowatch, a system whereby ten "nondescript monitors" would "sniff the air for fifteen lethal pathogens," with an alarming twenty-four-hour delay for processing results. Old-style radiation detectors were reportedly being used throughout the city. Two hundred distribution centers were also being planned so that as many as eight million people could receive emergency treatment in five to ten days' time, relying on the federal stockpile of vaccines and drugs. If a quarantine should prove necessary, city health officials were ready "to persuade New Yorkers exposed to a deadly infectious pathogen to stay at home."

But this lavish outdated display—even if it actually existed— was likely to be of little use. These science-fictionesque measures were designed for an almost inconceivable worst-case scenario. Instead of feeling protected, people I knew who read the *Times* article immediately broke into a cold sweat.

Old and Recurrent Threats

On Monday, August 2, 2004, a terror alert was issued that financial centers in some of our major cities, including New York, were under direct threat by al-Qaeda. Police presence increased visibly, traffic thickened, and people everywhere wondered whether they were about to be attacked. President Bush predictably announced, "We are a country in danger. We are doing everything we can to confront this danger."

The alert was based on the computer files and related information uncovered following the arrest of an al-Qaeda operative in Pakistan.

By Tuesday it was determined that much of the information released was in fact three or four years old, and there was no evidence that a terror plot was actually underway.

The *New York Times*, the *Washington Post*, and other major newspapers, after splattering the initial concerns over their front pages on Monday, on Tuesday sheepishly front-paged the qualifying information. And a Tuesday *Times* editorial read, "But it's unfortunate that it is necessary to fight suspicions of political timing, suspicions the administration has sown by misleading the public on security."

Once again the public appeared to have been thrown into a fight-or-flight mode unnecessarily. Once again, unlike animals, we were transmitting danger signals based on abstract information. Abstract risk assessment is an advantage for humans over animals only as long as we can learn to use it accurately.

Agenda-driven communication creates a problem with a basic mechanism such as fear. The al-Qaeda report was overpersonalized, the danger perceived was out of proportion to the real risk, and the fear response was useless or even maladaptive.

By Wednesday, government officials, including Tom Ridge, the secretary of homeland security at the time, tried to salvage the situation by saying that al-Qaeda took a long time to size up and stalk a potential target. But by this time, the public imagination was already diverted, though the fear of al-Qaeda remained just below the surface.

In fact, in a final preelection ad, the Bush campaign cast the terrorist threat as menacing wolves prowling through a shadowy forest, and tried to capitalize one last time on our fear. They knew well by this point that our attention has an on-and-off switch, but our fear does not.

5

DISASTERS:
REAL OR IMAGINED

If they can get you asking the wrong questions, they
don't have to worry about the answers.

—Thomas Pynchon

In August 2003, I was working in my office in New York
City when the lights went out. The phones went dead
too, and I silently counted off the minutes. At first I thought this
might be terrorism. I felt my way along the concrete-walled hallway
down seven floors to the lobby of the building, where the doormen
were listening to their battery-powered radio. It soon became clear
to them and me and almost everyone in the Northeast that this
wasn't any sort of terrorist attack, but the mother of all blackouts.

I joined the crowd on First Avenue, and the feeling was warm
and friendly, camaraderie offsetting fear and worry.

WAYS TO OFFSET FEAR

Since the blackout was a shared reality and wasn't simply speculative, like so many other hyped threats in the wake of 9/11, there

were useful actions to be taken. Certain practical ideas helped people respond calmly and without panic. The combination of no TV to hype the problem and simple preparations at home worked to help people stay calm. Here are practical precautions that helped many people avoid panic:

- It was useful for everyone to have available a land-line telephone that did not require electricity.

- If you weren't feeling well and you couldn't reach your physician, then it was appropriate to call 911.

- Opening the windows was prudent. In a power outage such as this it was wise to keep well hydrated. You could easily become dehydrated without realizing it. If your water supply was on an electrical pump and went off, you could use the ice and water in your refrigerator for several hours, as long as you avoided opening and closing the door frequently.

- It was important to continue taking most regular medicines, especially those for heart problems and high blood pressure.

Though the blackout of 2003 affected much of the Northeast, and a terrorist attack would likely affect only a small part of the population, the sudden civic paralysis during a terrorist attack would probably be far worse. The public may be stirred to greater hysteria if the full-court media press, including television and Internet, is available to egg them on. In terrorist attacks, panic is the greatest weapon.

The blackout brought out the best in New Yorkers. People calmly shared food and water on the stoops outside their darkened apartments. Since the blackout neutralized our TV screens, for once we could not be whipped into a frenzy by twenty-four-hour cable news reports.

Is it a coincidence that a blackout is the only kind of disaster that can't be endlessly dissected on TV? It's hard to come to any conclusion other than that, without the constant news crawl and the breathless speculation of news analysts, we just weren't as terrified.

Instead of being riveted to a disaster-magnifying TV screen, many of us rediscovered our staircases. Several of my invalid patients who could not use stairs waited patiently in their apartments and wisely rationed their ice and water, cooling themselves at regular intervals.

We learned to distinguish the luxuries from the necessities. Reading by candlelight in front of an open window, talking with your neighbor—as new habits go, these weren't all bad.

In my own particular apartment complex, people gathered around the doormen who were listening to the radio reports and giving us updates whenever we asked. Seeing them automatically take this role reminded me that doorpeople always have had the comforting role of go-to people.

An Organized Response Team

Ironically, the power returned to Long Island twelve hours earlier than to many parts of our powerhouse city. My wife and I collected our young children and drove the two hours out to our Sag Harbor house, arriving there with our thawing perishables midday on Friday, the second day of the blackout. What we found there was a well-organized collection of emergency responders, ready to help residents make it through the emergency without excess fear.

The Cove Deli, a tick on the odometer past my house, is an old-fashioned place to go to in Sag Harbor for unspoken comfort on a dark night. Any convenience store can offer bright lights, but the bleached white glow, the constant electrical hum, and the under-aged fidgety cashier who has read too many thrillers hardly offer comfort. The convenience store—because we have seen it through the eye of the security camera in too many crime movies and news reports—is part of the culture of fear.

In our Cove Deli the woman behind the counter has bleached her hair half purple with a streak of melon or mango, and she has tiny rings of silver displayed on earlobes and navel. Yet I feel confident that we can pass the time of day here, and ask about the weather and she'll know. She knows the neighborhood and its people, she is calm, and I know that in an emergency she'll know just how to get hold of the fire guys or the police guys or an ambulance. Feeling safe is all about context. If you were to transplant her into the eerie luminescence of the 7-Eleven, the feeling would be lost.

The fire department is the basis for a massive premium hike on our homeowner's policy because it isn't a paid group. Nevertheless, these firefighters are available for community support, they serve pancake breakfasts on Sunday, and they are razor-sharp responders in an emergency. These men are Sag Harbor's fear guardians, they help everyone feel more secure. It is their old-fashioned quality, not connected to time clocks, that defines them and reassures the citizens. These groups are an endangered species, though they can still be found in small towns throughout the country.

In Sag Harbor the local oldies radio station, WLNG-FM, occupies a one-story building on the cove. I never thought they were equipped for emergency broadcasting, but they do have a generator. During the blackout, while the Cove Deli was handing out free coffee and doughnuts, the firetrucks were patrolling the streets, and the radio station was broadcasting updates every fifteen minutes and telling people how to stay safe.

Radio stations have traditionally played a crucial role in informing citizens and defusing panic. Unfortunately, the commercial rush to gobble up local stations and convert everything to centralized broadcasting can undermine that role. Of course, not all local-run stations provide calm and not all nationally syndicated radio causes panic, but the problem of being out of touch with the community that you're supposed to be informing can be disastrous. In January 2002 in Minot, North Dakota, a terrible accident at a chemical plant released noxious ammonia gas into the air. People holed up in their basements and awaited information about whether it was safe to go out or not. There was supposed to be an emergency broadcast system in place, but it failed to work. Clear Channel, a national conglomerate, had bought up all the local stations in Minot, and although spokesmen then and since have denied culpability, they and only they were responsible for a radio blackout at a time of great need. The absence of information at a crucial time was so frightening, it was difficult for people in Minot to feel safe after that.

WHY SO CALM?

On the second day of the blackout, with the power long restored to Sag Harbor and the rest of eastern Long Island, I followed the cable news accounts of the struggle to return power to the industrial northeast corridor. During the later stages of the blackout, Con Ed was being asked to parcel out radio sound bite updates that unreliably estimated when the power might come back on in the parts of New York City that were still affected.

I recalled the blackout of 1965, the first of New York's three major blackouts, which was characterized by a ceremonial formality befitting disaster management in those days. Con Ed was called by its full name, Consolidated Edison, with spokesmen who I imagined wore tight-fitting suits with starched collars, and there were no sound bites, but rather clear and complete explanations about what was happening and when things might improve. Maybe I am romanticizing, but I recall those radio updates as more comforting. Today's updates are generally slick and more streamlined. WLNG is the exception.

We have gadgeted up to the max—we have so many air conditioners, electrical outlets, hair dryers, and blowers, we can no longer contemplate the source of our power. Even our water and our phones are tied into the electrical grid these days. Our grid is out of date, it includes old equipment that was built for much less usage than it gets, but we are oblivious, loading it up with every device we can think of. It is as if by controlling our environment completely, we can maintain our distance from the ultimate fear penetration—mortality recognition. But it is a false comfort. We simulate everlasting life with devices to keep us—artificially—from our fear of death.

Ultimately the grim reaper will find us in our climate-controlled cars and houses.

Like many, I was most able to appreciate our country's excessive use of power on the one day we had to do without it. Power is one of our false crutches. We are afraid to lose it. Given our increasing dependence on energy, one might expect the sudden loss of electricity to be a focus of our fears. And yet the 2003 blackout in the Northeast was met with relative calm. Why? One answer was the absence of the usual media hype, an important catalyst of panic. Another answer was that when we were compelled to forgo electricity, many of us learned we didn't really need it.

And this was why we weren't really afraid. The secret to the calm of the blackout was that we found the time to talk to each other and reassure each other the way we did before the grid took over.

Some pundits smartly postulated that we were calm only after we knew this wasn't a terrorist act. Others insisted that fear fatigue over 9/11 had finally set in and that we were calm during the blackout simply because fear had exhausted itself. But this assertion was wrong. The next several panics would prove this wasn't the case.

THE HURRICANE

If I am correct that television whips us into a frenzy over the slightest inconvenience, and that TV's absence during the blackout allowed us to return to a more solid and supportive community structure, this theory was also borne out in reverse during the next "catastrophe," a natural one, a month later. The great storm of September 2003, Hurricane Isabel, only rated a 2 on a scale of 5 by the time it came inland, whereas Hurricane Floyd, in 1999, was a 5 and did a lot more damage (over $6 billion in damage compared to $1 billion for Isabel). Yet Floyd wasn't perceived with nearly as much panic. Areas that Isabel didn't even touch, such as New York, were cowering in her shadow, because TV news, back in full throttle this time, projected an evil menace. Both the forecasting and the reaction to the storm were exaggerated. Weathermen and correspondents appeared worried and were shown being blown about by the wind.

This hyperbole was also present in many newspaper accounts, as print and broadcast media combined to alarm us. Page 2 of the *New York Daily News* reported it this way on September 19, 2003: "Hurricane Isabel raced inland from North Carolina last night before weakening to a tropical storm, leaving at least eight people dead, more than 2.5 million people without power, some 1,500 planes grounded and the nation's capital shut down."

And page 1 of the *New York Times* on September 20, 2003, reported: "Hurricane Isabel petered out over Canada last night, leaving a wide scar of destruction: nearly two dozen deaths, flooded cities in Virginia and Maryland, millions of people without power and tens of thousands of fallen trees that punctured roofs and blocked roads from North Carolina to New Jersey."

"A wide scar of destruction" was a hyperbolic phrase that simply didn't fit the facts, no matter how many people were inconvenienced by the storm. And "puncture" was a painful word that a reader could too easily personalize.

True, nationwide twenty-three people died because of Isabel, millions were without power for several days, and property damage was significant, affecting tens of millions, maybe more. People in the affected areas were right to take precautions, especially at a time when information was still evolving.

But a comparison between the blackout and the hurricane in the Northeast suggests that the reaction to the blackout was more orderly and less frenzied precisely because television itself was

71

blacked out. Not only was the hurricane not a risky storm to many who feared it, but it wasn't even really a hurricane by the time it reached the Northeast. Yet workers everywhere were going home early, the U.S. Congress had the day off, and the D.C. subway system was closed.

More than a thousand miles away from the storm, my patients were canceling their appointments for fear of the weather. Yet the Metro section of the *Times* reported the next day, "For all the apocalyptic forecasting, Hurricane Isabel moved through the New York region with more of a whimper than a bang . . . the fears of extensive flooding that prompted officials to declare emergencies and muster rescue vehicles for low-lying areas proved groundless."

Meanwhile, on the Outer Banks of North Carolina, where the storm really did cause some inconvenience, the overreaction was exponentially greater. The local police, to encourage recalcitrant citizens to depart, told people to write their names on their forearms in permanent marker to make their corpses easy to identify. They also collected names of next of kin.

Hurricane Isabel was personified by the news media as a massive potential killer, instead of the unthinking, unfeeling, rain and wind storm it was. It was too easy for John Doe on the street to accept the media spin as gospel and become unnecessarily frightened. Isabel was part of a fiction constructed by the news coverage itself. Reporters would seek outside points of view from experts, but these comments were rapidly recast in the context of the larger story of Isabel, by media definition a great consuming storm.

The facts were there to interpret differently: it was downgraded to level 2 by the time it hit North Carolina, weakened partly by a contrary gust of warm air while still at sea. Climbing up the coast, it was quickly reclassified as a tropical storm. We saw the new designation, tropical storm, and yet we continued to worry as the media encouraged this danger perception.

Of the twenty-three people who died from Isabel, most were in car accidents, a tiny minority challenging the power of the tropical storm. An off-duty policeman in Long Beach, New York, where the storm never really took hold, died swimming through strong waves in the middle of the night. It would be more accurate to classify his foolish death as unrelated to Isabel.

In serving as an authoritative source of information, while at the same time magnifying risk, the mainstream media—especially television—prey on our vulnerabilities and uncertainties, provoking us to be afraid. This is not to say that the media can't play a positive role in a true disaster. Accurate contextual forecasting can save many lives. In the wake of a true disaster, accurate reporting can also help people recover, while hype is overpersonalized and wounds the public psyche. The recent tsunami in Asia was historic in terms of the extensive media coverage of the rescue effort, but it was also magnified to the point where people in California and elsewhere expected the next set of monster waves to mount their shores at any moment.

FALSE EVIDENCE

Joey Reynolds, the host of a late-night talk show on WOR radio in New York, has anointed fear "False Evidence Assumed Risk." "Fear," he said to me, "occurs when you don't think you can get what you need." Reynolds said many people deal with their own fear of personal loss by making others afraid in their place. "And no matter how inaccurate, the greater the impact, the more powerful the scarer feels."

Reynolds is radio's version of the counter person at the deli, and he lulls thousands of anxious insomniacs to sleep every night with his peculiar lullabies. His guests are like guests in his living room, and he serves them food and coffee as any generous host would.

I asked Reynolds if he thought we could become used to this fear over time, become desensitized to it, and evolve into better-balanced human beings despite our fragmented media-driven lives. He laughed his knowing cackle and said he didn't see how we could.

Spinning Fear

Narratives are employed by the mainstream media to advance a story, embodying aspects of fiction in order to hold their audiences' attention. These narratives tend to be compatible with others already in circulation. According to Barry Glassner, prior to 2001, a "sick society" narrative predominated. In this story, heroes were hard to find, and villains were domestic. The story line was ultimately about the decline of Western civilization.

Post-9/11, there was a new narrative. In this story, people were pulling together to fight a common enemy, villains were from foreign lands, and Americans were the object of scorn of the rest of the world. In this narrative, former villains were now portrayed as heroes, including the previously criticized fire department and police.

By the middle of 2004, the media were growing weary of the new narrative. The country was dividing into factions, no longer pulling together, and our leaders were once again perceived by many as villains worth discrediting, and Western civilization was once again seen as declining.

Despite this shift in emphasis, one strategy remained the same throughout all the narratives: newspapers, television, and radio continued to exaggerate minor dangers.

6

FINDING THINGS TO
WORRY ABOUT

We are hard-wired in our brains to fear first, think
second.

—David Ropeik, director of risk communication at
the Harvard Center for Risk Analysis

The risk terrain has changed. As more of our sense of
what threatens us comes from the news media and
the Internet, we lose track of our former guides. Trustworthy
mentors who put things in perspective for us have been largely
replaced by the bright lights of computer and TV screens that
offer info fragments, alarming us more often than they reassure. I
call this new fear terrain the topography of worry. Go-to people
have almost disappeared. We have lost the ability to assess risk.
We worry so much about danger that doesn't exist that our ability
to judge real danger is impaired. We see terrorists where there are
none. But the terrorist we should fear the most comes disguised as
one of us, and we cannot recognize him.

THE PROPER USE OF FEAR

In 1997, Gavin de Becker published *The Gift of Fear*, a book about how to use fear properly. He described fears that protect. Perhaps most important, he warned against the destructive power of prolonged states of unremitting fear. "Far too many people are walking around in a constant state of vigilance, their intuition misinformed about what really poses danger. It needn't be so. . . . Real fear is a signal intended to be very brief, a mere servant of intuition."

Some of de Becker's examples are extreme. The experience of being stalked by a murderer, or of being famous and the vulnerable object of adoring fans, is not something that most of us can, or should try to, relate to. But many women have tried to break off a relationship only to have the jilted suitor stalk them. "There's a lesson in real-life stalking cases. The fact that a romantic pursuer is relentless doesn't mean you are special—it means he is troubled." This kind of fear radar is not hype but protective. If someone in an intimate relationship feels intuitively that he or she is at risk, it is often the case, especially if the partner has a history of violence. De Becker pointed out that a partner's "justifications for violence" and threats are always to be taken seriously.

De Becker wrote convincingly that recognizing real danger is the key to real safety. He told the story of a woman who had just been raped who somehow sensed that she was about to be killed. De Becker called it a survival signal—when the perpetrator closed the window just when he said he was about to leave, the victim's unconscious signaled her into a fight-or-flight mode, and she sneaked away just as he went into her kitchen to find a knife. The closed window was a sign that the perpetrator didn't want the noise of the murder to be overheard. Previous to this she had been submissive, controlled by the violence, but with the closing of the window, her unconscious was alerted. With no time left, she rallied to take back control and escape.

De Becker is an expert in telling the difference between "a real warning and mere words." "If your intuition is informed accurately, the danger signal will sound when it should. If you come to trust this fact, you'll not only be safer, but it will be possible to live life nearly free of fear."

In 2002, in the post-9/11 climate, de Becker wrote a follow-up book: *Fear Less*. He concluded that despite the terrorist attacks we could still feel safe, in part by understanding our enemies were not "superhuman," but "merely anti-human." "Occasionally effective, to be sure, but our enemies are not powerful or ubiquitous."

Many of us tend to think of the world in terms of good guys and bad guys. Bad guys help create our fears. Good guys help us feel protected. Unfortunately, our concern about bad guys is often blown out of proportion to the real danger they represent.

After 9/11, we went through an adjustment period. We recognized that violence could happen to us. Many of us began to imagine worst-case scenarios involving weapons and terrorists, or we were handed them by the media. Wrote de Becker, "But if a person feels fear constantly, there is no signal left for when it's really needed. Thus, the person who chooses to worry all the time or to persistently chew on unwarranted fears is actually making himself less safe . . . trusting intuition is the exact opposite of living in fear. When you honor intuitive signals and evaluate them without denial, you can actually relax, even in these troubled times."

Post-9/11, the group of people who were covered by the debris of the falling World Trade Center expanded to include practically the entire country, as we were all bombarded by media images of destruction and fear of further terrorism. This fear was contagious. Many of us vacillated between feelings of disbelief and panic. Hyped symptoms of posttraumatic stress that included helplessness, numbness, and withdrawal from daily activities lasted for weeks.

The TV generation that grew up in America watching Wile E. Coyote zoom unhindered off countless cartoon cliffs in Roadrunner episodes, and later became watchers of building-crushing flicks such as *The Towering Inferno* and *Independence Day*, experienced an initial detachment from the real events of September 11, 2001. To many baby boomers, the balls of fire and the thunderous crash didn't seem real. But as the news media continued their focus, the horror began to sink in, which helped fuel an outpouring of concern and generosity as people everywhere banded together. Yet the news coverage also caused countless people who had lost no one to feel vulnerable and afraid. This wasn't true posttraumatic stress, since most of us hadn't experienced the trauma directly, but many personalized it and felt helpless. It was only over time, by sticking to family, to work, to passions, that we began to live normal lives again.

Dr. Rachel Yehuda, an expert on posttraumatic stress, said she thinks we struggled as a society in this period because we felt entitled to live a trauma-free life. We said, "Why me?" whereas "in a previous generation, no one had the expectation that something wouldn't happen to them—in those days, it was 'Why not me?' Previously, no one thought that being exposed to a trauma was that unusual."

"Posttraumatic stress is a mismatch between what we think the world should be like, and what it is really like. We aren't prepared. In a culture where you're expecting people to hate you, you let go of it for a lot longer. In Europe, for example, Jews always had the thought that a certain percentage wouldn't survive because of anti-Semitism. There was a lower expectation of peaceful existence, so the trauma of threat was less."

Dr. Yehuda also indicated that many of our scientists and those who inform us do us a disservice by overdramatizing their concerns. This grandiosity is part of what causes the public to overperceive risks. "We scientists can't tolerate being cogs in a wheel. Technology allows us to look at things we never could before. But we need to learn to be excited by what we do without telling a premature story. We can alarm people unnecessarily. And then we're stuck with our story, right or wrong."

ASSESSING RISK

We need to learn how to see risk in perspective, without overreacting to imagined dangers. Unfortunately, there is no consensus about what constitutes proper risk assessment or the best way to accomplish it. There is disagreement about who is an expert on risk, and some authors don't trust so-called experts at all because of their hidden agendas.

Published in 2002, David Ropeik and George Gray's book *Risk* is a practical guide intended to counter the hysteria caused by inaccurate public health reporting. Like de Becker, these authors believe that "we live in a dangerous world. Yet it is also a world far safer in many ways than it has ever been. Life expectancy is up. Infant mortality is down. Diseases that only recently were mass killers have been all but eradicated. Advances in public health, medicine, environmental regulation, food safety, and worker protection have dramatically reduced many of the major risks we faced just a few decades ago."

Ropeik and Gray developed a risk meter, a way of converting uncertainty into calculable risk. This risk meter assesses the likelihood of exposure to a potential danger as well as the consequences if you are one of the unlucky victims. The list of risks is extensive. Accidents, alcohol, tobacco, and obesity top the list in terms of both prevalence and severity of outcome. On the other end of the spectrum, vaccines are deemed essentially safe, mad cow disease is too rare in humans to be a factor, mercury doesn't really affect most people, and pesticides have a minimal impact.

The book attempts to reorient the reader. The authors would see dangers demystified. Their goal was to cut the public loose from hype and decontaminate us from prior misconceptions.

But Cass Sunstein, a professor of law at the University of Chicago, distrusts authorities who approach us with a "we know what's best for you" attitude. In 2002, Sunstein published the book *Risk and Reason*, in which he suggested that it is not the expert or official, but the populist/consumer advocate who generally has our best interests at heart. Sunstein would likely distrust Ropeik and Gray's fear meters as simplistic and too easily politicized, preferring instead the judgment of the same consumer advocates that Ropeik and Gray might see as inaccurate. According to Sunstein, "Populists insist that the very characterization of risks involves no simple 'fact,' . . . In the populist view . . . any judgment about risk is subjective . . . for populists, ordinary intuitions have normative force."

Like Ropeik and Gray, Sunstein also observed that information about risk was easily distorted, but unlike the authors of *Risk*, Sunstein generally blamed the government. He wrote, "Public officials know that they might be severely punished for downplaying a risk that is perceived as serious or for calling attention to a hazard that is perceived as trivial . . . to avoid charges of insensitivity . . . he [the public official] may make speeches and promote policies that convey deep concern about the very waste spill that he actually considers harmless." The effective politician rides the waves from one created danger to the next: "Thus people might be fearful, for a time, about some risk—shark attacks, or air travel in the aftermath of a disaster—that produces no concern at all after a few months."

In the 2002 book *Risk Communication*, Drs. Granger Morgan, Baruch Fischhoff, and their coauthors suggested the need to integrate common beliefs with facts about risk. On the surface, this book seems to be an attempt to bring together the facts of Ropeik and Gray with the public intuition of Sunstein. The people who inform us need to consider "how the public intuitively thinks about the risks and . . . which aspects of the scientific literature actually matter to the public. Then those topics must be presented in a balanced, credible, and comprehensive manner."

If this declaration seems idealistic, it is because it relies on an agenda-free panel of public-minded experts. But learning to assess risk doesn't simply mean finding the right expert to listen to. We also have to take responsibility for our own fear meters. As Bruce Schneier, a world-respected security expert, wrote in his 2003 book *Beyond Fear*, "When you're living in fear, it's easy to let others make decisions for you. . . . To get beyond fear, you have to start thinking intelligently about the trade-offs you make. You have to start evaluating the risks you face." Taking responsibility for our own fear meter sometimes means disregarding public pronouncements of risks, while at other times accepting them.

But Schneier was concerned that we can too easily give up our freedom to a blanket authority that promises to handle our risk assessment for us but ultimately doesn't make us more secure, in part because this authority may tend to magnify threats. Like Sunstein, Schneier did not trust the usual experts and officials to advise us or protect us.

Wrote Schneier, "We are told that we are in graver danger than ever, and that we must change our lives in drastic and inconvenient ways in order to be secure. We are told that we must sacrifice privacy and anonymity and accept restrictions on our actions. We are told that the police need new far-reaching investigative powers, that domestic spying capabilities need to be instituted, and that we must spy on each other. . . . But the reality is that most of the changes we're being asked to endure won't result in good security. . . . Even in the worst neighborhoods, most people are safe. It's hard to find a terrorist, kidnapper, bank robber, because there simply aren't that many in our society."

All the authors I have cited here are only partly right. We can't trust our risk experts because their facts are amplified by the government, the media, and public advocates, each depending on different agendas. But this doesn't mean we can automatically trust our intuition either, which, as de Becker wrote, is too often "misinformed." Any resolution of this dichotomy between misinforming experts and misguided intuition must involve retraining in how to recognize danger.

FINDING THINGS TO FEAR

On September 24, 2003, Anne Applebaum addressed the American terrain of worry in a column titled "Finding Things to Fear" in the *Washington Post*. She too was arguing against the wisdom of our unschooled intuition.

81

She described how we have miscalculated risks in the post-9/11 world because of our continuing anxiety. "After Sept. 11, 2001, thousands of people in this country swore off airplanes and began driving cars, apparently believing that cars are safer. In fact, the number of deaths on U.S. highways in a typical year—more than 40,000—is more than double the number of people who have died in all commercial airplane accidents in the past 40 years. To put it differently, the odds of being killed in a terrorist incident in 2002 were 1 in 9 million. In that same year, the odds of dying in a traffic accident were about 1 in 7,000. By taking the precaution of not flying, many people died."

Indeed, we are far safer in America, but we feel more afraid. We Americans have dramatically reduced our risk in every area of life, and our life spans were 60 percent longer in 2000 than in 1900. We have thousands of safety devices, including smoke detectors, circuit breakers, and air bags. We are protected against everyday mishaps of all kinds. Yet if our fears aren't real, we invent them.

The flow of information about risk has grown steadily during the same period of time that we have grown safer. Government officials, scientists, marketers, and the media use risk as a way to get attention. We tend to believe people who tell us that we are in danger. But when a warning such as an orange alert proves fallacious, we are slow to lose faith in the authority who has warned us. It takes several false warnings before we begin to question a source. By that time it is often too late, as our fear apparatus has already been triggered.

THE GOOD GUYS—THEN

Without mentors, without people we can trust, we grow more fearful. Doctors are among the groups of former good guys who have been discredited by our culture of worry. At the outset of the twenty-first century, patients are frightened by the latest technologies, but even more so by the impersonal and robotic way medical information is sometimes delivered. In the context of today's fear-provoking parceling out of health factoids, a well-informed communicative caring physician—a throwback to an earlier time in history—can make a big difference in calming fears and providing perspective.

The television character Marcus Welby was a paradigm of the kind of physician I'm referring to, who above all else offered a dose of reassurance and perspective to the dispensing of treatment. It is no accident that the Welby TV show reruns faded from the screen over the years, and even with the propagation of cable stations, this old medical show is still rarely seen. It is no wonder that ratings-obsessed TV got rid of Welby for being out-of-date, realizing that today's time-constrained doctors have too little in common with the hand-holders of yesteryear.

Marcus Welby, M.D., at the time a very popular medical drama set in middle America, ran from 1969 to 1976 on ABC. Robert Young as Welby was a study in bedside manner. The creased brow of concern, the empathetic pat on the patient's shoulder, these Welby trademarks delivered the message that a family doctor could guide a patient caringly through life's crises. *Marcus Welby, M.D.* was a response to the beginning of the technological age. In an era that celebrated the invention of coronary bypass surgery, a revolutionary procedure that didn't require hand-holding, Welby believed in comforting the patient as much as curing the illness.

In a movie that emphasized Welby's obsolescence, *The Return of Marcus Welby*, in 1984, a hospital tried to cut the privileges of its oldest doctors, including Welby. He argued ineffectively that a patient would be lost among the CT scanners, the MRIs, and the multitude of pills.

In the worried post-9/11 world, there was a surge of volunteerism among physicians that brought back memories of the old Welby house-call days. Unfortunately, this return to an era of physician guidance was short-lived, and we all soon went back to rushing for clipped fees from one worried patient to the next.

But in 2005, I believe we need to bring back the image of smiling old Doc Welby. In his world, there was less withholding of information or ignoring the frightened patient. The doctor battled a puzzling illness until the diagnosis was made, and the patient was attended to until he or she felt comfortable.

THE GOOD GUYS—NOW

As fear of illness connects directly to our central fear of death, there is a crucial need to comfort patients. But there are many obstacles to overcome. The process promises to get harder the more patients an insurance company expects doctors to see in a shorter period of time. And for the patients, there is less comfort to be found in the doctor's office.

The daily squeeze hit me hardest the morning I saw a likable sixty-eight-year-old patient of mine waving at me through my waiting-room window. I'd been treating him for years, but he didn't have an appointment, and I barely recognized him with his newly bald head, yellowed skin, and shaking hands. My office staff wanted to turn him away because the day's schedule was already packed, but I sensed his desperation and made time for him. His cancer was far more advanced than Azziz's, and in the examination room, he told me that his oncologist had informed him bluntly that his cancer was incurable and then dismissed him. I was the man's internist, his gatekeeper to the medical world, and he had returned to me—not for expertise, but for simple warmth.

I ended up spending an hour with him and told him that he could come in again anytime, with or without an appointment. I would do my best to arrange palliative or comfort care by speaking with the oncologist or possibly helping the patient to change oncologists. Though his prognosis was abysmal, he looked visibly calmer for having someone to count on—and I felt good about this—until the swelling crowd in the waiting room reminded me that my other patients had what in their eyes were equally important problems and equally urgent claims on a doctor's ever-shrinking time.

Not surprisingly, rushing doctors leads to panicked patients. "I just want a doctor I can talk to," many say.

There doesn't seem to be an easy solution. Mark Aaronson, a founding partner of one of New York's top doctor-defending malpractice law firms, believes that the pressures of managed-care medicine help to create a threatening climate where "the patient is looked upon, if not as an enemy, then as a potential lawsuit."

"What to do about it?" I asked him.

He said, "You have to create an atmosphere that encourages patients to be open with you, and where it's not inappropriate to present any problem."

Struggling with their professional identity, many doctors try to find themselves in the famed physicians' Hippocratic Oath, which says, in part, "In every house where I come I will enter only for the good of my patients, keeping myself far from all intentional ill-doing and all seduction." An effective doctor has to maintain integrity in order to be trusted rather than feared.

THE BAD GUYS—NOW

These days, though we are often afraid of people who don't directly threaten us, at the same time, in the rare instance when we encounter someone who is truly dangerous, we may not know how to identify him. With all the unnecessary worry we experience, there is still no guarantee that the real bad guys won't slip by us. In fact, perhaps if we weren't casting such a wide safety net, we might be more likely to notice a clear danger signal, like a pilot in training who says he doesn't need to know how to land.

The good Arthur R. Droba, J.D., M.D., is an internist who performs insurance screening physicals for the FAA in Sarasota, Florida. He examined the 9/11 terrorist leader Mohammed Atta and okayed him to fly. Afterward, he couldn't remember his infamous patient, though his nurse had heard him say he felt Atta was a "bad man."

Droba's friend Arne Kruithof is the forty-year-old director of the flight school in Sarasota that trained Ziyad Al-Jarrah, one of the hijackers of Flight 93. Kruithof found this Machiavellian pilot-to-be honest, hardworking, well mannered, and intelligent.

Al-Jarrah's own father, the minister of social affairs in Lebanon, and his uncle, the director of a large bank, said they couldn't believe he had done such a thing.

Terrorists are hard to recognize. They don't wear the mark of Cain on their foreheads.

Kruithof said he felt horrible about not seeing Al-Jarrah's evil. "German intelligence had tracked him in Hamburg, meeting with Atta. He was in Afghanistan for a few weeks. He wasn't there on a charity mission."

I suggested that there is also a Dostoyevskian phenomenon to consider, the overintellectualization of political acts. In *Crime and Punishment*, the protagonist Raskolnikov kills an aged woman to test his theory that someone who makes others' lives miserable doesn't deserve to live.

Kruithof considered the comparison between Raskolnikov and his fledgling pilot. "When I looked into his eyes," he said finally, "I saw someone intelligent, perhaps too intelligent for our society. Someone who is bitter and cold. Someone who passes by an old man who can't walk anymore and decides the man should be subtracted from the equation for walking so slow. The cause was more important than the life."

I asked Kruithof if there is some way to pick out a terrorist, someone who intends you great harm. He paused, considering my question. In America we see terrorists everywhere we look, but he had known a real one.

"Al-Jarrah dressed well," he said. "He looked European. Good social manners. He was hard to spot. He was slow at times, but he trained up to a commercial level."

Kruithof sighed heavily. "You think it's someone you like, who you used to hang out with. It's hard for the brain to accept what happened."

The advisories are full of suggestions about how to protect oneself, how to recognize a likely suspect by the way he or she dresses or acts. But Kruithof witnessed up close the danger that we just imagine. He, like the rest of us, lacked an accurate fear radar. Meanwhile the terrorists continue to generate fear with an impact that extends well beyond their actual numbers. It is terrorism that infects us, not the terrorists themselves. The shadows they cast on us are longer than the shadows of real men.

7

PROFITING FROM FEAR

Tampering with prescription drugs could be a way for terrorists to launch an attack on Americans, according to acting Food and Drug Administration Commissioner Lester Crawford.

—Associated Press report, August 11, 2004

In the first years of the twenty-first century, we are filled with worry and dread in part because we have been taught to rely on false props to protect us. We tell one another that we have to look a certain way, eat certain foods, even swallow certain pills, in order to remain healthy and safe. We rely on an elaborate system of danger signals that have inspired the creation of an elaborate system of safety signals. Since both sets of signals are often inaccurate, we are unnecessarily unsettled and then falsely reassured. Our superstitions fall apart as soon as we encounter the slightest contradiction to our controlled world.

Aging and illness scare us because they are tied to the inevitability of death and suffering, our ultimate fears. Advertisements in the media rely on these fears to generate the need for products. These products feed billion-dollar industries, which in turn foster dependencies to keep themselves in business. We worship the illusions these products provide, and in so doing we think we can keep ourselves safe.

THE PROMISE OF PILLS

In America, we pay outlandish prices for cosmetic surgeries and for our medications. In fact, we are willing to pay any price if it helps keep us insulated from the inevitability of death. Manufacturers manipulate us by playing to this notion of keeping us beyond harm. Medications that work perfectly well are stampeded into disuse by the magic-elixir claims of the new drugs. These preparations are more expensive but often not worth the additional cost.

Europeans, in contrast, are not held hostage to the same extent. To cite one important example, Europeans are often able to use their entire populations as a cohort—a large group of patients with a common need—to compel drug manufacturers to charge far less than we pay here in the United States for the same drugs. It is essentially a take-it-or-leave-it approach, fueled by the courage to say no. So while the drug companies are forced to sell close to the margin in Europe, they make up the difference in the cowardly American market, inflating our domestic drug prices by an additional 2 to 3 percent per year, according to IMS Health, a market research firm in Fairfield, Connecticut.

The governments of France, Italy, and Spain boldly use direct price controls, limiting prices at the launch of a product and later controlling the amount of reimbursement once the drug is on the market. Spain and Britain also limit profitability on a drug-by-drug basis. The U.S. House Committee on Government Reform, in a 2001 report on prescription drug prices, found that as a result of controls, such drugs cost 31 percent to 48 percent less in Canada, France, Italy, Britain, Germany, and Japan than in the United States.

In the contemporary American climate of "me-too" drugs, new drugs that lower blood pressure or cholesterol or soothe the stomach compete with older, satisfactory products in the same class. The advertising ploy is invariably a "you can't do without this" approach, with high prices supposedly justified by the expense of research and development.

What the drug companies don't say is that the availability of an excessive number of duplicate products, aggressively promoted, only increases the perception of need. And we hardly feel safer once we realize that sheer numbers don't correspond to an increased ability to treat disease. The implicit rationale, if one product doesn't protect you from illness, why not try another one, is hardly comforting. With a new blockbuster drug, it isn't unusual for a manufacturer to budget $50 million to $100 million for advertising aimed at consumers, according to Rx Insight, a consulting group that advises drug companies. In 2000, for example, Pfizer spent $89.5 million trying to convince consumers that Viagra was essential to their well-being.

Meanwhile, tried and true antibiotics like penicillin and amoxicillin that cost pennies are overlooked in favor of new brand-name drugs. Zithromax and Levaquin, to name two, are given out in doctors' offices to almost every nervous patient with a cough. The ad-driven patients push for these expensive drugs, and doctors readily prescribe them.

 The United States and New Zealand are the only industrialized countries in the world that haven't banned direct-to-consumer pharmaceutical advertising. Western Europe has saved billions of dollars by not allowing this questionable form of seduction.

In America, extensive advertising has created a furor of religious zeal surrounding certain drugs. Every day I treat patients with ad-driven cravings for a drug.

In the United States, Lipitor, which brought Pfizer revenues of $8.6 billion worldwide in 2001, cost $2.38 per 10-milligram tablet wholesale in 2003—that is, the cost to pharmacies. The same pill was sold to French pharmacists for 75 cents. It cost 93 cents in Britain.

While the major drug companies are largely ineffective in dictating European prices, from time to time they threaten to stop supplying the drugs, but the European governments remain unafraid. In 2002, Germany's health ministry took a $200 million stipend from the world's largest drug companies so that it wouldn't cut prescription drug prices 4 percent across the board. Germany took the money yet went ahead with the price cut anyway, and because 80 percent of prescription drugs in that country are purchased by the national health insurance system, the drug companies had no choice but to accept the ministry's terms.

Europe accounts for just over 20 percent of the pharmaceutical industry's more than $400 billion world market, according to IMS Health. The United States accounts for 46 percent. But with our unregulated practices, driven by the American consumer's fear of going without, we are the source of more than 60 percent of the industry's profit. We are filling its coffers, rather than using our collective influence to negotiate better prices. We could certainly buy a lot more drugs at the prices Europeans pay for them.

Beyond the astronomical prices for the latest drugs, there is the worry of doing without medicines altogether. Advertising creates a heightened need for these drugs, and then patients discover they can't afford them, and the fear grows. Many of my patients, living on a fixed income from Social Security and a small pension, are perfect candidates for real prescription drug coverage. Many patients would sleep better at night knowing they could afford at least the most essential medicines.

But the Medicare drug plan—approved at the end of 2003—is another example of false reassurance causing yet more alarm once it is exposed as being inadequate. Under the new Medicare plan, patients are faced with high deductibles, $420 in yearly co-pays, and the prospect of $3,600 coming out of their pockets at top dollar prices just to receive $1,500 in coverage before more complete coverage kicks in. When I explained the details of the new plan, one patient simply shook his head. "Not for me, Doc," he said.

This poor paralyzed patient suffers from diabetes and hypertension, and he relies on the free samples in my closet to treat these conditions. When I run out of samples, his blood pressure shoots up. His blood sweetens and unsweetens, depending on whether I can offer him his diabetes pill or not.

The new drug coverage merely serves to extract top-drawer prices from larger groups of clients who couldn't afford the medicines before. Since Medicare isn't allowed to negotiate, the government will pay full price for the coverage they do provide, and the patients will then have to pay cash prices for their drugs when they reach the gap in coverage. Once patients realize this, they are bound to thrash around like fish out of water. In 2003 the New York Public Interest Research Group (NYPIRG) published a survey of one hundred pharmacies, revealing that cash consumers of prescription drugs paid 100 percent more on average for their medicines than the government paid for army or veteran supplies, and 130 percent more than Canada paid. Joel Eichel, the chief pharmacist at Bigelow Pharmacy in New York City, validated NYPIRG's finding that cash customers paid the highest prices for their drugs. Eichel cited as an example Lipitor, the cholesterol-lowering drug. In 2003, the government paid $41.12 for a month's supply of 10-milligram tablets. Eichel said that pharmacies paid just under $60 for a month's supply, but the cash customer paid $85.30. Eichel admitted that "cash customers are paying a price so that a retailer can make a profit."

So here is a manufacturer's dream: a pocket-lining system that falsely reassures. A drug company's ability to charge an outrageous price is a testament to the perceived indispensability of a drug. The more afraid we are to go without a drug, the more we are willing to pay for it.

This ballooning process of fear-induced propaganda can be traced back to 1981. At that time, "Ira Lassiter," a popular journalist who had been suffering from arthritis of the hips for many years, saw the first television ad for a pharmaceutical. This ad glamorized Motrin, one of the original arthritis drugs, and Ira became one of many who asked his physician at the time to pre-scribe it.

"The pill helped me," Ira said many years later. "But I thought it was supposed to cure me. When it didn't cure me, I became even more worried about what my arthritis might do to me." This cycle of worry is at the heart of what is wrong with the role of prescription drugs in modern medical practice.

Once the process had started, it was difficult to stop. In February 2002 the *New England Journal of Medicine* published a study showing that direct-to-consumer advertising constituted 16 percent of drug promotion spending. At the same time the National Institute for Health Care Management released a study showing that 2001 drug costs were up 17.1 percent from the year before, with most of the increases in four heavily advertised categories: arthritis, cholesterol, depression, and allergy. The Kaiser Family Foundation demonstrated an association between consumer advertising expenditures and drugs that were growing the fastest. The implication behind the advertising was that without a certain drug you couldn't be healthy, an essential fear tactic.

In 1997 the FDA issued a series of feeble guidelines that allowed TV ads with only a brief mention of side effects. According to Rx Insight, the drug companies refer to this as "liberation day."

After 1997 the drug companies struggled to create name recognition using extensive television and magazine ads. Doctors found themselves compelled to respond to nervous ad-driven questions rather than those of fundamental medical importance. A report from UCLA in 2000 concluded that the effects of this would be that "we will have a world of aggressive, distrustful and only partially informed patients and cowed physicians."

Surveys by the FDA in 1999 and 2003, and by Kaiser in 2001, showed that between 20 and 30 percent of consumers, or more than 50 million people, responded to these drug ads by questioning their doctors. But the same studies revealed that almost 60 percent of consumers felt that the warnings of potential side effects communicated by these ads were inadequate. Here was the cycle of fear. When patients experienced the side effects of their "nirvana" pills, they became more frightened, as false reassurance over time ultimately led to more fear.

Into the 1990s Ira Lassiter continued to suffer from arthritis of the hips, and he first came to me for his medical care five years ago. Ira became caught in the billion-dollar struggle between Merck and Pfizer over two drugs for arthritis, Vioxx and Celebrex. This minidrama played itself out in my office. Ira was a reasonable patient who readily followed a doctor's advice, yet the advertising wars over prescription drugs confused and frightened him. He asked to switch from Motrin to Vioxx as the result of a TV ad, and I accommodated him. Then I reassured Ira when Vioxx's competitors first ran campaigns to discredit it, until it turned out that the association with heart disease was legitimate. Ira stopped the drug long before it was taken off the market in September 2004, and then he switched to Celebrex when Pfizer hyped it in the wake of Merck's removing Vioxx from the shelves. The Vioxx removal scared millions of arthritis sufferers unnecessarily, as they careened back and forth from exaggerated expectations to worry that this pill might actually be harming them.

This process continued in December, when studies showed an apparent increased risk of heart disease in patients with a prolonged use of Celebrex or naproxen (Aleve). Ira, like many of my patients, fled from one drug to the other and soon was off both. The pendulum swung from panacea to panic, and drugs that were misperceived as lifesavers instantly became villains.

Of course the perception of risk was much greater than the real threat. The damning studies showed that a few people out of a thousand patients could be at risk to suffer a heart attack while on one of these drugs. And the patients in the studies had been taking high doses of the drug every day for several months, which was an extended use that didn't apply to most people who became afraid of the drug.

The very day that Vioxx was removed from the market back in

September 2004, a Pfizer representative was stationed in my office trying to convert me to the Celebrex faith.

"Have you no shame?" I asked her. "Don't you realize that these drugs have similar effects?"

"Celebrex doesn't have that problem," she retorted, without any scientific documentation to back up her assertion. When Celebrex advertising was pulled by Pfizer in December, this drug rep never acknowledged her mistake, but simply moved on to hyping the next product.

Drug companies were trying to create a fear that the "other guy" would hurt you while only they could help you. Perhaps the most down and dirty advertising war was occurring in the world of allergy. After years of sniffling miserably, many of my patients had settled on Claritin (Schering-Plough) as the antihistamine that provided the most relief while making them the least drowsy. But the patent on Claritin expired in 2002, and it went over the counter at one-third the price, two major defeats for Schering after it had spent a fortune successfully marketing this drug and turning it into a $3-billion-a-year product. Monopolizing the over-the-counter market for antihistamines might have been a consolation, but Johnson & Johnson had already applied for approval of its generic product and was beating Schering to the punch. So Schering developed a more potent drug, Clarinex, and began to knock its own product, Claritin, as not as effective. Schering also engaged in a multimedia billion-dollar advertising face-off with other drug companies—in particular, Pfizer (Zyrtec) and Aventis (Allegra)—over their products. Each manufacturer was claiming that the other guy's product wasn't as effective, made you sleepier, and had more side effects.

The drug companies do their best to undermine their competitors and to instill fear in any patient who happens to be taking the other guy's product. In 2002 the American Medical Association protested that the ads do nothing to educate either patients or physicians. Consumer advocacy groups and even health maintenance organizations lobbied Congress, but the drug company lobbyists outnumbered their opposition eleven to one. The FDA turned a blind eye.

"I saw an ad for an antidepressant during halftime of the Super Bowl," Ira Lassiter said. "It showed a beautiful person smiling, saying how much the medicine helped. Soon you'll have people asking you for the drug who aren't even depressed."

"Until they find out it ruins their sex lives, which they don't bother to say on TV," I replied.

Ira thought this over. "So then they'll ask you for another billion-dollar drug, Viagra, to compensate," he said, catching on to how the process works. "You'll grow dependent on the new pill too and be afraid to go without both."

A victim of advertising, Ira tried one anti-inflammatory medicine after another. But his hips ached, no matter what drug I prescribed.

"The expensive new pills don't work any better than the cheap old pills, and they may not be as safe," Ira concluded during one of his worst days, when his hips could interpret the humidity as well as any weather forecaster predicting rain. Ira was growing more and more cynical, and on the rare day when his symptoms eased and he felt well, he would claim that medications had nothing to do with it.

He would not consider hip surgery—probably because no hip prosthesis salesman came to my office to soft-sell him through it.

Despite his lack of success, Ira continued filling his gym bag with drug samples from my supply closet. There were fewer arthritis drugs there now, but there were still green boxes of Mobic, a newer nonsteroidal drug that had yet to be associated with safety issues. The samples were free, and Ira was a self-proclaimed addict.

On his most recent visit just before a trip out of town, Ira took samples of a red antibiotic to keep on hand for frequent sinus infections that I was also having trouble treating. When he called me a few days later with what sounded like another sinus infection, I told him to take the red antibiotic. When he called back to say he was feeling better, not only in terms of his sinuses, but also his hips, I finally sensed a breakthrough.

"Which arthritis pill are you taking now?" I asked eagerly.

"None of them."

"And your hips are better?"

I was ready to believe that his sinuses were better as a result of taking the red antibiotic. But I couldn't understand the sudden improvement in his hips.

"What are you taking besides the red pill?"

"Nothing. Just an aspirin every four or five hours, for the cold."

"Aspirin? That must be what's helping your hips!"

It was Ira who had had a breakthrough; he had broken through his prescription drug dependency.

From that moment on, Ira would have nothing to do with any of the fancy pills that modern medicine or its sales representatives could offer him. Cured of his penchant for the ads, he insisted on taking only aspirin for his hips. He was surprised to find out how cheap aspirin was and how well it could work.

In relying on his intuition, sometimes a patient is able to overcome an essential fear of illness that the glut of shiny pills continues to encourage. I relearned an old lesson: often an old-fashioned remedy works better and is more comforting to the patient than the latest hyped discovery.

As for Ira's sinuses, I soon learned that the new chemical had not helped me to cure them either. It turned out his sinuses had cleared that night not from any state-of-the-art, sports-car-red antibiotic but from the chicken soup and hot tea the hotel bellhop had brought up to his room.

The Antifear Drug

For a while after Ira's success I was smitten with aspirin, the old remedy, the simple comfort. Occurring in nature, costing mere pennies, with no one to hype it, aspirin is the antifear drug. It is useful without being misperceived as a cure-all.

The ancient Greeks used the bark of the willow tree to relieve pain and combat fever without knowing what it contained.

Maimonides also wrote of these effects in the twelfth century. But it wasn't until the nineteenth century that Johann Buchner, a German chemist, isolated an active glucoside from the bark, calling it salicin (after *Salix*, the Latin name for the willow tree). Sodium salicylate then became a useful medication to treat pain, particularly joint aches.

In 1897, Felix Hoffman, an employee at a German fabric-dyeing company known as Bayer, sought a chemical to lessen the misery of his father's arthritis. He came upon acetylsalicylic acid (ASA), produced by the company's chemists but then ignored. ASA proved to be quite effective for his father's pains, and it lacked the bitter taste and some of the stomach upset of sodium salicylate.

Bayer patented ASA and called it aspirin.

The chemical compound in aspirin—acetylsalicylic acid—is closely related to the salicylates found in fruit and vegetables. Berries are a good source. Herbs and spices and tea also contain high amounts.

So it turns out the food we farmed and gathered back when we couldn't buy everything in a store contained an essential chemical. Since the average American diet is now low in fruit and vegetables, aspirin takes its place.

Aspirin's effectiveness at preventing heart attacks and strokes is tied to its antiplatelet effects, the sticky blood components that initiate clots. Aspirin also works as an anti-inflammatory agent, blocking enzymes cyclooxygenase 1 and 2. These enzymes are necessary for the growth of intestinal cancer cells. In several studies a 40 percent reduction in the incidence of colon cancer has been shown in patients taking aspirin.

Another landmark study in the May 2004 *Journal of the American Medical Association* found that women taking aspirin daily had a 26 percent lower risk of developing estrogen-stimulated tumors, the most common type of breast cancer.

But aspirin is not a cure-all. It is poorly tolerated in patients with asthma or kidney disease. Stomach irritation and bleeding are common side effects. Hemorrhagic stroke occurs in one in every thousand regular aspirin takers. The public can still too easily fall into that familiar cycle of hype and disappointment, followed by worry. No medical crutch can carry the weight of all our illnesses, not even a basic remedy like aspirin.

The renewed interest in aspirin comes at a time when medical props are overglorified as tools to keep us from aging or getting sick. But even this old-time remedy, which has turned out to have major uses never before considered, is not effective in calming our deepest fears.

VACCINE FEARS

Vaccine fears cut both ways. Sometimes we feel afraid of the disease, while at other times we feel afraid of the vaccine. The concept of disease protection can be useful, if the protection offered is substantial. In fact, in the past vaccines have helped public health scientists to eradicate or diminish the threats of diseases such as smallpox and polio, thereby diminishing associated fears.

At other times, as with the flu vaccine shortage in the fall of 2004, we have come to covet a vaccine as a health panacea even when it offers at best only limited protection against a disease.

Sometimes, even while feeling protected, we have also been made to feel afraid of some of these same vaccines. Mercury-based vaccines like thimerosal, for example, have been suspected of potential neurotoxicity for years without proof. Two large epidemiological studies in the United States and Denmark didn't find a greater risk of autism in children who received thimerosal-containing vaccines. Recently a study from Columbia University *did* find that a mercury preservative used in vaccines may have caused some behavioral changes in a strain of mice. Still, showing that thimerosal or mercury-based vaccines can be associated with slight neurotoxicity in mice is not the same as proving an association with autism in humans.

Parents of autistic children naturally look for a cause-and-effect relationship associated with a potential threat. But what has been uncovered is not proof, especially at a time when the prevalence of autism appears to be increasing in part due to improved diagnostic sensitivity.

Vaccine manufacturers contribute to the hysteria by not screening their products carefully enough. Even if thimerosal has not been shown to cause autism, it still should have been removed as soon as some toxicity was shown. Instead, years of inaction contributed to a climate of fear. Despite the fact that a vaccine should be pure, vaccine manufacturers have also stubbornly persisted in using pooled bovine serum for their vaccines from regions of Europe where mad cow disease has been endemic. The manufacturers' refusal to carefully vet their product or to remove a questionable additive has fueled public distrust.

Unfortunately, the sense that scientific rigor and caution are not always applied to vaccine manufacture translates too easily into a distrust of all vaccines. There is a tendency to generalize a fear of one vaccine to a fear of every vaccine. Fears of autism and mercury shouldn't automatically extend to a distrust of any product a drug company brings to market.

FEAR IN OUR FOOD

Many of us are obsessed with certain methods of dieting, adhering to elaborate regimes that will transform us into our ideal selves. The goal of eternal beauty and youth that drives us is connected to our fear of death, as if superstitious ritual could keep us beyond harm. A study in October 2003 revealed that simply drinking eight glasses of water per day is just as good for losing weight as the cultlike ephedra, but of course water intake lacks the aura of self-sacrifice that is at the heart of modern dieting.

All of our most popular religions include food fasts or restrictions as a method of purging the soul. The Christians have Lent;

the Jews, Yom Kippur; the Muslims, Ramadan. We punish our-selves for our indiscretions. Our souls will rise, and later, if we are forgiven, we will be free from harm.

Popular diets such as Atkins are diets of contrition—they play into a cycle of punishment and reward that centers on a phobia of carbohydrates.

Carbohydrates are sinful foodstuffs under Atkins, and the man-date from the dietary gods is that carbs must be avoided at all costs. Atkins devotees fill plates with carcinogenic bacon, while sugar triggers their fear apparatus. It is as if verboten chocolate cake can somehow directly enter your coronary arteries and stop your heart on the spot, whereas fried eggs cannot.

Like fanatical religion, fanatical dieting means giving over con-trol to the directives of a zealot. Dietary prophets twist the termi-nology of weight loss until theirs seems to be the only true road to salvation. Their books rise on the best-seller lists as their followers become more and more fervent, feeling safe and comfortable only when following the "good word," and deeply afraid of choosing any other dietary path.

Yet many, as they obsess over the numbers, lose sight of the good health that is supposed to accompany a slimmer body. And others even lose sight of the weight, getting lost in the compulsive ritual of the process, as though, like religion, the details of dieting can some-how protect you. For those unfortunate souls who fail, they can still seek protection from a more powerful prophet—the plastic surgeon. The perils of obesity can be instantly circumvented. Lipo-suction or gastric stapling or even a simple tummy tuck represents a miracle cure for those newly converted to the cosmetic faith.

From Antibiotic Safety to Pill Dependency

Just a generation ago, when my parents were children, a single scratch on the arm could evolve into a life-threatening septic wound infection without the antibiotics available to stop it. This was a true danger. Yet people learned to live with this perilous risk, which statistically speaking, was still not an imminent threat to most people. A sense of relative safety kept people from panicking.

The discovery of antibiotics went a long way toward making people feel legitimately safer when it came to infections. Unfortunately, it wasn't long before antibiotics became part of the inflated danger/protector cascade. A need is created by drug company ads for each new medication as if it is just as lifesaving as penicillin. We develop pill dependencies, because we are told how crucial these pills are to our well-being—hormone replacement therapy is a prime example of a supposed panacea that left a trail of fear when its true effects were unmasked.

Medications such as aspirin or Lipitor prevent countless premature deaths, but most medications hyped as crucial really aren't. The overall result is a panicked, pill-popping public.

We are afraid to grow old, afraid to get sick. Today's pills put only a thin coating over our ultimate fear of death. Pills and plastic surgery are used to keep us looking and feeling like we imagine "the beautiful people" feel, for as long as possible.

The Real Danger of Cigarettes

Over the past half century, cancer has taken the place of infection in terms of its reputation for striking people down in the midst of good health. Cancer petrifies us. An earlier generation's worry about common infections has become this generation's fear of cancer.

Even though we can control some of the risks for cancer, such as cigarette smoke, diet, and environmental toxins, the way our ancestors might have avoided contaminated food and water, powerful industry and tobacco lobbies downplay the real risks of toxins and cigarettes. Instead, the media play up pseudodangers, while the real toxins that threaten us are obscured. We become more and more disoriented, afraid of going without pills that really don't protect us, not afraid enough of the poisons that put us at genuine risk.

Lobbyists have tried to convince legislators that tobacco smoke in the air doesn't threaten us, when in fact it contains thousands of different toxic chemicals including nicotine, carbon monoxide, hydrogen cyanide, and sulfur dioxide. Secondhand smoke is the third leading preventable cause of death in the United States, killing at least fifty thousand nonsmokers every year. In reports from the surgeon general, the Environmental Protection Agency, and the National Research Council, environmental tobacco smoke is identified as a causative factor in all respiratory illnesses including asthma, heart disease, pneumonia, and lung cancer.

Though many of the toxic particles of cigarette smoke are simply the by-products of a fire, they are found in much higher amounts in cigarette smoke than in emissions from fireplaces or gas stoves. Nevertheless, more public health warnings and restrictions are attached to heaters and grills than to cigarettes, another prime example of the public's attention being focused on the wrong dangers.

There is a deep-rooted public resistance to thinking that familiar objects are perilous. We tend to believe that an invisible remote pathogen like SARS or sarin gas can infiltrate our air more easily than a common cigarette.

Cigarettes are familiar props in our society. We saw them romanticized in movies, television ads, and glossy magazines, before promoting cigarettes was restricted. We are still slow to accept the danger of casual exposure. Even if most people have now accepted that smoking itself is dangerous, secondhand smoke is still tied to the dreamy images of our youth, wafts of it tickling our faces on a moonlit night.

People who are lulled into such a false sense of security are not brought fully awake until they experience a sudden chest pain or the frightening feeling of not being able to catch their breath.

Who to Turn To?

When a person becomes seriously ill, a trusted doctor can be very helpful. He or she can provide perspective on the illness, offering reassurance as well as proper context.

Unfortunately, doctors aren't always trustworthy, and patients don't always trust us. Without this kind of guidance, sudden illness is particularly frightening. It is a doctor's job to explain, yet many patients feel uninformed by their doctors. A study reported in the April 2004 *Archives of Internal Medicine* revealed that the majority of patients are interested in reviewing their medical chart because they are afraid that something is being kept from them. I rarely write notes in a patient's chart that I don't want them to be aware of, but my patients don't always believe this.

Patients have a right to know, and the information physicians provide needs to be understandable. Many of my patients worry about any lab or test result that is red-marked as abnormal no matter how inconsequential I say that result is. Often, patients worry the most who don't feel well informed to begin with.

We doctors do our patients a disservice when we aren't careful about the context of the information we provide. We may exaggerate the level of danger to protect ourselves from lawsuits in the event of an unlikely outcome.

Many of the secrets of illness and health are being communicated to a patient directly by his own body. Doctors are most effective as guides when we listen carefully to patients' symptoms and help them put these symptoms in the context of their illness in as straightforward a manner as possible. The more oblique we are, the more we hide behind a sanctimonious self-image, the less patients gain true perspective, and the more worried they become. We doctors can be feared along with the illness we are trying to treat.

Part II

BUGS DU JOUR

8

ANTHRAX

If and when another attack on American soil occurs, however, everything we know about the psychology of fear suggests that it will lead to extreme public panic that may be disproportionate to the actual casualties. The public responds emotionally to remote but terrifying threats, and this leads us to make choices about security that are not always rational. . . . The vicious cycle at this point should be clear. The public fixates on low-probability but vivid risks because of images we absorb from television and from politicians.

—Jeffrey Rosen, *The Naked Crowd*

Exactly a month after September 11, 2001, at a time when many of us felt vulnerable, a mysterious white powder began appearing in the mail rooms of major media outlets, from the *National Enquirer* in Boca Raton, Florida, to NBC News in New York. Attacking media centers, the national nervous system, is an instant way to broadcast a message of panic.

At first this message seemed to come right from the international terrorist group that had just destroyed the World Trade

Center. And by the time this no longer seemed to be the case, we were already afraid to open our mail. The anthrax scare—the disproportionate public reaction to a few letters—was a direct manifestation of our growing fear of terrorism.

The anthrax scare established a precedent, a pattern by which we would convert our unease into a specific threat. Each new public health risk from this point forward would reach the news media and initiate an overreaction on a nationwide basis. The government provides the information, and the media announce it. If we give our fear a name, we can feel that we are engaged in a plan to protect ourselves from it. The first name we gave our fear after 9/11 was anthrax.

Some of us understood that our perception had been warped by the built-in publicity of the moment when the media centers were hit. But then there was Kathy Nguyen, a Vietnamese woman from the Bronx who wasn't in the media and who wasn't a national figure or a senator, but who was just opening her mail. Nguyen's untimely death from an anthrax letter was seen as a warning that it could happen to any of us. This everyman scene affected only one person, but it was enough to petrify the public. The media broadcast Nguyen's fate until people everywhere were afraid.

It would have been far better if the information had been contained. This would have allowed our federal agencies to quietly prepare an integrated response to anthrax without alarming the public and inflating the risk before the facts were known.

Ever since then, we have been sent reeling from one bug du jour to another. The media megaphone alerts each time, and we wait expectantly for the latest hyped virus or bacteria to overtake us individually and collectively. When it doesn't, we forget and move on to the next bug. The media have no memory, nor do we, as a result. We do not gain perspective from the news, and we build on each overreaction until we have created a universal fear epidemic. Our collective sense of immunity is fragile, and we feel as threatened by the hyping of a tropical storm as by the latest virus.

A SIMPLE NASAL SWAB

On a cold morning early in November 2001, a black Lincoln limousine awaited me in the first light. It would take me to CNBC studios in Fort Lee, New Jersey, just over the George Washington Bridge.

Three weeks after the first anthrax letter appeared, I was going to CNBC to give Bob Sellers, then their morning anchor, an anthrax test on the air.

"If you have flu symptoms, and you think it could be anthrax, then it's almost certainly the flu and not anthrax," I said to the camera. "Anthrax is not contagious. But the fear of anthrax is."

I worried that by demonstrating the nasal swab test on the air, by swabbing Sellers's nostril with this ridiculously long Q-tip swab, I was sending the wrong public message. Teaching people the right way to get tested for anthrax was absurd, since the public risk of getting anthrax was infinitesimally low.

To my surprise, when we were finished, Bob Sellers asked me if *he* had anything to worry about. He explained that since NBC had been hit with the letter to Tom Brokaw, the mail rooms at CNBC had been sealed, and everyone worried that anthrax might be in their midst.

Sellers's producers as well as his coanchor listened carefully as I told them there was no evidence that they had any exposure to anthrax. They breathed easier.

I called Sellers two days later to tell him that his anthrax culture was negative. This CNBC visit was the first time I saw up close that some newspeople actually believe what they are reporting. True, in this case Sellers had a personal reason to be cautious, but I was also able to see that he lived with the same hype and worry that he was pushing onto us.

Even in the Internet age, the postal service serves as an important avenue of communication. The anthrax letters undermined our sense of well-being by attacking this basic need to be connected with the world around us. A positive feature of our lives turned into a random avenue of death. On top of this problem, the FBI and the CDC fumbled the anthrax investigation, contributing further to an erosion of our sense of safety. In retrospect, anthrax turned out to be a minor eruption, with only twenty-two cases and five deaths. But the handling of the crisis, with its misinformation and distortion, contributed to a widespread panic out of proportion to the risk at the time.

First we were told by the news media to be afraid of something that didn't truly threaten us. Then, once we were worried, we saw that our federal agencies weren't functioning effectively, which worried us further.

WHAT IS ANTHRAX?

Anthrax is a type of bacteria that doesn't move and lives in a capsule. It uses oxygen for energy and produces dormant spores that are hard to kill and can remain in the environment for years. Anthrax affects mostly animals, and humans can catch it mainly by contact with infected animals. In most humans, anthrax is a curable skin infection. There are hundreds of cases yearly in the Middle East. In the United States, there have been only three cases of naturally occurring anthrax reported between 1984 and 1993.

In the 1970s, epidemics of anthrax occurred in the former Soviet Union at Sverdlovsk due to a military accident, and on the farms of Zimbabwe due to animal contagion when the vaccination program was stopped there because of war.

Anthrax is not contagious but may be introduced into the skin of a victim via cuts or by biting flies. A red sore develops, which forms a black ulcer. In inhalation anthrax, the spores are breathed directly into the lungs and carried to the lymph nodes. A powerful toxin develops. Once in the bloodstream of an inhalation anthrax victim, the anthrax bacteria evade capture by white blood cells, and they multiply. But anthrax may be cured with an early and aggressive course of antibiotics.

In terms of bioterror, it is difficult to deploy anthrax on a large scale because of wind, and most of the anthrax in a bomb would be destroyed on detonation. Anthrax spores can persist in the environment but can also be removed by careful decontamination.

THE ANTHRAX FUMBLE

When the first anthrax-laden envelopes were received in October 2001, the FBI froze the Centers for Disease Control out of the high-profile investigation, according to CDC officials. That meant half the country's experts on bioattacks (the army employs the other half), and the only scientists with a special interest in public health were kept out of the loop. Then, to make matters worse, the CDC spread information it had received secondhand. All this resulted in a fumbled response that put some postal and media workers at serious risk and scared the public. The sense of inadequate protection against an overhyped threat contributed to the spread of panic.

The main problem was that the Centers for Disease Control, the government agency charged with protecting the public from disease, was never permitted to see or examine the anthrax letters. Without access, the CDC experts could not accurately assess the danger the letters posed.

Consequently, the public could not be properly informed. This mismanagement ultimately contributed to the growing fear when more people unexpectedly developed anthrax. The CDC flip-flopped from downplaying the risk to wallowing in worst-case scenarios in part because it didn't have solid information. This uncertainty spread fear.

The scare began on October 12, 2001, when NBC news anchor Tom Brokaw received an anthrax letter postmarked in Trenton, New Jersey. It was immediately turned over to the FBI. The CDC never examined it. Dr. Mitchell Cohen, the CDC's director of bacterial diseases and liaison to the FBI, said he saw only photographs of it. On the basis of media accounts and conference calls with the FBI, the CDC determined that the Brokaw letter was "only risky to those who opened it." By October 18, 2001, though, several New Jersey postal workers had suspicious skin sores, and Teresa Heller, a West Trenton letter carrier, and Richard Morgano, a Hamilton postal worker, had confirmed cases of skin anthrax. New Jersey's Hamilton postal distribution center, which had processed the Brokaw letter, was closed as a result of these cases, and hundreds of workers there were given precautionary antibiotics. Had the FBI allowed the CDC to examine the Brokaw letter on October 12, the CDC would have been in a better position to make assessments that might have led to an earlier closing of the Hamilton facility. The CDC might well have learned that this anthrax could spread beyond its envelope. Unfortunately, the FBI did not perform tests for leakage on the Brokaw letter. The CDC looked inept—watching TV for information like the rest of us. The public's lack of confidence in our health officials is part of the reason we panicked. Once we realized that the CDC had underestimated the risk, many of us no longer trusted their statements, and we quickly overestimated the risk.

A similar series of events occurred after Senator Tom Daschle's office received an anthrax letter on October 15, 2001. It had been handled by the Brentwood postal facility in Washington. Again, the CDC was not invited to examine the letter, and its doctors were unable to observe just how easily the anthrax it contained could become airborne and spread. Nor could they run a test checking for cross-contamination by putting this envelope with other uncontaminated envelopes in a mail sorter.

How was the CDC supposed to issue accurate directives if its doctors and lab specialists were kept away from the evidence? And when the authorities were once again found to be underestimating the danger, this again contributed to the panic.

All the anthrax letters were tested by the Bethesda-based U.S. Army Medical Research Institute on Infectious Disease. On October 16, 2001, microbiologists at the army lab counted more than a billion spores in the Daschle envelope and discovered the fine military grade of the powder, which should have alerted them right away to its potency. In a conference call that day with the FBI and the CDC, the army scientists described the powder as "going poof," an indication it could become airborne. Yet, according to the CDC's Cohen, the army and FBI officials didn't express concern that this could lead to the spread of the more deadly inhaled form of anthrax. In fact, Cohen said that the army scientists, having heard from FBI officials that the Daschle letter was supposedly well sealed, predicted limited spread—as they had with the Brokaw letter. Army scientists, who were not accustomed to making public health proclamations, wrongly reassured the CDC without sufficiently testing the spread potential of this potent anthrax. The CDC, in turn, blindly passed the information to the post office, claiming that there was no risk to postal employees and that mail-sorting equipment could be presumed safe. The CDC based much of its information on the few previous cases of anthrax caught from animals.

As with the Brokaw letter, the CDC wasn't given the opportunity to see firsthand the powerful powder of the Daschle letter, which was already working its way through Brentwood by the time the actual letter hit Daschle's office. Armed with such knowledge, the CDC could have acted more quickly in examining postal workers and providing antibiotics there. It might have even closed Brentwood days earlier. But Brentwood continued to operate until October 21, 2001, and two U.S. Postal Service workers there—Thomas Morris Jr. and Joseph Curseen Jr.—died from inhaled exposure due to contaminated equipment. Their deaths helped provoke the widespread panic that ensued, in part because it again appeared that the CDC—our disease protector—had fumbled. But according to Cohen, the CDC "based our assumptions [concerning the Daschle letter] on limited epidemiological information from the letter to Tom Brokaw that the greatest risk was to those who opened the letters." This misinformation, based on speculation, wasn't corrected in time.

The FBI also kept another piece of crucial evidence from the CDC. On October 19, 2001, the *New York Post* turned over to the bureau an anthrax letter it had received a week earlier. The letter had been stored unopened by a mail room worker. Though this envelope was not unsealed, three *Post* employees—including the opinion editor—acquired skin anthrax from handling the letter, which seemed to spread skin anthrax to anyone who touched it. Had the letter been shared with the CDC, its scientists could have tested seepage from the envelope and assessed the level of danger. If these cases had been prevented, the hysteria might well have died out sooner.

It wasn't until the last week in October 2001 that the FBI used DNA tracers and an electron microscope to discover that the anthrax could escape through tiny, 50-micron holes in the envelope, and that it became airborne if the envelope was compressed, shaken, or passed through a sorter. This knowledge, if available earlier, could have informed the CDC's evaluation of the situation and reinforced its image as a reliable source of information. Instead, by the end of October the public's imagination had been inflamed by the constant speculation that this anthrax could turn up anywhere.

In mid-November 2001, an envelope addressed to Senator Patrick Leahy and containing anthrax was discovered. Again the CDC wasn't included in the FBI-army examination, which once more showed an aggressive type of bacteria. The Leahy letter demonstrated leakage without a single lab test. As the letter was being carried from the FBI to the army lab, an embarrassingly large puddle of powder leaked from a hole in the envelope into the plastic bag containing it.

By this time four possibly preventable anthrax deaths—including Kathy Nguyen on October 29 and Ottilie Lundgren on November 11—had already occurred as a result of the mailings. Earlier precautions at the post office could have kept the deadly cross-contaminated mailings from ever reaching the last two women who died. Preventing these deaths could have significantly slowed the growing hysteria.

Clearly, there were holes in the safety net. Here's how biodefense was supposed to work: The army and the CDC had the only two top-response (Level D) microbiology laboratories in the country with the equipment and security clearance needed to study anthrax. When a federal crime involving contagion occurred, as with the anthrax mailings, the FBI automatically alerted the army lab. But the FBI had the power to expand the scope of the inquiry to include CDC experts. What was missed by one scientist might be discovered by another. And while the army's primary concern was biowarfare, the CDC was concerned with public health issues. In fact, Dr. Julie Gerberding, the CDC's then deputy director for infectious diseases (promoted after the anthrax fumble in part because of her boss's poor handling of it), admitted to Senator Chuck Grassley's staff during their investigation that the anthrax should have been seen before the CDC offered public health announcements.

While consulting for Grassley I determined that if the CDC was being left out, the postal service was being ignored. According to Deborah Wilhite, senior vice president for government relations at the postal service, "The different focuses of law enforcement and health organizations resulted in parties speaking different 'languages.'"

The FBI was in charge of this "tower of babel" team, and the army did the testing, while the CDC, known around Capitol Hill as the Rodney Dangerfield of federal agencies, was on the wrong end of conference calls. In contrast to the real Rodney Dangerfield, who famously got no respect, the CDC did not complain.

In the wake of the anthrax mailings, the CDC was to be more directly involved in bioterror defense planning. The new Department of Homeland Security intended to act as a liaison between the agencies. One could only hope that the FBI would become willing to cooperate, wouldn't automatically declare everything a crime scene, and wouldn't pirate away the evidence from other discerning scientific eyes.

Anthrax was the prototype for overreaction based on inadequate information. It set in motion a mode of public response that was always out of proportion to the public risk. After underestimating the anthrax risk to mail carriers and a few members of the media and public, the CDC never again wanted to be seen as underreacting. Instead, the CDC consistently overreacted and scared us unnecessarily. Every potential infection became an opportunity for a hyperbolic public health/media response. From the anthrax crisis onward, the CDC began to dramatize concerns at the earliest stage of a potential health crisis.

The anthrax letters cost five lives (including tabloid photo editor Robert Stevens of Boca Raton—the first death), with eighteen others sick and recovering, while at the same time scaring millions of people who were at zero risk.

Fear for Sale

The CDC had helped administer antibiotics to thirty thousand postal, media, and government workers who weren't anywhere near where the anthrax had been found. The antibiotic authorized for use, Cipro (three hundred dollars for a month's supply), was ten times more expensive than generic equivalents like doxycycline (thirty dollars for a month's supply), which had been tested and found to be equally effective against the anthrax bacteria. Examination of this particular anthrax strain revealed no drug resistance to any of these antibiotics, but the CDC wasn't told this by the army lab, and the more expensive Cipro continued to be used.

In the end, many more people got sick from the side effects of Cipro than from the noncontagious anthrax.

In New York, state and city health departments relied blindly on the guidance and the presence of the CDC. Expensive resources were marshaled to test large numbers of the population, with no real reason to believe that this was necessary. Labs were readied to perform nasal swab testing of all who might have been exposed to anthrax and blood cultures on those who might already be sick. (The blood cultures could supposedly help distinguish anthrax from flu.) The confusion about testing—who to test, how to test, how many to test—typified the lack of knowledge and the lack of communication between the CDC and the local agencies it was asked to inform.

With the anthrax scare, the public perception of a potential catastrophe was exacerbated by a growing awareness of governmental confusion, necessitating an additional expenditure just to combat hysteria.

Cipro Profits

In October 2001 every closet in my medical office was suddenly filled with samples of ciprofloxacin. For over a week, every patient phone call I received and almost every patient visit to my office included a frantic request for this ordinary antibiotic, which was intended primarily for use with bladder infections.

Physicians as well as patients were stockpiling the drug. One of my patients returned home to his wife, and instead of reassuring her with news of his normal test results, he bragged, "I've got it, I've got it," brandishing his hoard of Cipro samples. Another patient called me from Philadelphia to ask whether she should take Cipro to prevent anthrax. "No. Not unless you live inside the *National Enquirer* building in Boca Raton," I replied. Five minutes later she called me back frantically—her neighbor was returning from Boca, wheeling her possibly contaminated luggage down the hall—"No," I groaned. "No Cipro."

The Cipro manufacturer was stoking this frenzy and playing into public hysteria by promoting the drug. The drug reps dropped off hundreds of sample cartons at my office without saying why, though I could see them frowning whenever they heard me say, "I am not prescribing Cipro to prevent anthrax."

Why Cipro? What the drug company Bayer was not telling either patient or doctor was that Cipro's usefulness for prevention was speculative. It had not been shown to work better than other cheaper antibiotics like doxycycline or even good old penicillin.

Which was not to say that any of these antibiotics should have been prescribed. If too many people took it, resistance would develop, rendering the antibiotic less useful for common infections. Prolonged use of Cipro without a real treatment target or reasonable endpoint would cause significant side effects in a large population. Insomnia affected 5 percent of Cipro users, a fact that was of interest to the drug rep for Ambien who followed the Cipro rep into my office during the anthrax scare to encourage me to prescribe more sleeping pills.

A drug company was making a public display, attaching itself to the exact fear that was crippling us at the time. The well-dressed Cipro rep who visited my office, plying me with free lunches, was justifying the fear by acting as if he had the only treatment for it. This was what the drug company knew best, parasitism. Just one month post-9/11, we found our dread exploited by a monolith that couldn't resist an opportunity to make more money.

Doctoring Anthrax Fear

Anthrax was scary because it could kill. Thinking about it was connected to a fear of death.

The urge to stockpile an antibiotic was a prophylaxis against the fear. But if I allowed patients to have it, they would be more likely to take it unnecessarily, putting themselves at risk of side effects. If I prescribed it, I was condoning its use.

The antidote for anthrax fear was knowledge, corrective information, but this took time to work. In the meantime, back in the fall of 2001, people manifested their fears by checking their mail carefully, washing frequently, and calling their doctors with their concerns.

To calm short-term panic, sometimes it was necessary to administer tests to prove to a patient that she didn't have the disease. If this practice became too common, it would send the false message that more anthrax might be in the offing.

For those I couldn't reassure, for those who continued to believe they had anthrax or insisted on medication for anthrax despite all evidence to the contrary, I was compelled to admit defeat to the one condition that could take hold in spite of any medical intervention. Fueled incessantly by speculation, this condition, the tool of terrorists, was the fear itself.

By November 2001, twenty-two cases of anthrax seemed like twenty-two thousand to the public. Hysteria, the true contagion, was sweeping the country like crop dusting. I was discussing this with an opinion editor at the *New York Post* when I received a sudden e-mail back from him. "Forget all the people overreacting," he wrote. "Anthrax has hit my building and I have to get out."

Finally, someone in real danger. I offered him antibiotics. He stubbornly declined, returning to work at the newspaper. Meanwhile, multitudes of others who had come nowhere near anthrax were stockpiling Cipro.

Panic too easily blurred the distinction between the few at real risk and the vast majority who were at no risk. For a physician it was crucial to have a realistic concept of the likelihood of a disease's occurrence—I downplayed anthrax in 2001 precisely because I knew that the risk to my patients was so low.

I e-mailed the *Post* editor again, stating my theory that physicians had to develop reflexes to downplay worry in their patients.

"True. But I have a real reason to worry," he shot back.

He was right. I again offered him prophylactic antibiotics.

"I'm not taking antibiotics when I'm not sick," was his reply. He reminded me that I was the one saying that people shouldn't be taking antibiotics needlessly.

"But you're one of the few who need them," I wrote.

Those who followed the news closely in late 2001 know the rest. He noticed a red mark on his forehead, a sore that soon turned the color of cigarette ash. He saw his own doctor, and the biopsy came back positive for anthrax.

He started on Cipro, but then he didn't want to take the whole sixty-day course.

"You must," I wrote in an e-mail. "You're one of the few who really needs antibiotics."

"Okay," he replied. I'm not sure whether he completed the full sixty days, but he did get better.

The traditional reflexes of aggressive treatment when appropriate were just as important as the reflexes to counter undue fear.

The anthrax panic in the United States continued for weeks. A patient who was a Holocaust survivor said the anthrax worries caused him to remember his feelings of helplessness of long ago. Another patient complained that I was so busy asking about anthrax phobia that I almost forgot to treat her bronchitis. Several patients demanded flu shots—not because they needed them, which they did, but because they were afraid to confuse the flu with the symptoms of anthrax. I remember 2001 as the year when I first began to use flu shots to vaccinate against hysteria.

He Sleeps with His Boots On

I barely recognized the patient, though he had been coming to see me for almost ten years and I knew him well. It wasn't just that his appearance had changed, though the baseball cap pulled low over his eyes and the workman's shoes were not his usual attire.

Under the lights of my examination room, I realized that it was his manner that had altered the most: formerly confident, even strident, now he leaned against the counter, not wanting to sit. He hunched over, wringing his hands, looking toward the window every few seconds.

Seeing me, he seemed to calm, and I reminded him that the visit was a simple follow-up for a prostate infection. He needed to leave a urine sample and he could go, and I would call him in a few days with the results. He could stop taking his Cipro.

"I've renewed it," he whispered, though his voice usually boomed.

"Why renew it? I gave you the refill in case the infection flared up again and you couldn't reach me right away."

"Why should I stop now?" And then came the words that were supposed to explain everything: "There's a war on."

I could see him eyeing the closets in the examination room. Was he wondering what medicines were there? I put my hand on his shoulder and we looked at each other. I realized that I had always treated this patient more like a friend. He knew my home phone number; he was free to page me when I wasn't on call. We liked to talk about sports. It was painful to consider this new source of tension that had come between us.

In my consultation room I explained to the patient that the risks of taking this expensive antibiotic for an extended period far outweighed any benefit against an unlikely microbe (the *New York Post* editor being by far the exception). With prolonged use of the medicine this patient might develop diarrhea, rash, or insomnia.

"Insomnia," he said. "So what? I already can't sleep."

I reviewed my office notes and saw that a few years before he'd had a brief spell of anxiety related to a problem at work. He had declined medication, and the problem had resolved on its own.

"How about something to calm your nerves and help you sleep?"

The patient readily agreed this time. He was thirty-five and lived alone in a walk-up apartment six blocks from the World Trade Center site. He worked uptown at a communications firm and had been at work when the planes hit, but he had since returned to a smoky, soot-covered existence downtown, where he had to keep the windows closed and his telephone hadn't worked for weeks. He told me he spent the night sitting in a chair, fully clothed, in case he had to leave at a moment's notice.

I tried my best to reassure him. "Nothing else is likely to happen right now. The risk of anthrax is extraordinarily low. Don't you believe me?"

"Sure I believe you, Doc. But I just can't stop thinking about it."

Across my desk I could see his bulky bag, bulging open with a gas mask. He said he carried it wherever he went. I tried not to look at it. "Would you agree to see a therapist?"

"Are you saying I'm crazy?"

"Of course not. I'm worried that your reaction is causing you pain."

"I can handle it. Let's talk about something more important. The vaccine for anthrax. Can you get it?"

"It's not a very strong vaccine, and you can't get it here in America right now. If you insist on it, you can fly to England to get it."

"Are you crazy, Doc? Me get on a plane right now?"

The patient rose and headed to the front of the office. I felt that my "plane" suggestion, one month after September 11, had caused him to lose respect for me.

"Wait," I said. But he ignored me. He was heading for my supply closet at the front of the office. Without hesitation, he began rummaging through it. My nurse, who had never before seen a patient so boldly enter a private area of the office, seemed afraid to intervene. The patient knocked over pillboxes until he found the antibiotic he was looking for, and then he stuffed it into his pockets until my supply was exhausted. He left the office then, without saying goodbye to anyone.

I found myself ready to enter the hall after him, but my nurse wisely stopped me. "Let him go," she said.

THE NEW SAFETY NET

Just assigning billions of dollars to the terrorism problem and spreading the money around the country as was initiated by the federal government in the spring of 2002 did little more than spread the message that something might be in the offing.

Provisions for a national stockpile of antibiotics and vaccines were wasteful. These items were perishable, and no biological agent was capable of spreading through our populace overnight. Stockpiling was not a panacea; the country might temporarily feel more prepared psychologically, but to the tune of billions of wasted dollars.

In an op-ed in the *Chicago Tribune* in June 2002, I wrote, "But simply allotting massive monies and card-shuffling various agencies does not ensure an impenetrable safety net."

On June 29, 2002, the *New York Times* suddenly reported that the anthrax vaccine was being shifted to civilian uses amidst a sudden panic, with July 4 approaching, that a terrorist attack might be unleashed from Iraq, where "well over 2,650 gallons of liquid anthrax" were supposedly stored. Here in the United States, plans were hurriedly being made to stockpile the vaccine for civilian use.

But the vaccine was antiquated, cumbersome (requiring six doses), and not 100 percent effective. It was also known for its flu-like side effects. Other, more effective, better-tolerated vaccines were under investigation in Europe. And there was simply no evidence that anthrax was about to appear here.

"Yes, but should this vaccine be given to all Americans?" Connie Chung asked me on CNN.

"I don't think that's necessary," I replied.

The next day I received a scathing correspondence from the medical director of the vaccine manufacturer, Bioport, who stood to make great financial gains from the stockpiling of this vaccine. He protested that the vaccine was effective, not antiquated, and that its side effects were no different from those of any other vaccine.

He was wrong. The vaccine had been tested for effectiveness in a small group of wool-gathering shepherds, not the general population. The data on side effects clearly showed that at least 10 percent have muscle aches or flu symptoms—a significant number when there is no anthrax in sight. Plus, the Bioport vaccine was expensive, the federal supply price ($10.64) was expected to double, and civilians would be paying a lot more.

To Vaccinate or Not to Vaccinate?

As a bug du jour, anthrax fell out of the spotlight after that July 4 scare, except for a brief mention as part of a lineup of possibilities with the first trumped-up terror alerts in late 2002 and early 2003. Then there was an anthrax gap until the last day of 2003, when the *New York Times* reported on page 1 the FDA announcement that the anthrax vaccine protected against the inhaled form of the bacteria. This FDA declaration aided government efforts to restart the Pentagon's mandatory inoculation program for soldiers, which had been stalled by a federal injunction. What was the truth here—was there new scientific evidence on the effectiveness of the old vaccine? Should soldiers going into battle take it?

Mark S. Zaid, a lawyer who challenged the Pentagon's mandatory anthrax vaccine program, told the *Times* that the timing of the FDA announcement was driven by politics, not science. The FDA disagreed, claiming that numerous studies had shown the safety and effectiveness of the vaccine against inhaled anthrax.

The *Wall Street Journal* editorialized on January 2, 2004, that mandatory vaccination for the military was the right thing to do. But the editorial also revealed that the FDA had admitted that there were "too few inhalation anthrax cases to support an independent statistical analysis." The *Journal* argued illogically that soldiers refusing the anthrax vaccine would weaken and endanger their unit should the bacterium be used against them in battle, even though anthrax isn't contagious and none of it had been found in Iraq.

The *Journal* called the FDA declaration "a welcome blow to pseudoscientific hysteria." The editorial blamed the conspiracy mongers who had found a willing audience in the media, stoking an increasingly scared society. "A healthy approach to science and risk is critical if we're going to protect ourselves against threats going forward, especially those associated with bioterror."

The *Journal* was right to caution against vaccine hysteria, but the editorial was flawed. It was wrong to conflate a combat situation with the possibility of civilian bioterror. It was not clear, as the *Journal* suggested, that this was one of our safest vaccines or that its use, even in the military, was crucial. In fact, this vaccine was still in the process of being tested by the CDC. And better vaccines were under investigation, which the *Journal* failed to mention.

A volunteer army is not a prison. It was difficult to fault the six recruits who refused the vaccine. It was one thing to advise soldiers going overseas to take this vaccine, it was quite another to force, or even frighten, every member of the military into taking it.

9

INSECTS, POX, AND
LETHAL GAS

"Watch out for weapons of mass destruction!"

—Grandpa, on *Hey, Arnold!* seen on Cartoon
Network, January 2004

WEST NILE VIRUS

In the summer of 2002, the *New York Times*'s prominent coverage of West Nile virus helped contribute to a growing perception that a huge epidemic might be in the offing here in the United States. Dr. Lawrence K. Altman wrote in his column "The Doctor's World" on August 11, 2002, that "as West Nile fever spreads through the country . . . a virus carves a new ecological niche in a hemisphere where it has never been seen." The choice of words "spreads through the country," "carves," and "hemisphere where it has never been seen" exaggerated the extent of the disease. In fact, there were only 170 cases nationwide with only 11 deaths at the time of his writing, though the article made it seem like a lot more. On August 16, 2002, Altman's front-page headline read "Experts Expect Rapid Rise in West Nile Virus Cases," and the lead stated, "The number of cases of West Nile fever is expected to rise sharply in the next week. . . . If the current epidemic reflects experience, about 10 percent of the cases will be fatal."

Altman's and others' emphasis on fatalities helped provoke fear. West Nile did kill, but it was still a very rare disease. By this time, half the country was scratching and overheating in fall clothing. People were afraid to go into their backyards, expecting to encounter either a dead bird or a killer mosquito. Dr. Lyle Peterson, an epidemiologist at the CDC who is an expert in insect-borne diseases, helped spread the panic by speculating that most patients were hospitalized due to brain swelling, when in fact most people afflicted suffered a mild flu or no symptoms at all.

Anthrax narrowed the focus of our fear. After 9/11 we felt vulnerable to attack, and after anthrax we felt vulnerable to infectious agents. West Nile virus was the first bug du jour after anthrax, and the American public quickly transferred its unrealistic fear of the mail to a fear of mosquitoes. Each time we gave fear a name, there was a hope we could control the threat and thereby control the fear. But with each media-driven infection, our fear was soon well out of proportion to the actual risk. We had seen bird viruses of the same class (arboviruses) transmitted from the east to the west by mosquitoes before, yet we had never responded with the trepidation we felt for West Nile virus. These were viruses with a risk of sickness and death, but so were the other arboviruses that didn't scare us nearly as much as West Nile did.

There were cases of West Nile virus in 1999, 2000, and 2001, but it wasn't until after anthrax drew our attention to bacteria and viruses in 2002 that we began to worry about West Nile virus. The number of cases was on the rise, but hardly enough to justify the sudden hysteria.

What Is West Nile Virus?

West Nile virus is transmitted among wild birds by the *Culex pipiens* mosquito, otherwise known as the southern house mosquito.

It has traditionally been found in Africa, the Middle East, southern Europe, and Asia.

In humans, it frequently causes a fever without involving the brain, though it occasionally causes meningitis or brain swelling (encephalitis), especially in the very young and the very old. It is commonly associated with muscle aches, a rash on the trunk, headaches, and lymph node swelling, though most people who are infected have only a mild flu or no symptoms at all.

It is very difficult to catch West Nile virus, even in a region where it has been found. Less than 1 percent of *Culex* mosquitoes in the area have it, and less than 1 percent of those humans bitten by the culprit mosquito become seriously ill.

There is a vaccine that has been released for use in animals, and one is under investigation for use in humans. In the meantime, prevention of West Nile virus cases is best accomplished by removing stagnant water where mosquitoes breed.

Sending trucks trundling up and down streets at night, puffing pesticide fog into the air, as was done in the summer of 2002, is an extreme overreaction, since it knocks down mosquito populations for only a few days while killing wildlife, including some insects that kill mosquitoes. Fogging also may injure humans by aggravating asthma and other lung conditions. Much safer and more effective is larviciding, which attacks mosquito breeding sites and habitats.

The virus was first discovered in Uganda in 1937, and the first urban epidemic occurred in 1996 in Bucharest, Romania, with 393 cases, including 17 deaths. The first North American case appeared in 1999, when 62 cases occurred in New York City, 7 of which were fatal.

UNDER A SUDDEN MEDIA MICROSCOPE

John Barry, a scholar at the Center for Bioenvironmental Research, wrote in an op-ed in the *New York Times* on August 10, 2002, that "the emergence and spread of any new disease is something to take seriously, but the reaction to the West Nile virus has been character-ized not by seriousness but by hysteria. There has been no rational discussion of the threat and no information given about the likely future course of the disease." He went on to point out that it was really only a marginal threat and that it was similar to another mosquito-borne virus, St. Louis encephalitis, which had a variable number of cases every year, with a high of 1,967 in 1975. "And yet there has never been a national focus on this disease, no sudden expenditures of tens of millions of dollars, no media feeding frenzy and no talk of declaring a statewide emergency, as happened in Louisiana last week with the outbreak of the West Nile virus."

On August 13, 2002, the *Chicago Tribune* published an edito-rial, "Fighting Fear and West Nile," which put it in the minority of newspapers that were not overreacting to the overblown threat. The *Tribune* laudably stated that "the alarm—bordering on hyste-ria—over West Nile virus has thrown many local communities into turmoil. Officials report fielding hundreds of phone calls from worried homeowners who have spotted dead birds or who have been disturbed by media reports." The *Tribune* labeled Dr. Julie Gerberding, the director of the CDC, as part of the problem for calling the virus an "emerging infectious disease epidemic," despite the fact that medical experts throughout the United States saw no reason to panic. The *Tribune* was rightfully more con-cerned about the effects of the pesticide fogging than from the virus itself. By way of comparison, West Nile had killed eleven people so far that summer, whereas the flu kills thirty-six thou-sand per year.

In a letter to the *New York Times* that August, I wrote, "The West Nile virus has captured the public imagination. It causes a rash and other scary symptoms, including swollen lymph nodes, which other viruses in its class do not exhibit. Surely the virus can be contained through public health measures that have been use-ful in other similar outbreaks. If public information leads to more insect repellent, longer sleeves and less stagnant water in our backyards, so much the better. But more worrisome is the attempt to treat our hysteria with spraying: how much toxic insecticide will it take to calm our fears? . . . As with anthrax, when 30,000 people were treated with antibiotics and only 22 people were afflicted, the greater problem with West Nile is panic."

West Nile virus stayed in the headlines on the cable news networks and in the newspapers on into early September. Four transplant recipients appeared to have received the virus from donors. This opened up the real possibility that West Nile virus could be transmitted by transfused blood, a prospect that was later confirmed.

The cable news networks inflated this possibility hysterically, raising the question of whether our blood supply was safe. In fact, there was no rapid blood screening test for West Nile, but the blood supply was certainly safe. "Blood supply" is a misnomer, a panic-laden term, since it suggests that a bug can somehow make its way from one donor into all our transfused blood. There is no such reality, as the rule is one donor, one recipient, with no large-scale pooling of transfused blood.

Blood transfusions are often lifesaving, and the risks of getting any virus, especially West Nile, that way are very low. Malaria infects ninety-three people per year via blood transfusions, and millions every year overall, but malaria was not scaring us, because almost all of its killing took place overseas.

Blood transfusion was not a new mode of transmission for West Nile. In fact, it was expected, since mosquitoes take a blood meal when they bite someone.

As of early September, there were still only six hundred cases of West Nile virus nationwide with thirty-one deaths, though it felt like a lot more, thanks to the media coverage. But the fear began to die out as fall came and mosquito season ended.

There was no media memory. As West Nile faded in the fall, no one at any network or any newspaper thought to apologize for overstating the case. There were no retractions, no amendments, just simply no more front-page coverage and no more headlines on cable TV.

should stay?

The following summer, 2003, West Nile was having a slow season. It had infected over ten thousand horses the year before and now there was an animal vaccine, but this was reported only in a small article in a back section of the *Wall Street Journal*.

West Nile just wasn't on our list in 2003, and we didn't know whether it was back with a vengeance or not. We no longer heard about how many it killed. We were back out in our backyards with our short sleeves and our stagnant water. We were thinking about SARS and then the great blackout, followed by the hurricane. In the meantime, West Nile virus made an appearance in the western Plains states, and the CDC reported 6,411 cases of it, with 134 deaths. But we were no longer afraid of West Nile in 2003, and no one was paying attention. The media eye was focused elsewhere.

SMALLPOX

Medicine depends on probabilities: the probability of a disease occurring, the likelihood that it will spread or can be prevented, and the odds of a side effect coming from the prevention or treatment. A risk/benefit analysis weighs the risk of a disease against the risk of the intervention.

With smallpox, the greatest problem in the fall and winter of 2002 was an exaggerated sense of risk on all sides. The smallpox scare was a new category of absurd overreaction when compared with the previous public health hypes. Here was a disease that was being hyped even though it hadn't made anyone sick in the United States in over fifty years. Yet the public had to contend with two opposing fears: fear of smallpox and fear of the vaccine.

True, in its day, smallpox was a debilitating disease that left disfiguring scars. When untreated, it had a 30 percent mortality rate. But it mainly spread person to person by inhaled droplet after a victim was already showing fevers and obvious skin lesions and so was easily isolated. It had been fully eradicated here in the United States in 1949, and from the entire planet in the 1970s, when the immunization program ceased.

Nevertheless, in 2002, scientists and public health officials were talking about the ravages of smallpox as if it were a current problem, a running commentary that needlessly spread fear.

SMALLPOX, THE WEAPON

Ken Alibek, the former deputy director of Biopreparat, the Soviet biological weapons apparatus, admitted to the existence of large amounts of smallpox in the former Soviet Union, so there was reason to believe that some of the stockpiled virus might have found its way into the hands of rogue dictators or terrorists.

The risk of smallpox appearing in the United States was theoretical, yet the media—followed by the public—grew rapidly afraid of it. The amorphous sense of undefined danger contributed to the growing fear. David Goldston, a staffer on the House Science Committee, pointed out to me in late 2002 that "it's difficult to weigh the risks since the government hasn't given out information about the risks, even to the panel advising it on vaccination policy."

In 1797, when Edward Jenner invented the first smallpox vaccine by injecting its viral cousin, cowpox, into a human, he surely never dreamt his work would lead to a vaccination controversy more than two hundred years later. Yet in the fall of 2002 we were faced with a medical dilemma: should we vaccinate anyone against a disease that didn't currently exist? With two vaccines made from killed virus on the horizon—one of which was undergoing trials at the National Institutes of Health—should we use the outdated and more dangerous live-virus vaccine at all? And if so, who should receive it? Was anyone truly at risk?

The old live virus (Jennerian) vaccine had been quite useful at a time when vaccination still made sense. "It offers excellent protection," said Dr. Martin Blaser, an infectious disease specialist. "It is the reason why smallpox is no longer circulating in the world." This vaccine used a related virus (vaccinia) that was much weaker than smallpox but could occasionally cause skin problems, brain swelling, or could spread to patient contacts. It was also not safe to give it to someone who was either pregnant or without a working immune system.

Few talked about the newer, killed-virus vaccines. One of these vaccines had been given safely to over 300,000 people in Japan while smallpox was in the process of being eradicated there. The other—the vaccine the NIH was studying—had been given safely to 100,000 people in Turkey. The CDC Web site listed these facts, but then went on to call these vaccines untested. Were the only tests that mattered to our scientists those that involved Americans? Work was also proceeding on a third state-of-the-art recombinant vaccine, where smallpox DNA was produced using a bacteria such as *E. coli*. Recombinant vaccines were generally the safest and were used for hepatitis and other viruses. It was likely that one would soon be developed for smallpox.

The smallpox fearmongers maintained that, if it did occur here in the United States, it would probably spread first within the hospitals that were attempting to treat it. This was why during the smallpox hype of 2002, hospitals were at the center of the controversy. Some wanted the old vaccine, but most were refusing it. But of course it was difficult to apply any kind of meaningful risk analysis to hospitals in the absence of actual smallpox. Lacking was a public health strategy to help the public see this theoretical risk in perspective.

The Specter of an Ancient Scourge

As an ancient scourge, smallpox captures the dark side of our imaginations. Schoolchildren learn of it as the first bioweapon, distributed in blankets to Native American tribes by British troops during the French and Indian wars of the 1750s.

Yet in modern times smallpox never wiped out large populations at once the way influenza did. Smallpox had always been containable by public health measures. The vaccination program of the 1960s was undertaken largely to eradicate the disease worldwide and not because there was looming risk to a particular group.

The old smallpox vaccine has too many side effects to be used just to treat fear. The stockpiling of hundreds of thousands of doses of this old relic that began in late 2002 was excessive and unjustified.

By October of 2002, an absurd debate was raging about who should get the smallpox vaccine and who shouldn't. The *New York Times* reported on October 16, 2002, that "a panel of specialists advising the government on smallpox vaccinations recommended today offering the immunization to an estimated half-million emergency room and other hospital workers because of the possibility of a bioterrorist attack." This recommendation seemed arbitrary given that there was no reason to expect an imminent attack.

Over the next few months, the debate continued to rage: fear of smallpox versus fear of the vaccine. Finally, on December 13, President Bush veered from his previous pronouncements and stated in a speech that he was not recommending the old smallpox vaccinations for the entire population.

But at the end of 2002, the public was still riddled with unrealistic expectations concerning smallpox. In mid-December the *New England Journal of Medicine* released a survey showing that 65 percent of the population still believed that everyone should be vaccinated now! It was unfortunate to have to respond to this hysteria by continuing to magnify the small risks of the vaccine, countering one set of fears with another.

Before too much vaccinating could go on, smallpox faded from the limelight altogether and was replaced by the next bug du jour. If we finally came to see smallpox in perspective, it was only because something else took its place.

Nine months later, in October 2003, a little-noticed article appeared in *USA Today*, entitled "Smallpox Vaccination Plan 'Ceased.'" Anita Manning reported, "Less than a year after President Bush announced a smallpox vaccination plan to protect

Americans in the event of a terrorist attack, a fraction of the expected number of health workers have been immunized and the much ballyhooed program is dead in the water."

Ray Strikas, the director of smallpox preparedness and response at the CDC, issued this update. He believed that "the pace of vaccinations had dropped dramatically in April after well-publicized reports of unexpected heart problems associated with the vaccine."

So the CDC shipped 291,400 doses, but only 38,549 people were vaccinated, a significant waste. In fact, the whole smallpox preparedness program cost billions of dollars. Homeland Security Department spokesman Brian Roehrkasse said that the plan of vaccinating first responders had accomplished what it set out to do, but this seemed like a ridiculous assertion under the circumstances. Money foolishly spent was becoming an identifying feature of a bug du jour.

CHEMICAL WEAPONS

With the war with Iraq fast approaching in early 2003, terror alerts began appearing on our cable news screens like potholes on a high-speed highway. The concern was easy to trace: the Bush administration was focusing on the UN reports stating that large quantities of chemical and biological weapons were unaccounted for in Iraq. The prevailing rhetoric lumped all these weapons together under the ominous banner "Weapons of Mass Destruction," ignoring the great variance from one potential agent to the next.

In a scenario analogous to that of the bug du jour, the Bush administration created a link in early 2003 with our personal security here at home and suggested that these weapons could somehow be smuggled over here in large enough quantities to imperil our personal safety.

But this was fear perception, not real risk. Our expectation was pushed to an all-time high. We were thousands of miles away, yet we were told we were under siege. President Bush maintained that he would send the troops over there and eradicate the threat, eliminate the danger, before more terrorists could come here and get us.

In coordination with this expectation, the terror alerts began a month before the Iraq war.

CLOTHES FOR THE THYROID

While most of the focus in early 2003 was on chemical weapons, occasionally false fears of nuclear terrorism were trumpeted. Bizarrely, this was accompanied by an obsession with protecting the thyroid with potassium iodide pills. Scam companies were mass marketing and Internet spamming these pills—with the unsubstantiated claim that they had prevented thyroid cancer in Chernobyl in some children who had been serendipitously taking them at the time of the nuclear accident there.

In the event of a nuclear attack or terrorist-provoked plant accident, the theory is that if the thyroid fills up on potassium iodide, it won't have room to take up radiation, and so will be partly protected from fallout. But more crucial organs, including the heart, lungs, gastrointestinal tract, and bone marrow, will still be at risk. Taking this pill in the event of a nuclear attack or accident is like a man going out into a snowstorm wearing only a scarf.

As with Cipro, with potassium iodide scams, people may hoard pills that they will then be too quick to use.

ON CALL FOR FEAR

In early February 2003, when the terror alert was elevated to orange for the first time, people were petrified, and the specter was rising of chemical weapons threatening us from hidden places in Iraq.

It was interesting the way the media helped to generate fear and then went about trying to rein it in, as though TV was simultaneously sensationalistic and in the business of public service.

The NBC *Today* show's Ann Curry told me intensely off camera that we needed to give effective advice to people feeling stress. On camera I suggested that people forget about duct tape, antibiotics, and other specific preparations. Israel coped with daily terrorist threats by going about "business as usual." Here in the United States people could continue with their regular daily activities, focus on things besides the alerts, which, over time, would seem less traumatic. If worry about losing everything caused people to cherish their loved ones, I said, that at least was a good thing.

In my medical office, I began receiving the same worried phone calls from my patients that I had received during the fall of 2001. They told me they were not sleeping, were thinking constantly about bombs, or were rushing to buy emergency supplies. In the months after September 11, many of my patients had desperately sought gas masks and Cipro. In February 2003 these same patients were buying duct tape and plastic sheeting.

In Israel, most people are able to live relatively normal lives despite frequent suicide bombings and constant military conflict. Statistically, a walk to the supermarket in Israel is still far more likely to be uneventful than unsafe. For those in Israel who are well adjusted, the threat gradually begins to seem less imminent and more in keeping with the statistical likelihood of terrorism actually taking place. But even Israel is not completely immune. The sense of threat remains just below the surface, and it wears at people's good health.

In New York City in 2003, many people were more irritable or angry than usual. Such anxiety could come in different forms—including a racing heart, shortness of breath, chest pain, or indigestion. Such patients needed to seek out their physicians for evaluation and perhaps sedatives.

Risks and probabilities are the prime tools of the medical trade, used to assess the chances of a certain disease occurring. In 2003, as the fear of terrorism lingered, these medical tools became more useful in countering the hype.

CHOOSE YOUR POISON

The threat we face from chemical terrorist attacks has been greatly exaggerated. Nerve gas is very difficult to produce and to distribute; moreover, it dissipates rapidly. For example, sarin gas, when it was released in the jam-packed Tokyo subway system in 1995, spread a lot more fear than gas. (Only a dozen people actually died during that attack.) Unfortunately, media descriptions of sarin as a colorless, odorless gas that causes visual disturbance, seizures, and difficulty breathing cast it as a primal threat. It has an antidote—atropine, which has to be injected right away into the thigh or the heart in order to be effective. But actually keeping atropine close at hand *just in case* of an attack is more likely to lead a person to accidental self-injection rather than self-protection.

VX gas stays around longer and can stick to the skin, enter the pores, and block the nerves—but it would be just about impossible for clouds of VX gas to blow through the streets. A delivery system that could expose a massive number of citizens to nerve gas without the gas being destroyed by heat or dissipated by wind simply doesn't exist. Duct tape and plastic sheets? To protect us from what? How is a terrorist going to bring VX gas to my door?

In early 2003, pictures of the old World War I killers, lewisite and mustard gas, blistering agents, were being spliced from our old high school history books and indiscriminately broadcast on our cable TV screens. Vats of these lethal gases had been found previously in Iraq, the worry went.

Lewisite is colorless and smells like geraniums. Mustard gas is colorless and smells like horseradish. They cause the eyes and the skin and the lungs to burn. There is an antidote (British anti-lewisite), and one can quickly flush the skin with water or bleach. But who in the world needs this antidote?

Fear causes us to mythologize these weapons, which have already taken on enlarged significance in our imagination because some have been used in the past for evil purposes.

The *preparations* for an imagined attack—unlikely as it is—create a great deal of anxiety. And holding a gas mask or a roll of duct tape or a box of Cipro in your hands does not provide reassurance to a rational person.

"When do I use this tape or this gas mask?" my patients asked me in early 2003.

"You don't," I replied.

Duct tape to keep out nerve gas is far more likely to lie idle than to protect someone. A chemical suit and gas mask offer 100 percent protection, but they may also suffocate you if used improperly.

We fear terrorism in part because it is unpredictable. Cold War fears were easier to track and were tied to a single enormously visible enemy, the Soviet Union. During the forty-five years of the Cold War, we had time to adapt to these fears and to build up psychological defenses to them. In contrast, the fear of terrorism is a fear with an ever-changing face.

Talking over the radio about these trumped-up fears in the spring of 2003 had a surreal quality for me. Brian Lehrer's WNYC studio observed a library-like silence for his hourlong show on terrorism fears. Mittenlike headphones enveloped our ears as we spoke an inch away from the large felt microphones.

It wasn't obvious to host and listeners, but human fear is too often based solely on our imaginations.

Ask Doctor Marc

Readers of my Ask Dr. Marc column in the *Nation* shared their obsessions with me:

From Springdale, Pennsylvania: If a chemical or biological weapon were used in the United States, how long would the agent persist in the environment? Would sealing windows and doors with plastic sheeting and duct tape keep the germs or chemicals out long enough for the agent to be cleaned or diluted to nonlethal levels?

DR. MARC: Certainly, beware of a mailman in a full bodysuit and gas mask. Otherwise, I recommend going about your daily business. Chemical agents such as sarin would dissipate in minutes on their own long before they reached your duct-taped door. Even if by some unlucky miracle you were right nearby, your best bet would be to leave the area. As far as germs go, anthrax isn't contagious, smallpox spreads very slowly, and bubonic-plague infection requires fleas. Homeland Security notwithstanding, I can't imagine a scenario where it would be essential to duct tape yourself inside a room.

From San Bruno, California: Assume that you could seal a $10' \times 20' \times 8'$ room so that it's airtight, which as a general contractor I think I can do. How long would it be before lack of oxygen or buildup of CO_2 becomes a problem for two people?

DR. MARC: CO_2 is such a noxious gas, maybe terrorists should consider it. In the airtight room you describe, CO_2 would overcome you in a matter of hours, long before a terrorist could reach you with sarin.

From Durango, Colorado: If we were to create a "safe room" in our house with duct tape, etc., how would we determine when to come out, and how would we deal with the contaminated environment from that point on?

DR. MARC: If you're concerned about a contaminated environment, well, we already live in one, yet few of us have chosen to go into a "safe room" and live out our lives there. Imagine what would happen if we all put our safe rooms together and made a safe world.

From an unidentified location: Even asking what we should do to protect ourselves against a chemical attack plays into Bush's fear-mongering agenda. The more scared Americans are, the easier it will be to scrap civil liberties and prosecute the "endless war" Bush has talked about. I think acting as if the possibility of a chemical attack is great enough to be discussed in the Nation *actually unwittingly gives momentum to the Bush agenda.*

DR. MARC: I'd argue that it's better to oppose the fearmongering than to ignore it. Correcting misinformation, providing perspective, countering fear with probability, and learning the real risks: these are treatments for the condition of hysteria that our government has helped to foster. We are not powerless. We can resist being mobilized by fear, first, by realizing that isolated terrorist acts can't defeat us and, second, by puncturing propaganda like the empty balloon it is.

THE GUIDE TO FEAR

In its 2003 manual *New Yorker's Guide to Terrorism Preparedness and Response: Chemical, Biological, Radiological, and Nuclear*, the American Council of Science and Health extended its worst-case scenarioing to chemical weapons. Lewisite, mustard, arsine, cyanide, phosgene, sarin, tabin, VX, and many more were described in excruciating detail: what to do, what antidotes to take, how to protect oneself, all thoroughly described. Of course, in most cases there really isn't much a person can do, which gave the manual a morbid tone.

Manuals such as this one belong on the shelf, as they provoke fear and obsessive thinking about dangers that remain remote. Too much detailed information invariably carries with it the agenda that something is in the offing. Otherwise, what is the point of the manual? What is the point of gearing up, pulse rate rising, for something that either isn't going to happen or that we can't do much about?

Instead of relying on how-to manuals that provoke the public, preparation for an unlikely event should go on behind the scenes. Public health experts can help our leaders stockpile real perspective instead of perishable antibiotics, vaccines, and preparation kits. Leaders and their scientific advisers need to learn restraint; they need to stop justifying their programs by launching campaigns of hype that cause people to feel endangered all the time.

10

SARS

> It seemed . . . very easy to paint the worst-case scenario. I thought about this, how our minds naturally jump to picture the negative outcome and stall there. It is because the mind is frozen by fear, and fear overwhelms hope.
>
> —Jerome Groopman, M.D., *The Anatomy of Hope*

In April 2003 up rose SARS to grab the media megaphone. SARS, or Severe Acute Respiratory Syndrome, brought the panic over a potential infection to a new level. The global health alert and travel advisories that were meant to inhibit the dissemination of the virus also spread virulent fear by word of mouth. Public health agencies raised the stakes, then presumptively took credit for the resolution of the problem.

The government sounded its note of preparedness, wanting to seem proactive in another public panic situation where it was actually being reactive. The CDC, which had lost credibility with the anthrax bungle, rallied publicly with SARS and quarantined entire sections of the planet in response to a virus that demonstrated seven thousand cases worldwide. The CDC and the World

Health Organization (WHO) used fear to provoke compliance, talking about worst-case scenarios and viral mutations, and alarming the whole Western Hemisphere with a few cases that flew around a Toronto hotel.

But no one died of SARS in the United States in 2003, and people eventually grew tired of hearing about it. The CDC and the World Health Organization had restricted travel to and from Asia and Toronto based on the assumption that air travel could allow an emerging contagion to spread more easily. This theory was neither proven nor disproven. In fact, historically, isolating an afflicted patient has always been much more effective than quarantining a region. This principle had held true for plague, influenza, and many other contagious threats. People as they panic from an imposed quarantine can spread a bug. It is human nature to run away from perceived risk and human nature to make common mistakes when engaged in overinflated, hypervigilant activity. People who face heavy stigmatizing for being a suspected disease carrier are likely to lose their common sense altogether.

Nevertheless, when the incidence of SARS died down (as many emerging viruses had done before it), the health organizations were quick to give the credit to their worldwide advisory.

THE CHOKEHOLD

Back in early April 2003, President Bush granted Secretary of Health and Human Services Tommy Thompson the right to quarantine for SARS, thus giving a nudge to the trend that was spreading panic around the globe.

In its more than fifty years of existence, the WHO had never before issued a travel advisory or enacted a global surveillance network, as it did with SARS. In the United States, meanwhile, the CDC was publicly analyzing every conceivable case—another unprecedented reaction. SARS was a legitimate concern, but the response was being carried to an extreme. By April, the virus had infected about two thousand people worldwide and killed fewer than one hundred, compared to the yearly average influenza death toll of thirty-six thousand in the United States alone.

What was going on medically? The answer was complex, since the SARS corona virus was a cousin to the common cold, which spreads easily via sneezing or even touch. But whereas the cold was countered by most people's immune systems, SARS was new so our bodies hadn't yet had time to produce antibodies to it.

On the surface, a strong public health initiative seemed warranted. As Julie Gerberding, the director of the CDC, pointed out in the *New England Journal of Medicine*, the cooperation of the international scientific community in identifying the corona virus as the culprit in a matter of weeks was very impressive. But Gerberding didn't stop with the scientists. She wrote: "Even more impressive than the speed of scientific discovery in the global SARS outbreak is the almost instantaneous communication and information exchange that has supported every aspect of the response."

But this was problematic. For the most part, the result of all this communication was global panic and economic shutdown that seemed way out of proportion to the real threat.

Yes, the WHO pressure on the Chinese medical authorities to take their heads out of the sand, identify patients, and isolate true cases was impressive. But beyond the historically proven method of isolating infected patients, it was difficult to tell how much air travel and the mobility now available to people—and their diseases—increased the mandate for regional embargo. This was an issue to be considered, but it wasn't an automatic justification for planetwide sequestration.

The CDC appeared to be fully recovered from the public lambasting it had received over anthrax back in 2001. It had given itself a new face, with Gerberding as the new director giving speeches and press conferences at an unprecedented rate. SARS was a full-fledged international bug du jour, with news and media coverage beyond any predecessor. The WHO, which had never gotten involved in global tracking strategies to this extent before, was weighing in heavily on SARS. In part this was due to improved technology, greater scientific cooperation, and an increased interest in tracking infectious agents because of concern over possible bioterrorism.

But neither organization was really used to the spotlight, and they weren't considering sufficiently how their reactions might be perceived by a fragile public. There was too much emphasis on public statements and not as much on serological testing and antiviral strategies. SARS needed to be cured with laboratory work, not press conferences. Panic over SARS was public health run amok. All the public posturing took SARS out of its proper context and contributed to a scare that ultimately did more harm than the virus itself.

By focusing only on the worst-case scenarios regarding the spread of SARS, the World Health Organization and the Centers for Disease Control were in effect controlling the populace through fear. This helped to spread worldwide economic havoc—many estimates were that SARS cost over $30 billion to local economies worldwide. Toronto was cut off by the WHO travel advisory throughout much of April 2003.

Chinatowns were deserted in all the major cities, and people around the world were stigmatizing anyone who came from an Asian country.

In contrast to the rest of Asia, Vietnam's careful and quiet isolating of suspected patients seemed to be behind its success in limiting the spread of the virus. Quarantining hospitals where SARS had spread to health care workers, or designating certain centers as "SARS hospitals," was at the upper limit of what seemed reasonable. Monitoring of traffic from countries where SARS had been diagnosed, or emphasizing careful precautions in such countries, was also reasonable but was not the same thing as frightening everyone who may have traveled there or who wanted to do so.

The problem with AIDS information back in the 1980s had been the opposite kind of distortion: affected groups were marginalized, and the prevailing rhetoric had minimized the disease. With SARS, the propaganda was fear, suggesting that everyone could get it overnight, which was far from the case. This notion had a negative impact on many people. Physician/essayist Abraham Verghese, writing in the *New York Times Magazine*, attacked the transparent political agendas that had been applied to bioterror preparation but made an invalid assumption that none of this applied to SARS. Certainly, restricting movement was necessary with a known killer, but with SARS, people were restricted throughout the spring of 2003 just for having a cough. Many life insurance companies wouldn't grant a person a policy if he'd been anywhere near Asia in the past month. This was a vast overreaction.

The distinction had to be made between the need for global control of a virus before it got out of hand and the political agenda of people wanting to justify their jobs and project themselves as soothsayers. The machinery for public broadcasting that had been set up for bioterror prevention was being used indiscriminately for SARS. It was a blind assumption that speaking about SARS incessantly on TV would prevent its spread.

GALVANIZING FEAR

The greatest problem with SARS was that once again public health authorities were talking only in terms of worst-case scenarios, while striving to commit massive resources to their agendas. If you approach people where they feel the most vulnerable, as with health care and disease, it is easier to sign them up for a program purported to be in their interest. This is exactly what government officials do with bioterror to whip up public support for their antiterror programs. Make people afraid, make people feel they need you to protect them, and they allow you free rein with your agenda.

For SARS, fear was the central pathogen, where the risks of acquiring the new mutated cold virus were far less than the fear of being infected. Uncertainty about what the risk really was promoted the panic—seeing SARS in the news caused us to personalize it. We knew it came from an exotic animal in Asia, but we weren't sure which one, which scared us further.

In reality, SARS was a garden-variety respiratory cold virus, nothing sexy, nothing sinister. It was unsettling to consider that all this attention paid to SARS took attention away from influenza and other proven killers. Worldwide, malaria, dengue, and AIDS were diseases that infected millions each year and for which the protections in place were woefully inadequate.

Meanwhile, here in the United States panic from SARS replaced panic from bioterror, which replaced panic from West Nile virus. All this reaction represented resources being taken away from the yearly epidemics in order to fight the latest scare.

True, there were some troublesome aspects to SARS. It was a potentially life-threatening infection to which we had zero immunity. And for SARS we had no ready vaccine, like we did for the flu.

The lead question in doctor's offices throughout April 2003 was what people should do to protect themselves against SARS. The answer of course was to do absolutely nothing. The best vaccine for SARS was information, seeing the new disease in its context. At the time there were only thirty-five documented cases in the United States, and no one had died. We had to treat the perception that we could get SARS rather than any real risk of it. We needed to convert our uncertainty to a realistic understanding of our chances of getting the disease, which were extremely low for any given individual. Overpersonalization of a minuscule risk spreads panic—and when people panic, they tend to take *fewer* precautions.

How did a person know if he had SARS? The answer was that if he had a fever, muscle aches, and difficulty breathing, he *didn't* have SARS, but he probably had the flu.

A Fear of Asians

The small waiting room in my office three blocks from New York University Medical Center was just as congested as the rest of New York, with patients sitting practically on top of one another. As with the subway, it felt as if germs here might spread more quickly than at other places, and I always half-expected my patients to catch the bug their neighbor was harboring. But whether the risk of catching something from another patient was real or imagined, one thing was certain: the stress of living and working in the city made it seem so. Added to this mix, in the spring of 2003 we had the seemingly tangible risk of SARS. My waiting room was filled with patients, all brimming with the same question.

"Could I have SARS?" a patient blurted out. Unsolicited, an office secretary replied, "You must ask the doctor." Meanwhile, the thirteen-inch television set in the middle of the room was playing all SARS all the time and updating my patients on the virus every hour.

An Asian American architect, "Mr. Ho," had come to see me for the first time. No one sat next to him in the waiting room, and when he coughed, the room emptied out altogether.

In my examination room, Mr. Ho announced that he had just returned from Hong Kong. He traveled to China and Hong Kong on business every few weeks, but because of the effect of the SARS scare on the economy there, he had lost his latest architectural job and had had to come back. On the plane bringing him home, he said, no one would sit with him.

He came to me with a cough and symptoms of a cold, but no fever, no muscle aches, no difficulty breathing. Hearing this, I wanted to don a mask, but I put on gloves instead. My patient downplayed his symptoms, clearly realizing I—the doctor—might be worried about SARS.

"It's just a cold," he said. "It was going away, then it came back a little. It's only a tickle."

Without saying the magic word, I reassured him that what he

had sounded not like something sinister but like simple bronchitis. I gave him an antibiotic and sent him home.

Afterwards, I was suddenly nervous, thinking of my two young children. Doctors are not immune to worries about contagion. In my case the concern didn't go away completely until I had taken a shower and irrationally washed away the psychological remnant of my fear. It was the same thing I used to do for AIDS in the 1980s, scrubbing my hands after every encounter with every potential AIDS patient.

A week later, Ho returned to the office with a smile rather than a cough. During that week, the specter of SARS had spread through the world more rapidly than even the disease itself. Though not a single new case had been reported in our city, New Yorkers were increasingly frightened and increasingly wary.

Asia was more isolated than before, and Ho had no immediate prospect for work there. Back in New York, he thought people were taking into account his Asian features and avoiding him on the street. I could actually see this occurring in my waiting room, where the other patients now deliberately avoided not only him but anything he touched.

So why was Ho smiling? In my consultation room he confessed that he had actually been afraid he had SARS, but now that he knew he didn't, despite the fact that he was not working, he believed his future was bright.

SARS IN NEW YORK CITY

New Yorkers are a nervous bunch to begin with, and our doctors are no exception. Most of us, doctors and patients alike, are medical Zeligs; like Woody Allen's character, we take on the symptoms and even the personality of the latest threat. The stress of living in an overcrowded city distorts perceptions in the direction of fear.

The scientific literature analyzing the health of our city's residents shows that a disproportionately high percentage of New York teenagers suffer from eating disorders related to a higher level of stress. The same literature shows that proportionately more adults suffer from heart disease for the same reason. After studying this phenomenon, the journal *Psychosomatic Medicine* reported in 1999 that these conditions are due to the strain of life in New York itself.

New Yorkers try to compensate for the pressure we feel by paying more attention to our symptoms, to every itch and twinge, as if this vigilance might protect us from an ever hostile environment. Our fear management is neurotic. Forever on the verge of panic, we seek out doctors more often and try to use elaborate health care safety nets to protect us from the ultimate free fall. The *Journal of Urban Health* in December 2002 described how New York's megacity has built an elaborate health system.

Our megacity also has more media than anywhere else, and so we are more quickly saturated and prodded by the latest hype. We feel the strain earlier but then we use our extensive safety net to become desensitized more quickly to the latest bug du jour, only to find ourselves right on the front lines of the next scare. It's a real roller-coaster ride.

In the era of SARS fear, we eventually developed a new sort of schtick. Though New Yorkers always cough and kvetch, I'd never heard so much nervous coughing before. We always seem to be on the verge of catching something, or if not actually catching something, at least complaining that we might. In the spring of 2003, each raspy breath seemed more significant, each sniffling acquaintance seemed ominously afflicted.

My office phone rang continually with respiratory complaints. I knew better than to counter these concerns with the bald statistic of zero deaths from SARS in the United States. I didn't want to appear to be downplaying serious potential risk even if that risk was remote.

After a month of SARS hype, New Yorkers began building up an immunity to the fear.

According to the Centers for Disease Control, there were only two probable cases of SARS in New York City by May of 2003, cases that ultimately turned out not to be SARS. So our respiratory filters joined our gas masks and our stash of antibiotics in our tiny closets.

SARS When the Smoke Cleared

By July of 2003, long after it had dropped off the headline news, it was determined that SARS had infected 8,400 people, killing 774 worldwide, with 33 probable U.S. cases and no deaths. After analyzing all the data from this outbreak, the WHO concluded that SARS is not spread easily through the air, but requires large respiratory droplets.

The Associated Press reported in October that fear over the possible return of SARS was so great in the United States that even if it didn't appear, the CDC expected emergency rooms to be swamped with suspected cases. They were concerned that doctors with limited SARS experience could confuse early SARS with the flu.

"Whether the virus comes back this winter or not, we will be dealing with SARS," said Dr. James Hughes, the director of the National Center for Infectious Diseases of the Centers for Disease Control and Prevention. "When people start showing up with respiratory diseases, physicians will be thinking of SARS. I can tell you we're more prepared than before," Hughes said. "I think the global community can handle SARS if it's handled appropriately. I think enough lessons have been learned" in the previous outbreak. Research on a vaccine and antiviral treatments were already underway.

As of February 2004, the outbreak still hadn't happened, with only three cases in Asia and none on the North American continent. But the new viral bug du jour was flu, not SARS. Hughes was wrong. By early 2004, SARS seemed like a distant memory.

We really don't know what stopped the SARS outbreak in spring 2003. It may simply have run its course. It seems likely that hand washing and isolation of infected individuals helped, as the

Times suggested in an editorial in early November 2003. But there was no direct evidence that the *Times* was right to conclude that "such tactics, buttressed by quarantines and restricted air travel, stopped the epidemic last time."

It clearly cost billions of dollars, and ironically, the *Times* editorial ended by reversing itself and cautioning the future use of aggressive tactics for SARS with a "recognition of the costs of any large-scale shutdown of normal activities."

But thanks to SARS hysteria, the apparatus was now in place for massive worldwide overreactions. If a disease died down, the health organizations and the media would take credit for its defeat without a true scientific study to prove they were right. If a disease seemed to get out of hand, the news media would continue to report it without ever acknowledging the way they—the media— were instantly altering the public's sense of risk.

In China, Zhong Nanshan, a scientist who had dealt with the first SARS outbreak, had a more practical plan. He urged people just to avoid spitting in public and eating wild animals.

11

FLU

"The fear in the hearts of people just withered them," said Susanna Turner, a hospital volunteer. "They were afraid to go out, afraid to do anything. . . . If you asked a neighbor for help, they wouldn't do so because they weren't taking any chances."

—John Barry, *The Great Influenza: The Epic Story of the Deadliest Plague in History*

TV Docs

In early December 2003, TV and radio across the country relentlessly covered the "flu outbreak." Practicing physicians appeared on multiple stations to respond to sudden concerns.

Marvin Scott, the WB11 weekend anchor in New York, a man with a classic sonorous TV voice, a square chin, and the pockmarks of a veteran newsman, seemed insulted that I didn't recognize him.

He rushed into my pale blue consultation room on the winter-cold afternoon of December 10 with his cameraman and his agenda ready. Some children had died, and he seemed to want me to say that all parents should be concerned. His first question was about what parents should be doing to protect their kids.

I cautioned that parents shouldn't overreact. The sniffles your child complained of might well be the common cold, whereas flu tends to manifest itself with sudden high fevers, chills, severe muscle aches, and headaches.

"Eleven children have died in one state," he said dramatically. "The number is climbing. Is this an epidemic?"

Scott's questions wouldn't go on TV, only my answers, wrapped together in a sixty-second sound bite. It was important for me not to utter a single phrase that might play into the hype. I told him that young deaths were clearly a tragedy, but not an epidemic.

"Should parents be keeping their kids out of schools?"

"Parents should be encouraging hand washing and should always keep sick kids at home. But flu is far from widespread enough to consider closing schools."

"What should parents do?"

"All day long my office telephone rings with nervous parents wanting to get flu shots for their kids."

"What do you tell them?"

"I tell parents that flu shots are not strictly necessary unless their kids have asthma or another chronic illness."

By the time he left my office, Marvin Scott seemed calmer. He had a hype bias, but he was open to fresh facts.

It was true that children were dying—twenty or thirty by December 12. How many the total number would be wasn't yet known. Still, the danger to any of us or our kids remained far less than it seemed.

Flu perception was far worse than the reality. Here is what I told my patients: schools closed for blizzards, not flurries. Our 2003 flu was a flurry, not a storm. Since we were on a heightened flu alert, we were likely to mistake every cough or sneeze for that bad bug, but doctors could usually tell whether their patients were overreacting or actually required immediate attention.

The Yearly Outbreak

Before 2003, flu was an underappreciated ho-hum domestic killer. It was traditionally robbed of the attention it deserved by the latest bug du jour. Thirty-six thousand people died of the flu in the United States yearly, but many didn't get the vaccine who should have. In previous years, the flu simply didn't worry enough people.

In the fall of 2003, all of that changed overnight, as talking-head doctors told TV viewers why they should worry: it was an earlier season then usual, a worse flu bug than usual, and the vaccine didn't really cover this flu, which appeared to be a killer of children. But the true epidemic was not from flu virus but flu fear.

The CDC and the WHO, now assuming the go-to position with every potential contagion, once again seized the media megaphone as soon as a few children started to die of flu in late November. I received hundreds of phone calls from healthy patients demanding the flu shot, a vaccine that was rapidly becoming scarce. One healthy young patient, whom I hadn't seen in over two years, called urgently for a shot because her sister was afraid to let her visit the newborn baby two days hence without one. I was able to slow her down only by pointing out that two days wasn't sufficient time for the shot to work. Even at the height of the concern, no one knew whether the flu season was going to be any worse than in prior years, when the media paid little attention.

Scares One Group, Kills Another

While 70 to 80 million had received the flu vaccine the year before in the United States, another 70 million were advised to receive it but didn't. Health care workers, those with respiratory or chronic illnesses, pregnant women, the elderly, and anyone who might come in close contact with the flu are on the CDC's recommended list to be vaccinated. Influenza affects 20 percent of the U.S. population in a given year, and over 200,000 people are hospitalized on average. The yearly flu vaccine is generally 40 to 60 percent effective at preventing the flu.

The Centers for Disease Control reported 85 million doses of the vaccine available in 2003, as the vaccine manufacturers based their year's supply on the previous year's usage. In 2002, they had had to discard over 10 million unused doses, and they weren't about to repeat that costly move in 2003. This way of determining supply inevitably led to a shortage in a year when the devastating deaths were broadcast and hyped by the media. By early December 2003, people were clamoring for the vaccine even as supplies of it ran short.

The World Health Organization has a global influenza surveillance system involving 112 regional influenza centers. These centers study the early patterns of the year's flu in Asia and South America. The WHO then makes its best guess of what the predominant strains would be here and makes up the vaccine for the most common serotypes. Unfortunately in 2003, the Fujian strain of influenza A, which was going to cause a lot of the havoc, wasn't included in the vaccine because of difficulty getting it to reproduce in the culture medium.

FLU HISTORY

The flu is an ancient scourge, tracing its origins back at least to the days of Hippocrates, who recorded an outbreak of an illness that began with a cough, followed by pneumonia and other symptoms, at Perinthus in ancient Greece in 400 B.C.

There were several pandemics (disease spreading widely over a large region) in the eighteenth century, but the most massive outbreak ever occurred in 1918, when more people in the world died of the Spanish flu (50 million) than died in World War I, with over 600,000 deaths from the flu in the United States alone.

In 1968, the Hong Kong flu killed 700,000 people worldwide, and this may well have set us up for the swine flu panic of 1976, when the outbreak wasn't large, but the rush vaccination program led to 100,000 cases of Guillain-Barré syndrome, a form of paralysis. Luckily, the current version of the flu vaccine is much safer than the one used in 1976.

A pandemic occurs when a new strain of influenza is created by mutation and species-jumping from bird or pig to human. Influenza experts agree that another pandemic is likely to happen at some point. Epidemiological models project that in industrialized countries alone, the next such scourge is likely to result in 57 million to 132 million outpatient visits and 1 million to 2.3 million hospitalizations, and 280,000 to 650,000 deaths over less than two years, or at least five to ten times what we tend to experience in an average flu year. However, these models don't take into sufficient account that a quickly developed vaccine may slow spread. A "herd immunity" may also have occurred from prior vaccination or exposure to similar flu strains.

The impact of the next flu blight is likely to be greatest in developing countries where health care resources are strained and the general population is weakened by poor health and nutrition. So the WHO and the CDC work at expanding the flu surveillance and containment network.

One reason for the potential panic out of proportion to the risk is that it is almost impossible to predict when this pandemic might occur. The event occurs only about once in fifty years, but the more we see it discussed in the media, the more we personalize the uncertainty, convincing ourselves irrationally that *every year* will be *the* year.

THE MAKING OF A BUG DU JOUR

Before 2003, flu was underappreciated. It was a widely held, yet poorly acted upon, public health perception that we needed more vaccinations, more isolation of those who were sick, and more hand washing. When I first saw flu hit the headlines, I hoped that the sudden attention would shed light on these basic precautions. Unfortunately, the flu scare of 2003 did not necessarily lead to proper prevention, but as with all bugs du jour, it involved significant expense.

By mid-December, influenza had completed its transition from ho-hum killer to whopping bug du jour. By December 12, it was all over the Internet that the flu had spread to all fifty states. Flu did this every year, though usually not until January, and in previous years most people who didn't have the flu paid little attention.

Dr. Julie Gerberding, the director of the CDC, was the official spokesperson for the flu, as she had been for every bug du jour since anthrax. She seemed to have gained at least some insight since SARS and was now attempting to be the voice of reason. Still, as always, she addressed the phenomenon without acknowledging that the perception of a scourge was a media creation. "I think what we're seeing is a natural response to concerns about a serious flu season," she said on December 12 on NBC's *Today* show. "But we also need to remember that for almost everyone, flu is not such a serious disease. We don't need to panic or assume that the worst-case scenario is going to happen to everyone. Most of us will get through this fine," she said.

Meanwhile, thousands all over the country lined up for flu shots wherever they could find them, mostly in response to the spreading fear. The federal government announced that it was scrambling to ship 100,000 adult vaccine doses to combat the shortages, hoping to head off what they felt could become one of the worst flu outbreaks in years, and 150,000 child vaccines were expected in January. The government, by wanting to show that it was preparing, helped spread the sense of urgency. Around the country, schools began to shut down. Emergency rooms were filling with sick children, many of whom just had colds. Doctors' offices were forced to turn away droves of people seeking flu shots. An Internet poll of 30,000 people reported 57 percent who said nothing more could be done, but 43 percent who felt this vaccine didn't offer adequate protection. Both of the vaccine manufacturers, Chiron and Aventis, had shipped their entire supply, though Aventis had set aside 250,000 doses that it was giving to the CDC for distribution. The CDC also managed to procure 375,000 more doses from Great Britain.

Gerberding said the CDC was recommending doctors give high-risk groups top priority for shots.

Despite the severity of the early outbreak, health experts were still not able to predict just how bad the flu season would be! The season could still just be peaking early.

SURPRISE ENDING

In mid-December, the government continued its rush to find extra vaccine doses (as it had in 1976) to help quell the panic it had helped to create. Dr. Walt Orenstein, the director of the CDC's National Immunization Program, fanned the fear flames by announcing that this was still looking like a bad flu season for children. Ninety-two children die in an average flu year. It was still too early to tell whether this number would be exceeded in the 2003–2004 season, though parents everywhere, fueled by media hype, continued to act like it.

The buzz among doctors was that it was highly unusual for healthy children to be dying from this flu. This unscientific observation, though it concerned only a few dozen patients nationwide, helped to spread the panic. Then suddenly, the news media stopped reporting on the flu. The CDC was just starting to use the word *epidemic* when the media showed its attention deficit and veered away.

The flu willies of 2003 were actually treated inadvertently by the capture of Saddam Hussein. On the morning of December 14, 2003, Paul Bremer, the U.S. administrator of Iraq, announced, "Ladies and gentlemen, we got him." The message was that because this evil man had been captured, the world was by definition much safer. The news media broadcast this central message for more than a week to the exclusion of any fear messages. The famous video footage of Saddam's mouth yielding to a tongue depressor replaced all images of sick children lying on hospital gurneys. The sense of relief we felt carried over to many aspects of our lives. We went through a "feeling safe" week and lumped the flu into the group of things we were automatically feeling safer from. Flu was displaced from the headlines, so we stopped thinking about it. It briefly seemed as if nothing deadly at all could take place now that the world's worst monster was in custody.

Seeing safety in these simplistic terms—that the world, with a broken-down Saddam snaked out of his hole, was suddenly safe where it hadn't been before—was a distortion, a perversion of the facts. It was as if the military's accomplishment was somehow a cure for all our ills, and for all potential ills, including influenza.

In reality, we were no more and no less susceptible to the risk of this year's flu than the day before Saddam's capture when the flu was all over the Internet, the Associated Press, and the top of the cable shows' news cycles 24/7. The sudden transition from palpable panic to utter disregard served to underline the extent to which our fears were manipulated and were ultimately unrelated to actual dangers.

"There is no firm line dividing what's an epidemic and what's not an epidemic," Gerberding emphasized on December 19, when people were no longer listening. "But I think when you look at maps with widespread activity in thirty-six states, we regard it from a commonsense perspective as an epidemic." The CDC said its emergency operations center had been up and running for two weeks, but rather than be alarmed by this announcement, the media barely covered it, and those people who knew about it ignored it.

Anthrax, West Nile virus, and SARS had driven people wild with worry while actually killing fewer than a thousand people combined in the Western Hemisphere. Influenza, a proven killer of thirty-six thousand people per year in the United States alone, was first ignored, then obsessed over, and then ignored again.

If there was a silver lining to all this fear-induced distortion, it was that increased public awareness might help the health care system contain the flu in the future—provided that some awareness of the real disease remained once the roving eye of the media had moved on.

12

COWS, BIRDS, AND
HUMANS

When it comes to scares, to paraphrase an old proverb,
reports of exaggerated risks can be halfway around
the world before the truth gets its boots on. . . . The
key here is to make our own decisions based on science,
not fear. . . . If we only spent as much time focusing
on real, significant risks (for example, cigarette smoking, skipping our influenza vaccine, overexposure to
sunlight, etc.) as we do to a minuscule risk like BSE in
beef, our nation would be even healthier than we
are today.

—Dr. Elizabeth Whelan, president of the American
Council on Science and Health, in the *New York
Sun*, December 26, 2003

MAD COW DISEASE

In late December 2003, as the excitement and the safe feeling over
the capture of Saddam Hussein were ebbing, a new bug du jour
was surfacing. While at the time we Americans tried to downplay
terror, calling the multicolored alerts the "boy who cried wolf,"

we became instantly afraid of beef—all because of a single infected cow. Humans were reacting like Esther Sabban's stressed rats; the suppression of one fear led to an exaggerated response to the next perceived danger that came along. Since 9/11, we have tended to panic over each conceivable contagion.

With mad cow disease, we were getting a taste of our own medicine. For over a decade we had banned European beef from our shores, cautioned our people not to eat meat when they traveled there, and refused even to allow our travelers to donate blood when they returned here. In May 2003, when a single case of mad cow disease appeared in Canada, the United States Department of Agriculture (USDA) immediately banned *all* Canadian cattle from crossing our border. Now, when a single U.S. cow was discovered—after it had already been killed and used for beef—to have mad cow disease (bovine spongiform encephalopathy, or BSE), over a dozen other countries, including meat-careful Japan and Korea, banned our beef. The entire world was petrified of mad cow disease, for reasons that I will explain later in this chapter. Canada quickly paid us back, banning our beef immediately in much the same way we had banned theirs earlier in the year. The USDA wanted to claim that this sick cow had somehow crossed the border from Canada into Washington State, but at first no one believed them. By the time they managed to show that indeed this cow had infiltrated us from Alberta, it was too late—hysteria had hit and we were branded.

The *New York Times*, which had practically ignored the flu willies two weeks before, perhaps because they hadn't broken the story in the first place, was all over this one, front-paging it every day for most of the week, giving a history of mad cow in Britain, tracing the effects on the meat industry, and detailing the USDA's paltry attempts to safeguard the meat we ate.

At the same time, cattle growers, industry representatives, and the agriculture secretary, Ann Veneman, went out of their way to assure Americans of the continued safety of American beef. Their assurances were justified in terms of the extremely low risk of mad cow, though by the time the results came back on the few cows they did test for BSE, the cows had already been made into hamburgers and hot dogs that were zooming toward people's dinner plates.

This single case of mad cow exposed the holes in the American system of meat production and disease testing. We were right to be concerned about the safety of our beef, though we were misdirected toward mad cow disease. The sick Holstein that prompted the panic hadn't been able to walk, yet like so many other downer cows, it hadn't been tested or banned before slaughter.

Once again, discovering the holes in one of our protective nets helped make us feel unsafe.

In 2002, according to Secretary Veneman, the USDA inspected only 20,526 cattle out of a herd of 35 million. In contrast, Japan tested all its cows, 1.2 million in 2002, and in Western Europe, they tested all cattle over two years old, all sick cattle, and a small screening percentage of healthy ones (10 million cows tested in 2002).

On Christmas Eve 2003, the sudden hysteria over the mad cow case caused Tyson meat packing and McDonald's to lose over 5 percent of their stock value in a single day. Supermarkets removed meat from their shelves.

What Is Mad Cow?

At the heart of the problem was a tiny protein known as a prion, a protein that can mutate and misfold into a lethal form, eating away at the brain, causing madness, wasting, and death. Dr. Stanley Prusiner discovered this agent in 1988 and won a Nobel Prize for his work. He proposed that this particle is also an infectious agent. Because it is an impossible-to-stop monotonic killer that starts off as an innocent protein, it has frightened the public despite being extremely rare.

Animals that eat infected tissues can contract the disease, setting off an epidemic when vegetarian animals are forced by humans to eat one another via rendered meats. But these misfolded proteins can also arise spontaneously in cattle and other animals, including man, where the rare disease of progressive dementia and muscle jerks is known as Creutzfeldt-Jakob disease, or CJD.

Scrapies is the version of the disease in sheep, causing severe wasting and madness. Unfortunately, sheep brains were part of the meal fed to cows in Europe in the late 1980s and early 1990s, when the disease became endemic in cows.

Because of the lag time of several years between contamination and infection, cases can be missed. Not every animal that has died a progressive demented death has been properly diagnosed. This uncertainty is part of what scares us.

But the risk of acquiring mad cow disease from the meat we eat has always been very low because of a built-in protection that the news media has failed to emphasize. The direct transmission from animal to human involves crossing an effective species barrier. This means that though there were several thousand infected animals in Europe in the 1980s and early 1990s, and though millions of humans ate beef, the number of people known to have acquired mad cow from eating beef (known as variant CJD) was very small. Even though the United Kingdom had 39,000 newly infected cows per year at peak, and 180,000 cases during the worst ten-year period, which was 90 percent of the world's total, only 140 people have actually been infected with the variant CJD so far, and 120 have died.

But the media focus on the mystery and deadliness of the disease has made it seem like a lot more deaths.

FROM COW TO HUMAN: FEAR IN EUROPE

In the 1990s, the British government responded to the growing epidemic among cows by banning the use of meat-and-bone meal, and the number of cattle with mad cow disease decreased dramatically.

But in 1996, health officials in Great Britain became alarmed by the discovery of an apparent link between mad cow disease in animals and a new variant of CJD in humans. Whereas the spontaneous human form of prion disease primarily affected the elderly, the new variant (vCJD) affected people in their late teens and twenties. In August 1996, a British coroner ruled that a twenty-year-old British vegetarian who died from variant Creutzfeldt-Jakob disease caught it from eating beefburgers as a child, starting the nationwide panic.

VCJD is a rapidly progressive disease—its symptoms include emotional distress or confusion, and, ultimately, dementia, loss of muscle control, and death within a year.

The primitive fear of catching a fatal disease from an animal coupled with the horror of the disease itself helped fuel the panic. Once isolated cases began occurring, worried people lost sight of the fact that the risk of catching the disease on a person-by-person basis was still almost nonexistent.

In the mid-1990s, responding to the growing panic, the European Union banned Britain from exporting beef. In Britain, some restaurants struck red meat from their menus, and many consumers refused to buy cow-based food even for their pets. The sale of any beef attached to the bone, which could contain prions, was outlawed in Europe for several years.

Even though the number of human cases remained quite small, the British government felt compelled to put in place a variety of safety measures: it ordered 4.5 million cattle destroyed, banned animal-component feed or fertilizer, and instituted the tracking and testing program.

These measures paid off handsomely at least in terms of cows. In 2003 there were only 148 confirmed cases in cows, well down from a peak of 36,680 in 1992, when one out of every twenty cows in Great Britain had the disease. The preventative and regulatory measures helped to revive the industry. The European Union ban against British beef was dropped in mid-1999.

However, a four-thousand-page report released in 2000 found that the British government had initially misled the public for a decade by failing to emphasize the possibility that the disease could be passed on to humans. Once a case appeared, this lack of information and preparation became the focus, rather than the limited risk. The public mistrust that resulted helped sustain the panic. It took several years before the systematic inspection of animals and the decreasing numbers of afflicted cows helped to relieve the public's fears.

The British experience illustrated how true diligence can diminish the public's fear response while misinformation enhances it. If you could trust your leaders to begin with, you would be much less likely to engage your fear apparatus unnecessarily.

MAD COW PRODUCTS

On this side of the ocean, beginning in 1989 the USDA banned the importation of cows, sheep, and goats and their products from Great Britain, and from all of Europe beginning in 1997. But outrageously, the FDA did not have similar success in banning these products from vaccines, soaps, and gel caps. The FDA has also had difficulty enforcing cow feed regulations here at home.

In January 2004, *Newsday*'s Kathleen Kerr reported that "in the last six years the FDA has sent 63 warning letters to companies involved in the cattle industry detailing unsafe practices— ranging from sloppy clean-up methods in feed mills to improper labeling."

At the same time, fetal calf serum from the United Kingdom has been used in the production of vaccines, including the period in the mid-1980s when the incidence of BSE in calves was as high as 1 in 2,000. Since the sera from approximately 1,500 calves are pooled together, this makes it theoretically possible that if 1 in 2,000 calves was infected, any given serum pool might be infected.

The FDA has stressed that the risks of getting mad cow disease from a bovine product are remote and strictly theoretical. But the same FDA has shown an inability to effectively restrict bovine products. The FDA repeatedly recommends that vaccine manufacturers stop using bovine materials from BSE-affected countries, but no one is listening. Furthermore, capsules used in countless medications have been made using gelatin ground from cow bones—including those from countries where mad cow disease was endemic.

Time has shown that our fear of mad cow disease was overblown, which was fortunate, given the ineptitude of the food-protecting agencies struggling to save us from it.

FEELING SAFE: BEYOND THE NUMERICAL RISK

On December 31, 2003, the *New York Times* reported that the USDA had issued new, tougher regulations. Animals tested for BSE would no longer be marked "inspected and passed" until test results were confirmed. This pending meat would not enter the food supply. Downer cows, which were sick or could not walk, would also be banned. The creation of a nationwide animal tracking system was planned.

On January 2, 2004, Eric Schlosser, the author of *Fast Food Nation*, wrote an op-ed in the *New York Times* pointing out that Agriculture Secretary Ann Veneman, who responded to the mad cow crisis by "reassuring the world that American beef is safe," was also former director of public relations for the National Cattlemen's Beef Association and was therefore quite biased. "For too long the emphasis has been on commerce, at the expense of safety," Schlosser wrote. Further, despite the new regulations, there was still no plan on the part of the USDA to begin the kind of large-scale beef-screening program as was in place in Europe or Japan. Schlosser recommended the creation of a new agency that would lack the USDA's agenda of promoting American meat worldwide. The new agency would be a real food safety agency.

But as mad cow faded from the public consciousness, the American public began to return to its habit of indiscriminate beef consumption.

Fear could be positive if it led to more careful scrutiny of our beef. Fear of a single cow infecting us isn't justified, but attention to the overall safety of our beef is.

Mad cow disease was now rare in cows and practically nonexistent in humans, but bacteria like *E. coli* were more prevalent and potentially risky. Unfortunately, news media overcome by hysteria weren't about to scratch below the surface to consider the real danger.

BIRD FLU

By the end of January 2004, it was clear that the human flu had peaked and petered out. Ironically, it turned out to be a mild flu season. The CDC reported that this year's mismatched vaccine had not succeeded in diminishing flu symptoms. The disease had simply run its yearly course. Increased attention to influenza, of a less frenzied type, could be helpful in the future, but the media-induced hysteria and the rush to vaccinate had not been productive.

We bounced from one bug du jour to the next, without perspective, without even a memory of how the past bug du jour had suddenly and unceremoniously been dumped from the media spotlight, deflating all its supposed dangers.

By January 24, 2004, we suddenly began hearing about the avian flu, the new potential bug du jour. After practically ignoring human flu, this time the *New York Times* provided extensive front-page coverage, creating a sense of immediacy and sweeping importance: "The announcement, made by the Thai government on Friday, has deepened fears of a global epidemic if the virus combines with another that can be transmitted from person to person."

The Thai government had supposedly suppressed the information about the sick chickens for weeks in order to protect its poultry industry, as China had suppressed information about patients sick with SARS the year before to protect tourism. Once uncovered, suppression stoked fears.

The City of New York Department of Health and Mental

Hygiene suddenly issued a new advisory on January 28, alerting health care providers to widespread outbreaks of avian influenza A in domestic poultry and wild birds in ten countries in Asia, where by the beginning of February avian flu had infected over twenty humans among bird handlers and their relatives, killing fourteen people. If you'd traveled to Asia recently and returned to New York with respiratory symptoms, you were being asked to report to the health department. But human-to-human transmission was extremely unlikely. The virus was routinely killed when a chicken was cooked. If this public health alert expanded, panic was sure to result.

A *New York Times* editorial on Friday, January 30, acknowledged that "the threat to Americans is virtually nonexistent," but went on to state that "health officials are rushing to prepare a seed virus for vaccine production, but full-scale production could take months." The problem with this sort of rhetoric was that while professing calm, it simultaneously spread fear. People could wrongly conclude from this that something terrible *might* be in the offing. Hype breeds fear, unless a person is trained to assess risk independently.

NOT ON OUR SHORES

Despite the fact that not a single infected bird had escaped the Asian continent, Lee Jong-Wook, WHO director general, had also helped to spread chicken phobia on January 28 with the statement "This is a serious global threat to human health." In fact, the bird flu was not such a threat, despite being a serious disease in birds. We would all worry less if we understood the difference between *potential* and *actual* risk.

As an American bug du jour, the avian flu would not have the same fear impact as the others did as long as it didn't jump to humans and cross the ocean. But if it infected even a single American, we might then wrongly conclude that it threatened all of us here.

Meanwhile, over in Asia, the virus was creating havoc, bringing up memories of SARS even if the victims this time around were birds, with few people. Over 100 million chickens, crows, and ducks died across Asia, mostly from government-ordered slaughters rather than from the disease. It was difficult to know whether this much bird carnage was necessary in order to prevent a significant spread to humans, or whether it was a way of treating the fear. But even as a protective gesture it backfired, as vivid television and newspaper images of unprotected people throwing dead chickens into pits or stuffing them live into sacks was enough to spread further hysteria and begin to cause economic shutdown, as it did with SARS.

Here in the United States, thousands of chickens were being killed in Delaware for another unrelated bird flu. (Ironically, China was now banning our chickens just as Japan was banning our beef.)

The excessive killing of birds was public health posturing, a gesture meant to show us that we were being protected. But obviously, no scientific study had been done to determine how many chickens needed to be killed to prevent significant spread of a bird flu, even among birds.

Another key factor keeping Americans from full-blown bird panic in early 2004 was that we weren't yet ready to consider another influenza. We were desensitized to flu viruses for the time being. According to Dr. Sabban, an expert in stress models, it would take a different kind of bug to make us hysterical again so soon.

Avian flu didn't quite capture our negative imagination. Asian birds didn't scare us here the way exotic cats did with SARS. Exotic cats were unfamiliar and made us feel uneasy, whereas Asian birds looked just like our own birds.

But in Asia, avian flu pushed the SARS fear button. The *Wall Street Journal* provided a stirring front-page headline on January 28, 2004: "Bird-flu Outbreak Revives Concerns Stirred by SARS."

This article described the poor public health conditions that had been the same for SARS: "animals and people living in close and sometimes unsanitary quarters; poor regulation of livestock; and ill-equipped public health workers hamstrung by local governments so anxious to avoid panic and economic pain that their actions border on a coverup."

Dr. Julie Gerberding of the CDC was quoted in the article, saying "This could be a very serious problem if the epidemic in Asia is not contained." Which epidemic was that? Was she trying to inflame us with the double-digit human deaths? Or perhaps she meant to say the "chicken epidemic?"

The *Journal* backed up its front-page story with another story headlined "Scientists Rush to Create Vaccine for Bird Flu—Just in Case." What was all this rushing about?

The *Journal* article provided the apparent answer in a box insert, "Some experts worry the virus could morph into a human superflu, as in the pandemic of 1918–1920." Here was scary 1918, invoked again. And the ultimate drama: "We have to think about the potential for a significant population die-off," said Dr. David Fedson, formerly of the vaccine maker Aventis. Was Dr. Fedson being mercenary or was he just going overboard? He was referring, after all, to the human population.

BIRD TO HUMAN

In a March 2004 article published in *Science*, the Spanish flu of 1918, which had infected close to a billion people around the world, killing 50 million, was determined to have made the jump from birds to humans by a slight change of the structure of the spikelike molecules known as hemagglutinins by which the virus attaches itself to body cells.

The 1918 Spanish flu pandemic is taken very seriously by epidemiologists, since it killed more people than any other single outbreak of disease, surpassing even the Black Death of the Middle Ages. In fact, it is thought that the virus played a role in ending

World War I, as soldiers were too sick to fight, and more men on both sides died of flu than were killed by weapons.

But the 2004 bird flu had a different molecular structure than the 1918 bug, and there was no direct evidence that it was about to mutate and pass from human to human. Bringing the old scourge to light to scare the public into some kind of "vigilance," when there was nothing definite in the offing, was problematic.

Yet this was what John Barry, the author of *The Great Influenza: The Epic Story of the Deadliest Plague in History*, urged everyone to do in his op-ed in *USA Today* on February 10, 2004. "A public information effort must be launched to convince people of the threat and heighten cooperation. From the perspectives of public health and national security, the bird flu in Asia already should have the full attention of every government in the world. The risks are too great to do otherwise." Cooperation among scientists was one thing. But "to convince people of the threat" meant to alarm them unnecessarily.

Unbelievably, it was the television rather than the print media that seemed to be sending a more reasoned message, for the first time I could point to since September 11, 2001. The cable news coverage of the bird flu didn't appear to be as extensive as what the *New York Times* or the *Wall Street Journal* provided. A producer at CNN told me that they didn't "want to appear to be sensationalizing the story."

But I suspected the lack of TV coverage had more to do with flu fatigue and lack of focus on other countries than it did with a sense of public responsibility. If the American public was ending up with the right perspective for once, it was for the wrong reasons.

THE WORLDWIDE LABORATORY

By this time, great scientists studying the worldwide laboratory were becoming too interested in the latest bug in the news. With publicized contagions, our public health experts easily set aside the rigor of their training and fell into a trap of hype. Public health had gotten too entangled with the media, and infectious disease experts had begun automatically using the media megaphone to broadcast their message.

It is true that an avian flu, if it morphs into a human-to-human virus, can cause another worldwide epidemic like the one in 1918. But many viruses and bacteria have the *potential* to harm, and it is up to public health agencies to distinguish between potential and actual. Disease information is contextual—it is never an all-or-nothing situation as portrayed in the news.

Regardless, the CDC continued its public demonstrations of vigilance. Led by Dr. Gerberding, it responded quickly with multiple press conferences to each new perceived threat. This did a disservice to standard killers like malaria and AIDS, which infected and killed millions each year but were largely ignored. Public health resources were unjustly transferred to the latest potential threat in the news.

The WHO had zoomed to the fore, with its new director Lee Jong-Wook embarrassing the Thais for keeping their sick birds under wraps. But where was the same effort on behalf of the real killers, malaria and dengue, AIDS and schistosomiasis? And what about malnutrition? More people have died of hunger than of all these diseases combined. Public health attention to the latest potential killer instead of the known killers is not only an "epidemic" of misinformation, it is also a form of politically expedient job justification.

Public health experts continued to use words like "vigilance" and "rush to a vaccine" when describing a needed reaction to the bird flu. These were the same words they used for SARS, and before that smallpox, and before that West Nile virus. These aren't informative words; they don't give us any special insight into a health risk, and they don't help us to distinguish a potential risk from an ongoing risk. Beyond misdirecting us away from real health risks, public health sound bites also provide wrong information. Clearly, an epidemiological need to track an emerging disease before it gets out of hand is not the same thing as saying the entire public is already at risk.

Part of the problem is that lab scientists who have never been trained in public speaking are suddenly clipped and quoted in the newspapers or thrust onto the television screens and asked to provide three-minute descriptions of something they may have spent a lifetime studying. There is a pressure to make it sound important or exciting, and this pressure leads easily to distortion and overstatement.

So we stockpiled millions of doses of smallpox vaccine in preparation for an attack that didn't come, to protect us against a bug that hadn't made anyone sick here since 1949. When the moment of fear and worry is upon us, our public health experts make us worry more. Unfortunately, in the case of smallpox, these vaccines were perishable, and since hardly anyone agreed to take them, this meant that millions of dollars worth of prevention had to be thrown away.

The criteria for publishing a paper in a top scientific journal are stiff. Researchers have to study the requisite number of patients to make sure the study is statistically significant. Often studies are double-blind, which means one can't know who receives which treatment ahead of time. There is a need for careful controls, and all data must be checked and rechecked. No self-respecting scientist would have it any other way. Why should the criteria be less stringent when scientists inform the public about these same health issues?

THE SEQUEL: FLU VACCINE 2004

In August 2004, Dr. Gerberding of the CDC stated that "the time to be complacent about the flu is over."

Dr. Anthony Fauci, the head of the National Institute for Allergy and Infectious Diseases, said on CNN, "There is really a full-court press going on now to develop" flu vaccines that protect against many strains of the virus, including the current bird flu. Fauci, a world leader in infectious diseases, spoke with his usual gravitas, which unfortunately gave the impression that an outbreak was looming.

Without evidence, and with minimal risk, the cycle of worry was restarting, and it was using as an unwitting mouthpiece one of our most dedicated scientists.

THE GOLDEN SHOT

In fall 2004, the year's first flu-related death came not from the disease, but from an elderly woman who fell while waiting in line for the vaccine. This unfortunate event added to the annals of illness, where panic has always killed far more than the disease that caused it. With the announcement that 50 million influenza vaccines from the manufacturer Chiron wouldn't be available in the United States because of possible contamination, the CDC was put in an instant quandary, its credibility once again damaged. From pushing the yearly flu vaccine accelerator pedal, urging everyone to get a shot, they suddenly had to slam on the brakes, their reassurances, of course, sounding hollow.

"Take a deep breath, this is not an emergency," Dr. Gerberding said, trying to change her persona instantly from apocalyptic to therapeutic.

The sudden panic of people with fear memory from last year's flu, primed for the shot but now with nowhere to go for it, was likely to cause a stampede of shot-seekers. The CDC had created a new monster. The frantic healthy folks could easily beat out the elderly short-of-breath patients who really need the vaccine to protect them from serious illness. The CDC's attempts to referee this problem were bound to be ineffective.

The whole flu-shot fiasco was an example of inadequate preparation coupled with overinflated expectation and a fear of going without. One of the main reasons that a shortage like this could occur is that drug manufacturers are not anxious to produce vaccines in the first place. Vaccines are costly. Without a patent to uphold high prices, the profit margins for generic vaccines are narrow. Plus, proper sterilization methods are quite expensive and cut into the profit margin further. The chicken-egg culture medium still being used to produce vaccines needs to be replaced by the latest in genetic engineering, but the changeover involves another billion-dollar expense.

Forget altruism, or concern for patients—they are simply not part of the drug company equation. Drug companies are not eager to make a product they can't make a lot of money on.

The only workable solution to prevent the panic of a sudden shortage is for the government to step in and support and subsidize the manufacture of this vaccine. The plan of buying back unused vaccines isn't sufficient. It is far more important to ensure production of an adequate number of vaccines in the first place.

Instead, Congress only approved half of the $100 million requested in 2003 to develop better flu vaccines and improve the distribution system.

The British did not end up with the same kind of shortage despite the Chiron manufacturing disaster on their soil, because they rely on a diversity of manufacturers, and the government purchases the entire supply itself, so the public needn't worry.

In contrast, in late October 2004, U.S. health authorities began scrambling to make up some of our lost doses from other countries' stockpiles. Canada had 2 million doses of surplus vaccine to make available for U.S. use, according to David Butler-Jones, Canada's public health officer. But there was difficulty licensing them for use in the United States in time for the 2004 flu season. There were six manufacturers in the world who produced 200 million doses for other nations in 2004, while only two, Chiron and Aventis, were entirely responsible for our 100 million doses.

In Germany, there is not the same urgent push for the flu vaccine. A study carried out by Berlin's Robert Koch Institute in

November 2003 showed that the average influenza vaccination rate in Germany is only 23.7 percent. The numbers are somewhat higher for those over sixty, but Germans overall appear to be less fearful of the flu than we are here in the United States, despite the fact that a comparable percentage, five to eight thousand people, die of the flu in Germany every year. In 2004, Germany had 20 million doses of the vaccine available for its use, and didn't report a shortage.

The difference in flu fear between countries may be cultural. A ninety-year-old woman I know in northern Germany not only doesn't believe in flu shots, but she believes in an ice-cold shower in the morning and open windows in the bedrooms without heat even in the winter. Yet, she is no more irrational than those who believe the flu shot is a panacea.

In the United States, the rush for the 2004 shot was based on fear, not on medical science. The well-publicized scarcity created a sudden sense of need. And by the time the smoke cleared in January of yet another mild flu season, there was an embarrassing surplus of shots that people no longer wanted. By this time the attention of the news media was diverted to the deadly tsunami on the other side of the world, and no one was thinking about the flu except for the few who had it.

BIOTERROR INSTEAD OF FLU

Instead of preparing for the flu, our government has been busy spending billions of dollars stockpiling millions of doses of anthrax vaccine (with no use for it in the foreseeable future), and over two hundred thousand doses of smallpox vaccine (without a single case occurring here since 1949). These actions have been taken at least partly so that Homeland Security can look like it takes the threat of biological agents seriously. A bioterror attack would likely only affect hundreds or, worst-case, thousands at once, yet the expensive preparations are for millions of potential victims.

Bioport makes the only current anthrax vaccine, an unwieldy six-dose process that many military recruits have complained gives them a flulike syndrome. But fearing an anthrax attack since 2001, the U.S. government has contracted with this company for 75 million doses of the vaccine. Since the vaccine is perishable, and there is no anthrax here, most of what is produced is thrown away. Similarly, panicked over smallpox in 2002 and 2003, the government purchased 291,400 doses of the antiquated live virus vaccines, discarding 90 percent of them due to fear of side effects and lack of need.

Meanwhile, the CDC has determined that at least 185 million Americans could benefit from flu vaccine, either because they are at risk of getting very sick or are in close contact with those who are.

Yet with the shortage in 2004, the available supply of flu vaccine that year was only about 54 million doses. The CDC was soon begging Aventis to produce more, but the company made available only 1 million additional doses. Was this all it could make, or all it *would* make? No one I spoke to at the manufacturer was able to provide an answer.

Instead of the government spending all its vaccine money on the production of nearly useless bioterror vaccines, a more substantial flu subsidy could lead to the consistent availability of at least 100 million doses, which would calm nerves and perhaps even save lives.

Who Gets the Shot?

The waiting room of my office was filling with frantic healthy patients who had come in without appointments, all yearning for the coveted 2004 vaccine. My phone was ringing incessantly with the same question. *Does he have it yet?* I told most callers no, though I had scrounged and begged my usual supplier for five vials, enough for fifty of my sickest patients. But I didn't tell anyone this, trying to avoid a stampede.

The flu vaccine is useful, but it is not the key to good health. Plenty of people make it through the winter safely without it.

Most of my patients would do fine without a shot in 2004, but knowing that there was a scarcity had clouded people's reason.

I offered my elderly and chronically ill patients a vaccine against pneumonia, which I had in ample supply, but even when they took it, they hardly seemed reassured by my observation that it was often pneumonia that made flu patients the sickest. The lucky few who did get the flu shot didn't flinch from the needle puncture, but sighed with an almost palpable relief as the protective serum surged into their muscle. For the others I stressed hand washing and isolating those with the flu, but driven by the news, frantic shot seekers ignored this calmer perspective.

In 2004 I was bound by public health authorities to give the vaccine I did have to the very old, the very young, the very sick, pregnant women, and health care workers. This was a good policy, because I had so little.

Within this policy, I set my own sub-policy—to give it only to those who already had an appointment and the sickest who called in. Like many other doctors, I had set aside office visits in the early fall to give these vaccinations, and I had neither enough appointments left nor flu shots for the panicked many.

I reassured those who weren't at great risk, and I saved some of my fifty shots for my office staff, my pregnant wife, and my elderly parents. For the first time in years I was compelled to ration supplies, which caused me to properly consider which patients were most susceptible to serious infection.

I declined to charge higher rates for giving an older patient the shot. An unethical doctor could make money in a hurry under these panicked circumstances, but he could also go to jail for Medicare fraud.

One night, I made a rare house call, taking a vial to Long Island. One of my chronically ill patients was an old friend who was housebound with a bad leg, and I drove out to see him. He was relieved to see the syringe, the alcohol pad, and, especially, the vial. But afterward, as I was getting ready to leave, he stopped me.

"Can my wife have one too?"

On cue, she was standing in the doorway, a woman in her early fifties, eager for a flu shot, but not qualifying for one.

"No," I said. "I can lose my license for giving this out to the wrong people. Think of the people who are really at risk."

She was ready to give up, but he wasn't. "Can't you make an exception?" he pleaded.

The tension was so great that I actually dropped the precious vial. I thought I heard it crack when it hit the floor, and I felt certain I had broken it. They both peered at me anxiously as I bent to pick up the magic elixir and retrieved it as it was rolling away. Luckily, the contents were intact.

"Okay," I said nervously. "Maybe she qualifies. You're at high risk, and she's a close contact. I can give her a shot."

They sighed, thanked me repeatedly, more than they had the last time he was treated successfully for pneumonia.

I felt good, like a medical Robin Hood.

It was only afterward, driving home, that I thought of my dwindling supply and considered a fragile wheezy patient with an office appointment a few weeks hence who wouldn't be able to get a shot because of the one I'd just given away.

Part III

HEALING FEAR

13

THE FEAR PROPHETS

> God is with me, I shall not fear.
>
> —Adon Olom prayer

Fear of the unknown and fear of death are primary fears, and they lead many people to religion. There is comfort to be found in the notion of a greater being who controls destiny. If a person makes peace with his or her god, then an inner serenity may be achieved.

Religion has worked well for many who struggle with deep questions that have no ready answers. If a patient suddenly receives a terminal diagnosis, her faith may sustain her through the harrowing process of dying.

Christianity and Judaism have taught that fearing God is the way to deal with the ultimate fear of death. We needn't fear death, instead we should revere God. A central passage in Jewish teachings states, "Raisheet chochmah yirat Adonoy—The beginning of wisdom is the awe of God" (Psalms 111:10).

In Christian theology, the principle of a loving God driving out the fear of the world is discussed in 1 John: "God is love . . . there is no fear in love. But perfect love drives out [worldly] fear, because fear has to do with punishment. The one who fears is not made perfect in love" (1 John 4:16b–18).

In the name of God throughout history, rather than preaching love and devotion, religious leaders have often used threats of retribution to get their followers to conform. (If you don't follow these rules, you may burn in hell.) Without doubt, religions can invoke fear as well as dispel it, but in times of tragedy and nervousness, many still turn to religion for comfort.

But religious leaders are not always equipped to handle day-to-day worries, superstitions, or unrealistic fears. In today's climate of fragmented and misguided information, an anxious alienated public may invoke spiritual platitudes that are difficult to apply to worldly concerns.

Priests, ministers, and rabbis are religion's go-to people, but they are not soothsayers. Nevertheless, the more nervous people become, worried out of proportion to real risks, frightened of hyped dangers, the more people present their clergy with questions that men of the cloth may not always be able to answer. God's representatives may grow weary, overwhelmed by their congregants' earthly panic.

A Rabbi

About a month after Ephraim Azziz's operative date to remove the tiny cancer at the top of his lung, I received a phone call on Saturday evening, just after dusk. He had decided to call me at the conclusion of the Sabbath. His voice was still a hoarse whisper, not immediately recognizable.

"Thank you, doctor," he whispered. "You found it very early. Stage IA. These things usually kill you by the time they're found. But no lymph nodes. No spread. I'm clean. Some chemo and hopefully I'm done. Thank God."

I recalled showing his CT scan to my office mate, Dr. Madison, and how the disorganization at NYU before his needle biopsy had led him to have his surgery at the Memorial Sloan-Kettering

Cancer Center. I hadn't expected to hear from him again after that.

"It's a good thing you came in when you did," I said, "and we decided not to wait on the CT scan. How are you feeling?"

"I'm weak. Very weak."

Two weeks later Azziz was back in my office examination room, covered with perspiration, breathing shallowly, and appearing fatigued. His hair had turned a new shade of gray, and his familiar tiny glasses were now crooked and greased. But a quick physical showed me that his vital signs were stable, his lungs were clear, and he had a normal temperature.

Despite his discomfort, it was clear to me that the purpose of his visit was not strictly medical—he was still under the direct care of the surgeon, but he was coming to me for reassurance.

He was in too much pain to sit straight on my blue office couch, so he half-sat, half-lounged.

"Let me tell you something, doctor," he said. "You are a man of science, not mysticism." His heavily accented voice added intrigue to his statement.

"I hope I am open-minded," I said.

"You know I am observant, a regular congregant at my synagogue. Do you know of the Rachamim? The mystical rabbis?"

"The Kabbalists," I said, and he smiled.

"Twelve years ago a Kabbalistic rabbi, as you call it, told me that I was supposed to die, but that God was going to have compassion on me. I've always remembered that. Now, you know it was two weeks before Rosh Hashanah, two weeks before I was to be inscribed in the book of life for the year, a week before you ordered the fateful CT scan, and I had a big fight with my wife. We came home from synagogue and she was upset. She said we had no life except the shul. We argued about it, and I went out again, but I had nowhere else to go, so I returned to the synagogue. It was the end of Shabbat, and I saw that there was a mystical rabbi there, famous from Israel, and there was a long line of people waiting to hear what he had to say. I stood at the end of the line, and by the time he got to me it was very dark outside. When he saw me, I could tell that he was startled. He told me that he was going to give me a new name, Mordecai."

"Why a new name?"

Azziz smiled slowly. "It is a tradition. It signifies a new life. Right away, he was telling me that I required a new identity. Sometimes things don't go right, he said. He said that he would write me a blessing on parchment and mail it to me from Israel."

"What happened?"

"When I got the results of the CT scan, I knew this was what he had meant. My wife said it was superstition, that these rabbis were just fortune-tellers, but I didn't agree. I telephoned the rabbi in Israel. I asked if he remembered me, and he did. I asked him what he saw, why he gave me another name. Here's what he said: 'In reincarnation, sometimes you come into this world with a sentence, something hanging over you from a previous life. But God gives you the means to undo that sentence, a medicine to treat it with. Your life has been spared,' the mystical rabbi told me. 'God will have compassion on you and there will be a new life for you, and everything will be okay.'

"I told him then the results of the CT scan, and he didn't seem surprised. He said again that I would be okay. The day of the operation, his letter arrived, with the parchment and the blessing."

We doctors had contributed to Azziz's well-being by discovering his cancer, then providing information that brought perspective and the hope appropriate with cancer that was found early. A doctor had swiftly removed the cancer with his scalpel and brought the chance for a cure.

But in the end Azziz was most comforted by the notion that both his illness and his recovery had been preordained, knowable only by the prescient powers of the mystical rabbis. Giving over control to their vision had helped him to make the difficult transition from apparent health to life-threatening illness in a short period of time. He'd been nervous and fearful, but he'd managed to cope.

Embracing this fateful view allowed him to take some of the responsibility away from cigarettes. But tobacco deserved no such pardon. The virile Marlboro Man images of smoking that corporate advertising had put over on us for so many years had a lot more to do with Azziz's cancer than the inevitability of fate.

Azziz was experiencing a fear that eclipsed even the usual fear of disease. Images of organ-wrenching cancer deaths have imbued it with a stigma that is difficult to face without becoming fatalistic. Azziz's fear was out of proportion to the risk of even cancer, because of the Internet and media hype and misinformation that had conditioned him. Cancer info-bites petrify people. It was unfortunate that the only relief for Azziz was to be found in the reassuring words and miraculous vision of an all-knowing mystic. In a world of such isolation, these were the only tools Azziz could find to help him regain his purpose.

Two Priests

Two priests were patients in my practice for several years, though I didn't connect them in my mind. They both served as chaplains to the New York City Fire Department, but they rarely met at FDNY functions, and not once in my office waiting room. They were different kinds of men. Father Mychal Judge, a Franciscan friar who lacked a parish, was a public figure who provided succor to firefighters as well as to everyone from the homeless to the famous. He served on soup lines and was also a regular guest at both Gracie Mansion and the Clinton White House.

A visit to my medical office from Judge meant a waiting room confessional involving Judge and several of my patients. Getting him to confide in me wasn't as easy. He accepted the samples of blood pressure medications I gave him, but he didn't seem concerned for his health, only for the health of others. Judge said he was not afraid of getting sick or of dying.

Father "John Henderson," on the other hand, was a private man. He too had high blood pressure and accepted samples, but beyond this, the similarity to Judge seemed to end. Henderson had his own parish in the heart of working man's Brooklyn; he was usually to be found in his study reading, or in the rectory, or meeting with his congregants. He was involved with the fire department only when they called him, sometimes when Judge was out of town visiting various dignitaries, including the Clintons.

Judge was not a favorite of Cardinal O'Connor, because Judge frequently upstaged him—and there was the time when a bereaved widow insisted that Friar Judge rather than the cardinal perform the funeral services for her husband at St. Patrick's Cathedral.

When Judge required sudden surgery for abdominal pain, he didn't show fear or worry, even after the surgeon took out a perfectly normal gall bladder and left in a festering part of the colon. Judge went through the second surgery without placing blame. He said he would ask God to forgive the surgeon's mistake. Judge was a clear example of how a person could stay centered, not allowing his perspective to be altered by panic.

I was hoping that the day would come when I could reassure Father Judge the way he did others, but he didn't require it from me. When his insurance lapsed, he didn't come to my office for many months, not wanting to accept my charity. When he died suddenly in the World Trade Center rescue operations on 9/11, it was with courage rather than fear.

Surely Judge, if he had lived, would have remained a go-to person in our hysteria-ridden times. While he was alive, he was a sponge for others' fear as well as a role model for courage.

The Fear Counselor

After Father Judge died, Father Henderson became very busy. He was compelled to ignore his own parish, taking Judge's prominent place amid complaints that this unassuming padre was no Father Judge. Henderson was the first to admit it.

But he had his own style, and he worked tirelessly through the evenings and late into the night calming the shocked and bereaved survivors of 9/11, the families, and the firefighters. He officiated at many of the funerals, but because of his halting speech, it was lost on many who attended just how eloquent his sermons were.

Henderson lacked Judge's flamboyance, but not his purpose, and his faith salved many psychic wounds. He helped people who were frightened to retain control of their lives by continuing to work and care for their families. He encouraged people to stay within their usual patterns of living.

I think that Henderson expected the complaints to slow down, as people readjusted to the post-9/11 world. Instead, with a continued high volume of calls he began to grow more and more uneasy. He no longer slept well at night, and he frequently forgot to shave. He also began to question the nature of the complaints. People were worried about another attack, they were worried about toxins in the air, they were worried about every bug du jour, and they were worried about their children's future. All this was understandable, but Henderson recognized that his role was transforming into that of a therapist. People were consulting him and needing to speak to him about worries that had little to do with his being a priest.

One night in April 2003, he returned home to his empty silent room at the church rectory at 2 A.M., and as he lay in his bed sleeplessly thinking, an old regret pained him—he didn't have a family. His life was becoming a collection of the frets and fears of his congregants.

The next day, Henderson appeared in my office in the late afternoon without an appointment, just before my staff was about to leave for the day. Seeing one of her favorite patients arrive bundled in an overcoat that was too heavy for the mild spring weather, my office nurse quickly ushered him into one of the examining rooms.

Henderson didn't speak. His blood pressure was normal and his physical exam and EKG unremarkable. I told him to dress, and he followed me to my pale blue brick consultation room. Sitting on the couch across from me, he stared out the window toward the Empire State Building.

"What's the matter, John?" I asked. "Why are you here?"

When he looked at me, he began wringing his hands until they reddened.

"I haven't been sleeping," he said slowly.

"Why not?"

"I'm out all evening. The whole city is in a panic. They're geared up for something, but they don't know what it is or when it's going to come. They can't seem to calm down."

I wasn't sure whether he was referring to a specific scare. SARS was just becoming "newsworthy" at the time of this office visit but wasn't yet in full swing.

"Who is afraid?"

"It's everyone. Not just the orphans and widows, not just the firefighters or their families. People stop me on the street: 'Father, can you help me?' 'Father, can I please talk to you?'"

"What do you tell them?"

He smiled. We had known each other for many years, and he was comfortable with my bluntness.

"Come on, Doc. You know what I tell them. I tell them to have faith. I tell them that everything is beyond their control, that they have to give their worries over to a merciful creator."

"Does this help them?"

"It helps them. But does it help me?! I absorb this, and then I can't sleep at night. I have my faith but it's not always enough. And what are they worried about? They worry about bombs and threats that haven't happened and may never happen. My parishioners, the firefighters, their families, their doubts overwhelm me. What am I supposed to do?"

This was more than he had said to me in all the years I'd known him. I'd met Father Henderson in 1993 following the stroke of his brother, Thomas, an accomplished botanist. I'd cared for Thomas through a blood clot in his leg, two bouts of pneumonia, and ultimately, the pancreatic cancer in 1999 that took his life. John brought his brother in his wheelchair to most of his doctors' visits.

At home, he injected him with morphine to control the pain. In the end, he helped his brother accept his death.

Even in the period of grief following this, John didn't appear as somber as he did now.

"Are you depressed?" I asked.

He thought about it. "No."

"Anxious, overwhelmed?"

"That's more like it."

"I can give you a mild tranquilizer at night called Klonopin that will help you break the cycle. You might be a little sleepy from it in the morning, but a cup of coffee will counter that."

He nodded that he would take the prescription.

"Father, do you know what you're afraid of?"

Henderson smiled.

"I'm not afraid of dying. Every day I pray for acceptance of my fate. But most who turn to me for help are afraid of dying. I think that's where their vulnerability comes from. People are in a panic every day now, they feel out of control. Their specific fears may be made up by the politicians or the TV, but it feels real to them. And I think I am absorbing this worry. I absorb it by osmosis, and it becomes difficult for me to control."

"What do you do?"

He sighed. "Back when I was a kid and something would frighten me, I remember coming home alone at night and seeing my father sitting in the warm kitchen, reading his paper and drinking his tea the way he did every night to relax. He would just wink at me, and I would be reassured. The apprehension would be gone, knowing he was the last stop for me."

"What do you do now?"

"I came here to see you today."

Father Henderson stood up then, and we shook hands.

"Thanks, Doc," he said.

"I want to see you again in two weeks," I said. "And don't reschedule."

John wouldn't go for psychotherapy, but he continued to come to see me in this manner, over several weeks. He rarely needed to take the Klonopin, and after five visits, he said he felt better.

I was flattered, realizing that the earthly comfort John was seeking was simply to know that he could confide in someone. In my office, where the staff treated him warmly, he could be diverted from the chaos of war anxiety. He had absorbed the irrational fears until he was radioactive with them.

Father Henderson and his enduring faith had always provided a haven for others from fear. His parish was for many their only consolation. When he was overwhelmed, however, my office was his haven, like the kitchen of his childhood. I served as a reminder of the comfort his father had provided on those days when a son came home frightened on a dark night.

THE FEAR PROPHET

Of all the speakers at the fear conference at the New School in February 2004, Tom Pyszczynski, the originator of terror management theory, was the most unassuming, the most soft-spoken, and yet his central idea stayed with me most vividly. His long white hair flowing to his shoulders like a postmodern wizard's, he spoke about all fear emanating from a central fear of death.

If this is true for animals, it is truer for humans, who, like our animal predecessors, can be instinctively petrified of death and, in addition, be petrified by the contemplation of death. Pyszczynski, a psychologist, saw the basic human need to sublimate this central fear in culture and society. But when the society we build for ourselves begins to deteriorate, as this one has, it no longer absorbs our fears. Our safety net of information and communicated risk is suspect. We are frightened for our lives beyond any realistic danger by those we've appointed as our protectors.

For many, faith is the only consolation. Faith takes the worry away and transfers it to a higher Being who is controlling the world. Any sense of control we have is illusory. And yet, we obsess on control and fear its loss.

These days our culture of worry is a growing weed that feeds on manufactured dangers and threatens to become its own cult. Traditional religion may not be a match for it. Religion works best when it engages the unanswerable questions, where faith is paramount in coping with the uncertainty of death. But religion has become overloaded with today's obsessive worry and no longer serves as a reliable cure for fear.

14

IS THERE A
CURE FOR FEAR?

I liberated myself from the fear by creating these
works. Their creation had the purpose of healing
myself.

—Japanese artist Yayoi Kusama in an interview

Nor should we forget that courage is contagious, that
it overcomes the silence and fear that estrange people
from one another.

—Paul Rogat Loeb, *The Impossible Will
Take a Little While: A Citizen's Guide to
Hope in a Time of Fear*

If fear is no longer protective, if it has been transformed from an adaptive tool into a symptomatic illness, then we have to find a way to cure it.

The spread of fear has reached epidemic proportions. The
national media broadcast threats and warp our perspective. The
sense of immediate danger is highly contagious.

To slow the spread of fear, it is necessary to "vaccinate" with reason those who aren't yet afflicted. A population that is slow to react hysterically helps contain fear. But lasting immunity to the epidemic of fear is difficult to attain. The biochemistry is built into our brains, waiting to be triggered.

Once fear has been elicited, it is stored deep in the emotional memory, ready to emerge whenever the so-called danger recurs.

In early 2004, months before she broke her leg, my daughter, Rebecca, was taking a bath. She was almost three years old, the time when the brain circuitry completes its wiring of the "safety center" in the prefrontal cortex. She had never before experienced the bubble effect, and when the Jacuzzi device in the tub turned on automatically, I was on the other side of the apartment. By the time I rushed back to the tub, she was petrified, standing straight up, bright red from crying.

For months afterward, she was afraid to take a bath at all. I tried to appeal to her newly working brain center to suppress the fear that this tub would always bring the scary bubbles, but the fear response was too strong.

This is the reality that we encounter in America in the twenty-first century. Once alerted, once afraid, it is hard to turn the switch back to the off position. The news signals danger, and we instantly fear it. A person living in a small town in the heartland who watches cable news may experience the fear almost as much as a big-city dweller who has an infinitely greater risk of witnessing terrorism up close. An absurd confirmation of this manufactured TV fear comes when Homeland Security allocates funds to protect people against terrorism at a rate of 25 dollars per person in New York, and just over 60 dollars per person in Wyoming (in 2004).

Of course, one simple cure is to turn off the TV.

A NEW EQUATION

There is no standard treatment for fear in part because the symptoms vary from one person to the next. A person may feel destined to a certain bad outcome and have a greater sense of foreboding because of a certain family tendency. Some people more easily trigger a fight-or-flight flood of hormones than others.

My wife's mother has a severe case of multiple sclerosis and has been confined to a wheelchair for almost twenty years. Six years ago, my wife's brother developed a mild case of MS, and my wife then confided in me her fear, practically a conviction, that she would be next. Every time she brings up her perception that MS is her destiny, I try to counter it with the bald statistic that only 4 percent of first-degree relatives are at risk for the disease. "There is a 96 percent chance that you won't get it," I say, but for my wife, as for many others, the perception rests with the 4 percent. Empathy for her mother and a natural tendency to personalize her experience create the fear and the conviction.

Recurrent or unremitting fear has the same effect on the human body that running an engine persistently at 80 to 100 mph has on a car. For a person who is always on the alert, who suffers from a too easily triggered and sustained fight-or-flight response, the result is a burned-out body. Many illnesses are more likely to occur as a result, including heart disease, cancer, stroke, and depression. What we have most to fear are not the exotic diseases that scare us, but the ordinary killers such as heart attacks that develop as a result of our unremitting worries.

We are scaring ourselves about the wrong things in a way that is clearly a terrorist's delight. (We do much of their work for them.) In 2001, terrorists killed 2,978 people in the United States, including the 5 from anthrax, and we have been obsessed with terrorism and the supposed risks ever since.

Meanwhile, according to the CDC, in 2001 heart disease killed 700,142 here; cancer 553,768; accidents 101,537; and suicide 30,622. Murders (not including 9/11) accounted for 17,330 deaths that year. The number of children who died in their infancy in 2001 was 27,801, and their deaths were no less horrible or frightening for those involved than the attack on the World Trade Center.

Of course the societal impact of 9/11 was unmatched.

We need to be reeducated as a prerequisite to healing fear. We tend to overpersonalize much of the information we receive. We need a new sense of proportion to correct this.

THE FEAR VACCINE

How calm can a patient be these days?

Can we be reeducated not to trigger our fear, or will there instead be a simple pill that cures us all, or a fear vaccine? Oh, how we love our miracle cures.

In a study by Jonathan Kipnis et al. in Israel published in the *Proceedings of the National Academy of Sciences* in May 2004, the authors gave an immunological vaccine to mice in whom they had previously induced psychosis. This chemical cocktail bolstered the nerve cells, and the state of panic and paranoia ended. The mice were once again able to perform their usual tasks.

The implication of these results is that immunological "vaccines" could have a role in reversing fear. If this supposition proves to be true, instead of learning healthier contexts, we will be able to obscure our hysteria with immunology.

Fear vaccines raise similar ethical issues as medicating an entire society with beta blockers or other antianxiety treatments. As our fear grows, the reach for soothing salves is typical of American consumerism. It is one thing to employ sophisticated technologies to heal the sick, to control psychosis, or to bolster a nerve fiber in a troubled brain. It is another to bottle the latest preventative and market it widely to treat all fear.

A CHEMICAL CURE

As I discussed in chapter 2, Joe Ledoux has determined that fear memory in rats is deeply rooted and predominates over other types of rational memory. Ledoux showed that when rats are given the medicine anisomycin, their fear memory is blocked. Based

197

on these results, Roger Pitman, a professor of psychiatry at Harvard, theorized that administering the beta-blocker drug propranolol can also block fear memory and blunt the fight-or-flight response.

In 2002, Pitman and his group looked at the effects of giving propranolol within six hours of a traumatic event (mostly car accidents). One month afterward, he was able to determine a significantly lower incidence of posttraumatic stress disorder than in the control group. Larry Cahill, at the Irvine, California, memory center, also tested the effects of propranolol on humans and found that it prevented people from recalling a gory story better than a bland story.

But blunting fear memory with medication is not the same thing as retraining the brain. It seems fruitless to provoke fear unnecessarily and then have to develop drugs to reverse it.

Or as the President's Council on Bioethics wrote in the 2003 book *Beyond Therapy*, "Use of memory-blunters at the time of traumatic events could interfere with the normal psychic work . . . there is a danger that our new pharmacological remedies will keep us 'bright' or impassive in the face of things that ought to trouble, sadden, outrage, or inspire us—that our medicated souls will stay flat no matter what happens to us or around us."

Descartes argued in *The Passions of the Soul* that "all the harm they [the passions] can cause consists in their fortifying and conserving those thoughts more than is needed, or in fortifying and conserving others which ought not to be fixed there." Descartes was referring to the damaging effects of negative emotions. He felt we could become obsessed with our own dark thoughts. Almost four hundred years later, we as a society may be even more susceptible to these fears.

I described the work of Rachel Yehuda earlier in this book. Dr. Yehuda has concluded that PTSD is too much in vogue in a way that harms us. Many people who simply read or hear about a trauma think they are suffering from it. Unnecessary anguish is often an overreaction to another person's trauma. We stimulate our voyeuristic suffering and then find we may have to medicate ourselves to cool down.

Our fear-for-profit culture is too ready to latch on to the next drug to regulate us. Imagine the drug company ears pricking up to this new role for beta blockers. The new drug company TV ad is sure to be, "Are you stressed? Do you experience posttraumatic stress? Try this . . ."

Pills become our crutches. Drug ads and our popular culture teach us to treat our cholesterol with pills rather than diet; our obesity responds to amphetamines rather than exercise; we clog our coronary arteries thoughtlessly and then "Roto-Rooter" them open. We come to depend on these treatments. We are *afraid* to do without them.

This medication dependency is not that dissimilar to many of our other product dependencies. We deplete the world's oil reserves built from millions of years of organic decay, and pollute the skies with our engines. All because we are afraid of the dark, or the cold, or the heat. We lead temperature-controlled, environment-controlled lives. We are afraid of aging, so we plastic-surgerize our bodies to the best approximation of youth that we can obtain.

All this environmental control stems back to our ultimate fear of death. We hide behind the illusion provided by technology, but ultimately, fear of death seeps through. True culture, art, philosophy, and science provide better depositories for human angst. Religious faith can help us to cope with our fear of death, but it can also be misappropriated by superstitious fears, as demonstrated in the last chapter.

In twenty-first-century America, we worship the god of wealth. We medicate ourselves with the emotional anesthesia of materialism, but our fears seep in and overtake us anyway.

THE POLITICS OF UNHEALING

I attended Medical Grand Rounds at New York University in March 2004 given by Dr. Julie Gerberding of the CDC. She spoke in a soft voice and appeared surprisingly nervous. Her cropped hair was the same heavily hair-sprayed salt-and-pepper bonnet that comes across on the TV screen. In person her face seemed rounder, though she continued to speak in the same pointed sound bites.

I watched her from the back of the auditorium. She said she was glad to be back among white-coat clinicians, since this had been her own background before joining the CDC. It was clear to me that she saw herself as a kind of healer in the public realm. The CDC was, after all, an agency intended to protect the public from health care dangers.

Gerberding, rather than present herself strictly as a scientist, tried to act the part of the head of a consumer-friendly group, a go-to person for public concerns. "As scientists deal with data, the public deals with values. Our role is to translate information into relevant knowledge that helps people make choices." She seemed sincere. Her soft voice and mild gestures helped to emphasize her apparent concern.

But Dr. Gerberding failed to consider that if the public was being hyped into a pseudoconcern by the media, then the CDC's concentrated involvement and public declarations also sent the wrong message. She said, "Like with bird flu, we know there is a serious threat of it jumping to humans. But do we need to worry about it on a day to day basis? It's our job to worry. We will worry for you."

Gerberding was not one to downplay sufficiently. Her public display of worrying always made us worry more. In fact, she was now associated with these diseases she'd helped to hype—SARS, smallpox, West Nile, and anthrax. "We were in a SARS mode," she said excitedly. "The public health system was able to step up to the plate. The CDC was protecting people in a transforming world."

This self-aggrandizing statement hadn't been proven. Had the CDC done more to contain the disease, or more to extend the hype? How could the public trust Dr. Gerberding unless she was able to give us a true perspective on diseases, differentiating between those that kill and those with only the potential to do so?

The same week that Gerberding was speaking at NYU, "Plan to

Battle AIDS Worldwide Is Falling Short" was a headline on the front page of the *New York Times*. An unstated factor in the public health reality was the constant reshuffling of priorities away from AIDS and toward the bug du jour. The article stated that "three years after the United Nations declared a worldwide offensive against AIDS and 14 months after President Bush promised $15 billion for AIDS treatment in poor countries, shortages of money and battles over patents have kept antiretroviral drugs from reaching more than 90 percent of the poor people who need them."

AIDS is a massive worldwide killer, but we just aren't as afraid of it here in the United States as we should be. The media, informed by the CDC, the WHO, and other experts, stoke our latest bug du jour fear fires to the detriment of the worldwide AIDS epidemic.

The CDC is not supposed to be a public relations firm for the government. It is a group of scientists, and when they talk too much about a trumped-up danger it has the effect of validating it. Preventing fear means developing a strategy that emphasizes that you aren't going to get a disease just because someone else a thousand miles away from you has gotten it. Preventing fear means learning that if there are holes in the so-called safety net, it matters only if the threat itself is real.

Instead, we are too often warned about things that don't threaten us, while at the same time, ho-hum killers that can really get us—the overuse of Tylenol and Advil, for example—are being ignored in our medicine cabinets.

Treating fear means gaining a real perspective on danger, redirecting our attention to those diseases that really can kill us, and developing a well-reasoned response to these real threats.

TERRORISM

Dr. Pachter, my neighbor and the director of the trauma service at NYU/Bellevue, still does not believe that proper medical preparations are in place against terrorism. I met him in the hallway between our apartments one evening in late March 2004.

"Are we prepared?" I asked.

"Nope," he said.

"Who is in charge?"

"No one," he said.

Dr. Pachter speaks sparely, and is known around the hospital as a gruff surgeon who is also a skilled craftsman. But I know him as a kind and deeply spiritual man. His eyes express his feelings even when he doesn't say anything. One afternoon he invited me into his apartment and without ceremony handed me a beautiful gift for my son Joshua.

Dr. Pachter has been involved in trying to integrate our hospitals into an emergency response plan for a terrorist attack.

"All we talk about is terrorism," I said to him that evening in March. "Everyone worries and exaggerates it. Maybe if we were prepared, we'd feel calmer."

"None of the hospitals speak to each other. There is no system in place in terms of who would do what, where the patients would go. Nothing has changed since September 11. At that time we had an array of stretchers lined up at Chelsea Piers downtown, but not a single respirator, and only one intubation kit. A bunch of volunteers standing around, not knowing what to do."

"Isn't it more organized now? Isn't there a strategy?"

"More equipment, maybe. A strategy? No."

Meetings took place, and the newspapers reported on them. But for a practical man like Pachter, whose presence made me feel secure in our own little apartment enclave, there was not a satisfactory medical safety net in place for New York City in 2004. If a limited attack actually happened and we didn't respond effectively, fear would become rampant.

On April 4, 2004, a *New York Times* front-page article lent further credence to Pachter's position, detailing the disagreements between the police, fire, and office of emergency management departments in New York City over who was really in charge. "The city still lacks what many experts say is the most basic and essential tool for handling disasters: a formal agreement governing what city agency will lead the response at the scene of any cata-strophic accident or terrorist strike."

Less focus on the unlikely, less exaggeration of potential impact, but more behind-the-scenes cooperation, would create a climate where, if something did happen, we might not overreact to it as easily.

HEALING HYPOCHONDRIACS

Living in a climate of fear, we are becoming a society of hypochon-driacs. Many people worry excessively over the slightest symp-tom, often convinced that they are sick. As Mary Duenwald wrote in the *New York Times* in March 2004, "They make frequent doc-tors' appointments, demand unnecessary tests and can drive their friends and relatives—not to mention their physicians—to distrac-tion with a seemingly endless search for reassurance."

According to the American Psychiatric Association, a hypochon-driac is a patient who fears that he has a serious disease for at least six months despite doctors' attempts to reassure him that he is healthy. This definition is beginning to apply to more and more of us.

The ancient Greeks coined the term *hypochondria* to refer to melancholy symptoms that they associated with certain organs in men beneath the rib cage. In women, symptoms of "hysteria" were related to problems with the womb. It wasn't until the seven-teenth century that physicians began to realize that these fears originated in the brain.

At the end of the twentieth century, when Ledoux and others began to map our fear circuitry, they uncovered the neural network of fear that involves the body's organs as well as the brain. So the Greeks weren't completely wrong in their beliefs.

Can the process that leads to hypochondria be reversed? Dr. Arthur Barsky of Harvard published a study in the *Journal of the American Medical Association* in March 2004 looking at the effect of teaching hypochondriacs to pay less attention to their symptoms. The results were analyzed at six-month and one-year intervals.

Patients were taught to suspend their usual ways of responding to their fears, which included searching the Internet, taking their own vital signs, and scheduling excessive doctors' appointments. Doctors were coached to see their patients only for regular appointments and not to schedule tests as a knee-jerk response.

In this *JAMA* study, Barsky observed that patients receiving this therapy "had significantly lower levels of hypochondriacal symptoms, beliefs, and attitudes . . . and health-related anxiety. They also had significantly less impairment of . . . activities of daily living."

In my medical practice, I have observed that many patients who aren't the full-blown hypochondriacs of Barsky's study share a fear of death that often overwhelms their ability to reason. I have found that many of these patients do better when they keep a sense of control rather than have strict limits imposed on them. Over time, these limits may not decrease fear as Barsky's study suggests. I have found that giving over this control to a physician is comforting only when a patient feels that this is her choice. Many patients who insist on reviewing their blood test results become even more apprehensive if a doctor tries to withhold these results. Deconditioning may be somewhat helpful, but primitive emotions like fear will find new outlets unless dealt with on a deeper level.

Recently, I had a visit from my patient "Zeke," whose father had died from an abdominal aneurysm. All of Zeke's siblings were suddenly worried that they too had aneurysms. I reassured Zeke that it didn't tend to run in families, which helped some. I listened to Zeke's abdomen and found no noisy bruits to correspond to an aneurysm, which reassured him further. Ultimately it took an abdominal ultrasound to completely reassure him that he didn't have an aneurysm, a test that Barsky might have considered excessive, but it did the trick. Though Zeke wasn't a textbook hypochondriac, his fears were extended by grieving in a way that required extra reassurance.

Hypochondriacs are people with an excessive fear of death translated into a multitude of neuroses about life. We all have these fears, but for some they are more overwhelming than for others. And illness isn't the only direct metaphor for death. Legal hypochondriacs are those of us who are always calling our lawyers and worrying about the possibility of suing or being sued—I am one of those people for whom a lawsuit represents death. Luckily, my lawyer is a close friend and doesn't charge for my calls.

My wife is a financial hypochondriac, which means that she worries that everything will cost more money that we have. For her, bankruptcy means death. Our accountant handles my wife's concerns but then sends us large bills for the service, which worries her further.

Mostly, we are becoming a society of hypochondriacs, not just for medical reasons, but because of preoccupations in all aspects of our lives. We build elaborate safety nets for the wrong things, and then we panic when these nets are found to be ineffective.

Healing this rampant fear means all of us becoming our own filters for information, not simply parroting what we hear on TV. We need to be deconditioned, decontaminated, and decompressed from the high-pressure misinformation that is being shot into our brains. Once purged, once healed of our programmed fears, and with the help of knowledgeable go-to people who really care about us, we can reappraise the safety of our lives.

ANTIDOTES FOR FEAR

MACBETH: Canst thou not minister to a mind diseas'd,
   Pluck from the memory a rooted sorrow,
   Raze out the rooted troubles of the brain,
   And with some sweet oblivious antidote,
   Cleanse the stuff'd bosom of that perilous stuff
   Which weighs upon the heart?
DOCTOR: Therein the patient
   Must minister to himself.

For years, I have tried to help people handle their disease fears without knowing if I am succeeding or not. In studying the fear circuitry of the brain, I have now come to appreciate that teaching might not automatically lead to learning. Fear is a deep-rooted emotion, difficult for the brain to control. Sometimes its triggering can't be avoided. My daughter's experience with the bubbles as well as with her broken leg educated me that if fear is unlearned, it is because a new emotion replaces it. This healing occurs at its own rate of speed and a parent, or a doctor, has little control over it.

Fear is an important factor in illness that hasn't been well accounted for. Physical, as well as psychological, breakdown occurs at an accelerated rate under the pressure of persistent fear. Science now has the brain-mapping and chemical-testing prowess to help determine exactly how this happens. Unfortunately, we still have a long way to go before we stop unnecessarily triggering the fear circuit in the first place.

Once triggered, fear is personal and too often intractable. People may fear anyone or anything they perceive as alien, from terrorism to atheism to crime to disease to noise. But all of this fear of the "other" ultimately stems from a fear of obliteration or death.

To conquer fear we must return it to its primitive place as an instinct. We must stop overpersonalizing it. We must regain our footing with regular sleep, regular meals, regular entertainment, regular exercise, and regular work. We must resist those who choose the wrong danger, hype the need to respond, and then bungle the response—making the threat seem even more real. We must replace our unreal fears with real courage.

CURING A MIDLIFE CRISIS

One patient revealed to me how fear could be healed.

"Joel Enrand" was suffering from depression, weight gain, high cholesterol, and elevated blood pressure. Many studies in the medical literature predicted these conditions would get worse if left untreated.

Mr. Enrand was a police detective and had endured the stress of many undercover investigations. He had just turned forty, and he planned to retire from the police force in five more years with a good pension. In the meantime, he was finding his job more and more difficult to perform. He had been married for almost twenty years and his son was a young teenager.

His mental deterioration may have been gradual, but it was during an office visit in midsummer that I noticed the change. Formerly a clap-you-on-the-shoulder type, on this visit he was timid, speaking too softly to be understood. His curly hair had become an untrimmed shrub, and the office scale recorded a thirty-pound weight gain on his muscular frame. I noticed that his rough-skinned face and neck had reddened, which may have been from the direct effect of stress hormones.

"I can't sleep," he said.

"Why not?"

"Things aren't so good with my wife."

He described a home situation that had devolved into screaming fights in front of his son. She yelled at him for coming home late. He yelled at her for yelling. She accused him of being with other women. He denied it. My instinct was to believe him.

I suggested that he see a therapist for the anxiety. He refused, saying he wasn't crazy.

I offered to treat his anxiety with Valium and Prozac. For his rising blood pressure I had in mind Lisinopril, a pill that dilates arteries, and for his high cholesterol I offered the ever-popular Lipitor (my patient looked nothing like the smiling healthy people advertising cholesterol drugs on TV). Once his blood pressure was under control, I could add an amphetamine for his obesity, and if his blood pressure rose as a result, I would increase the blood pressure medicine to compensate.

He showed little interest in these suggestions.

I was hoping that he would at least look to me to help him through this period of stress. Instead, he stopped coming to his appointments altogether, and when I called him on the phone, it was apparent that though he was suffering miserably, he wasn't about to listen to me.

I finally managed to convince him to see me one more time, and knowing this might be his final visit, I knew I had to rethink my approach. Trying to force him onto medications only underlined his deterioration, offered him a crutch, and made him identify himself as sick. Perhaps he felt that if he admitted to this weakness, he might break down altogether.

During our next meeting, Enrand admitted that he had an overriding fear of losing everything—his health, his job, his family. Most of all, with paralyzing middle-of-the-night bouts of sleepless fright, he was afraid he was losing his mind.

"You're not crazy," I said, and on hearing this, the tiny muscles around his eyes relaxed.

I realized then that fear was his illness, not the high blood pressure, obesity, or cholesterol that developed as a result. Perhaps his apprehension would diminish if he was able to continue his life and not lose what he feared losing.

I watched him, offering nothing. I had no choice now but to allow him to remain in control, as bit by bit he reinstituted his disciplines. He continued working. He refused couples therapy, but I think he was reassured by the simple fact that his wife stayed with him.

He finally asked me for Valium to take in the middle of the night, as his one medicine to break the cycle of worry. He began to admit he was depressed, but he still wouldn't take an antidepressant. I think he took pride in fighting depression without pills, and used this pride to help rebuild his self-esteem.

In the mornings, he willed himself to jog three miles before work. He ate two to three meals per day but didn't binge. He allowed himself two cigars per week, calling them his one vice.

He missed many doctor's visits but called me every few weeks. When he did come, I examined him and recorded his improving blood pressure. I suspected I was recording the physiological effects of a diminishing fear. Mostly I just sat and talked with him in my consultation room.

There was a correlation between his returning well-being and his personal grooming. On the same visit where I noticed his hair was combed and trimmed in the old fashion, he told me that things were better between him and his wife; he was no longer sleeping on the couch; he was no longer staying out late at night.

He began to enjoy his cronies at work again, the brief interludes of clowning and kidding. He talked with enthusiasm about tracking down the evidence that the DA needed to convict a notorious child molester.

Six months after reluctantly agreeing to Enrand's method, I measured his blood pressure and discovered it was back down to normal without treatment. My office scale indicated that he had lost thirty pounds over that time. His cholesterol was back below 190. Now he was sleeping through the night without Valium.

Looking at him sitting relaxed on the couch across from me, I knew that I would be seeing him less often, whether I scheduled appointments for him or not.

"My courage is back, Doc," he said.

He looked at me and I was glad to see the return of his purposeful expression.

"Things were happening to me. I latched onto the worry. I could feel it, like it was real. It gripped me, and it grew."

"But you fought it?"

"Just by sticking to routines, rituals, they replaced the doubts little by little. When I saw I was getting my life back, I started to enjoy the routines."

Enrand hesitated. "Most importantly," he said, "I'd always wanted to be a dad, and I loved my son more than anything, and I knew I was responsible for him. He needed me, and I grew stronger by refusing to let go of him."

Now that Enrand had passed through his midlife crisis, we both realized that he'd been doing the doctoring. He'd learned to treat—not physical illness—but fear.

In the end, his plan was far better than mine. He lost weight, his blood pressure and cholesterol went down, and his spirits and his marriage improved. I suspected that his stress hormones, which were responsible for his high blood pressure and anxiety, were now diminished.

I was merely a witness to this change, though I learned a big lesson. Committing him to three or four new pills might have led me to the erroneous conclusion that the medicines were responsible for his improvement, rather than his courage. And once started, how would I have known when to stop them?

AFTERWORD

We cannot maintain our historic self-confidence as a
people if we generate public panic.

—Jimmy Carter, Boston, July 26, 2004

The Event

Driving south on the FDR Drive just after ten o'clock
in the morning, I receive a page from my answering
service, but I am unable to answer it because the circuits are suddenly busy. I notice a line of ambulances from hospitals all over
New York City exiting at Twenty-third Street, bound for Bellevue
Hospital. They are not responding to 911 calls, but to one massive
emergency moment.

The bright red-and-white-striped ambulances of Metropolitan
Hospital line up behind the black-and-orange sleek emergency
vans of New York Presbyterian, following the squat ice-cream-
truck-looking EMS vehicles on a line to command central, designated at Bellevue.

When I reach the hospital, I find it transforming before my eyes
into a major MASH unit. The emergency room proper is designated
for triage, the emergency ward is filling with gowned surgeons and

211

surgical equipment intended for early stabilization of patients, and the second floor is being set aside for those with walk-in injuries.

On floor six, formerly the rehab area, a team of skilled phlebotomists is assembling to draw blood and take blood donations. Off to the side, there is a decontamination area, with a variety of antidotes and full body suits.

Upstairs, the ward residents are busily discharging all the stable patients to free up beds for expected admissions.

In a few hours the hospital will be almost emptied of its patients. Even the ICU is being cleared, as patients on respirators are moved to the wards, freeing up space for the worst victims of a possible catastrophe.

At the front area where the ambulances come in, doctors and nurses dressed in scrubs mill about expectantly. People I have known for years, who have undergone many changes in job description, from primary care to administrator, even to retirement, now stand shoulder to shoulder, awaiting the potential patients.

"I haven't drawn blood in years," the director of ambulatory medical services says to me. "But I'm ready."

THE AGENCIES

Bellevue's CBPP (chemical and biological preparation program) is meeting hourly, trying to develop a strategy. The actual terrorist tool hasn't yet been divulged even to the Terrorism Response Units. All that the upper echelon at Bellevue knows is that a tip has been received by one of our federal intelligence agencies, probably the FBI.

CBPP does not include preparations for a nuclear attack. Perhaps this is because the devastation from even a suitcase bomb would be so great that Bellevue would see few survivors. More likely, it is because the government has devoted most of its rhetoric and resources to everything besides nuclear, and the media have been ignoring nuclear threats in the same way that they hype airports but not seaports. Anthrax and smallpox hype have set in motion a mode of response that is misdirected and heavily weighted toward biological weapons. The public has been taught to obsess on a created fear of bacterial and viral warfare that is well out of proportion to the real risk. In the meantime, there is no training for radiation poisoning in our emergency disaster program, no lead-lined fallout shelters in our survival plans. The federal and local governments beef up the military and the police, but our coast guard remains undermanned, and our seaports are mostly undefended.

The federal government has been frighteningly ineffective in keeping track of nuclear material and weaponry around the world.

Police with sniffing dogs and radiation detectors are suddenly everywhere, and the police commissioner announces that people on the streets should avoid anyone who looks the least bit suspicious.

The Centers for Disease Control is concerned about possible contagion and orders a quarantine—there will be no travel to or from Manhattan until further notice. The bridges and tunnels are closed. Masses attempt to cross the Brooklyn Bridge and the Fifty-ninth Street Bridge to escape on foot, but they are stopped and pushed back by police barriers.

THE MEDIA

The major networks break into their soap operas with special news reports every twenty minutes, while the cable networks carry complete live coverage. There is a news team from each network stationed outside command central at Bellevue Hospital. The news producers eye each passing physician trying to identify who is in charge.

Disaster and terrorism experts are hired instantly as cable news analysts, and they speculate on FOX, CNN, and MSNBC all through the day about the identity of the weapon of mass destruction. Flipping channels back and forth on the TV in Bellevue's concrete lobby, I can see there is no consensus. There are strong assertions for and against chemical, biological, or nuclear. Nuclear is mentioned, but more for completeness' sake than because any of the pundits or commentators are convinced that this old foe is truly the "weapon du jour."

The news coverage shows continual shots of the harbor and the Statue of Liberty, transmitting the subliminal information that the nineteenth-century gift from France remains a symbolic target.

The police commissioner holds a press conference to announce that every possible method is being used to catch the terrorists, though he can't disclose what these methods are or who the terrorists might be. The mayor repeats this statement in a clip that is shown over and over on all the stations. He is running for reelection next year, and though his popularity has been plummeting with all the trouble in the public schools, his current robust appearance on TV makes his handlers suddenly hopeful about his chances.

The impending disaster's importance is defined by the cable media's decision to cover it 24/7. The politicians are lining up to be seen pontificating on the significance of the news.

THE PROFITEERS

People are becoming so afraid that they can't concentrate on their work. The news that the bridges and tunnels remain closed causes a great claustrophobic fright. Businesses close down and send their employees home. Schools are closed and children mill about in the parks and on the streets. The hardware stores are flooded with people buying gas masks, duct tape, and respiratory masks. Cipro is disappearing from the shelves of all the pharmacies, though none of the pharmacists know where the customers have gotten the Cipro prescriptions so quickly. There is no time to check for forgeries.

Roving gangs of consumers are desperate for these supplies, despite their lack of knowledge of which WMD this really is. A potassium iodide manufacturer is selling millions of pills over the Internet, despite the medicine's limited use—protecting only the thyroid—in the event of a real nuclear attack.

Sleeping pill and sedative manufacturers are gearing up for a serious boost to their sales. In the meantime, pharmacies throughout the city have run out of Valium and Xanax, while supplies of other sedatives are running low.

THE OUTCOME

As the day goes on and nothing further happens, it slowly begins to dawn on those of us stationed at Bellevue Hospital that the onslaught of patients may never come. In the meantime, the wail of ambulance sirens continues to echo through the streets.

At 2 P.M. the bridges and tunnels are reopened, which goes a long way to calming the traumatized masses. By the time the news media actually deliver the message that the report is a hoax, a fraudulent memo given to Homeland Security by an unreliable source, most people are already beyond the first blush of panic. This has been by far the worst of all the terror alerts, and it will keep people nervous for a long time. Too many "boy who cried wolf" reports will ultimately cause people to disregard the initial report of a real attack, if a real attack ever comes.

At night, Bellevue is a ghost hospital, its emptied unlit rooms looming over a stunned crowd on First Avenue. Bellevue's doctors and nurses are still huddled together unnecessarily in the hospital's vacant emergency room.

ORSON WELLES REVISITED

The above events are a hoax, not only on the city of New York, but also on you, the careful reader of this volume. This fallacious terror warning has not yet taken place, but I believe it can happen just this way any day. We are all suckers for a scary story, and too willing to believe one.

On October 30, 1938, Halloween Eve, when Orson Welles

announced on national radio that "the Martians are coming," it was too easily accepted as true. The original broadcast was produced by CBS and affiliates, and performed by a single production company, the Mercury Theatre. The so-called mass panic that resulted was nothing compared with what we deal with today. Since then, we have become far more gullible, relying as we do on hyperbolic news reports and speeches that sound like they were written by someone on steroids. It is a sad state of affairs when the public is constantly cowed, shocked and awed, manipulated to be afraid, then diverted from remembering that nothing bad actually happened. The single note of terror, September 11, 2001, is played over and over to juice up the audience.

Realizing that we are conned into being afraid is the first step toward learning a new set of skills to assess risk. Fear must be reserved for real danger. Each step away from false worry is a step toward true health.

BIBLIOGRAPHY

INTRODUCTION: THE FEAR EPIDEMIC

Allison, Graham. *Nuclear Terrorism: The Ultimate Preventable Catastrophe.* New York: Henry Holt, 2004.

Broad, William J. "In a Lonely Stand, a Scientist Takes on National Security Dogma." *New York Times,* June 29, 2004.

Corradi, Juan, Patrica Weiss Fagen, and Manuel Antonio Garreton. *Fear at the Edge: State Terror and Resistance in Latin America.* Berkeley: University of California Press, 1992.

Department of Energy, Office of Inspector General. "Activities Involving Biological Select Agents." IG-0492, Feb. 2, 2001.

Dershowitz, Alan M. "There's a Way for Israel to Deal with Terrorism." *New York Daily News,* Mar. 15, 2002.

Jernigan, D. B., P. L. Raghunathan, B. P. Bell, et al. "Investigation of Bioterrorism-Related Anthrax, United States, 2001 Epidemiologic Findings." *Emerging Infectious Diseases* 8 (Oct. 2002): 1019–28.

Kahn, Laura H. "Biodefense Research: Can Secrecy and Safety Coexist?" *Biosecurity and Bioterrorism: Biodefense Strategy, Practice, and Science* 2, no. 2 (2004): 81–85.

Kelley, M., and J. Coghlan. "Mixing Bugs and Bombs." *Bulletin of Atomic Scientists* 59, no. 5 (Sept./Oct. 2003): 25–31.

Kellman, Barry. "Biological Terrorism: Legal Measures for Preventing Catastrophe." *Harvard Journal of Law and Public Policy* 24, no. 2 (Spring 2001): 417.

Kertesz, Imre. *Fateless.* Evanston, Ill.: Northwestern University Press, 1992.

Kristof, Nicholas. "The Nuclear Shadow." *New York Times,* Aug. 14, 2004.

Melamed, Samueal. "Association of Fear of Terror with Low-Grade Inflammation among Apparently Healthy Employed Adults." *Psychosomatic Medicine* 66, no. 4 (Aug. 2004): 484–91.

Merkin, Daphne. "The Way We Live Now: 8-15-04; Terror-Filled." *New York Times Magazine,* Aug. 15, 2004.

Spencer, Jane, and Cynthia Crossen. "Why Do Americans Believe Danger Lurks Everywhere?" *Wall Street Journal,* Apr. 24, 2003.

217

Steinberg, Jonathan S., et al. "Increased Incidence of Life-Threatening Ventricular Arrhythmias in Implantable Defibrillator Patients after the World Trade Center Attack." *Journal of the American College of Cardiology* 44, no. 6 (Sept. 15, 2004): 1261–64.

Tierno, Philip M. *Protect Yourself against Bioterrorism.* New York: Pocket Books, 2002.

———. *The Secret Life of Germs: Observations and Lessons from a Microbe Hunter.* New York: Pocket Books, 2001.

Interviews

Clarke, Betsy, and Mary Furth. Supervisors at International Red Cross, Family Assistance Center. Sept. 27, 2001.

Corradi, Juan E., PhD. Professor of Sociology, New York University. Dec. 2003.

Tierno, Philip, Jr., PhD. Director of Clinical Microbiology, New York University Medical Center. Mar. 11, 2003.

Tuchman, Marcel, MD. Professor of Medicine, New York University Medical School. Jan. 9, 2004.

1. WHY ARE WE SO AFRAID?

American Psychiatric Association. *Diagnostic and Statistical Manual of Mental Disorders,* 4th ed. Arlington, Va.: American Psychiatric Association, 1994.

Bradley, Walter. *Neurology in Clinical Practice.* Burlington, Vt.: Butterworth-Heinemann, 1996.

Braunwald, Eugene, et al. *Harrison's Principles of Internal Medicine,* 15th ed. New York: McGraw-Hill, 2001.

Fox, James Alan, and Jack Levin. "Media Exaggerate Sniper Threat." *USA Today,* Dec. 9, 2003.

Low, Phillip. *Clinical Autonomic Disorders.* Philadelphia: Lippincott Williams & Wilkins, 1997.

Siegel, Marc. "When Doctors Say Don't and the Patient Says Do." *New York Times,* Oct. 29, 2002.

2. IT WORKS FOR ANIMALS BUT NOT FOR US

Barad, Mark, Chris Cain, and Ashley Blouin. "L-type Voltage Gated Calcium Channels Are Required for Extinction of Fear." *The Journal of Neuroscience* 22, no. 20 (Oct. 15, 2002): 9113–21.

Ekman, Paul. *Emotions Revealed: Recognizing Faces and Feelings to Improve Communication and Emotional Life.* New York: Times Books, 2003.

Garcia, Rene, Richard Thompson, Michel Baudry, and Rose Marie Vouimba. "The Amygdala Modulates Prefrontal Cortex Activity Relative to Conditioned Fear." *Nature* 402 (Nov. 18, 1999): 294–96.

Ledoux, Joseph. *The Emotional Brain: The Mysterious Underpinnings of Emotional Life.* New York: Simon and Schuster, 1996.

McCarty, Richard, Greti Aguilera, Esther L. Sabban, and Richard Kvetnansky, eds. *Stress: Neural, Endocrine, and Molecular Studies.* Boca Raton, Fla.: CRC Press, 2002.

Meagher, Mary W., Randolph C. Arnau, and Jamie L. Rudy. "Pain and Emotion: Effects of Affective Picture Modulation." *Psychosomatic Medicine* 63 (2001): 79–90.

Milad, M. R., and G. J. Quirk. "Neurons in Medial Prefrontal Cortex Signal Memory for Fear Extinction." *Nature* 240 (Nov. 7, 2002): 70–74.

Olsson, Andreas, and Elizabeth A. Phelps. "Learned Fear of 'Unseen' Faces after Pavlovian, Observational, and Instructed Fear." *Psychological Science* 15, no. 12 (Dec. 2004): 822–28.

Phelps, Elizabeth. "Extinction Learning in Humans: Role of the Amygdala and vmPFC." *Neuron* 43 (Sept. 16, 2004): 897–905.

Sabban, Esther L., and Richard Kvetnansky. "Stress-Triggered Activation of Gene Expression in Catecholaminergic Systems: Dynamics of Transcriptional Events." *Trends in Neurosciences* 24, no. 2 (Feb. 2001).

Sapolsky, Robert M. "Glucocorticoids and Hippocampal Atrophy in Neuropsychiatric Disorders." *Archives of General Psychiatry* 57, no. 10 (2000): 925–35.

———. *A Primate's Memoir: A Neuroscientist's Unconventional Life among the Baboons.* New York: Scribner, 2001.

Shumyatsky, G. P., G. Malleret, S. Vronskaya, M. Hatton, L. Hampton, J. F. Battey, C. Dulac, E. R. Kandel, and V. Y. Bolshakov. "Identification of a Signaling Network in Lateral Nucleus of Amygdala Important for Inhibiting Memory Specifically Related to Learned Fear." *Cell* 111, no. 6 (Dec. 13, 2002): 905–18.

Interviews

Jolly, Chris, PhD. Professor of Anthropology, New York University. Dec. 18, 2003.

Ledoux, Joseph, PhD. Professor of Neuroscience, New York University. Dec. 17, 2003.

Mann, John, MD. Director of Neuroscience, New York State Psychiatric Institute. Jan. 22, 2004.

Phelps, Elizabeth, PhD. Associate Professor of Psychology and Neuroscience, New York University. Dec. 30, 2004.

Sabban, Esther, PhD. Professor and Graduate Program Director, New York Medical College. Dec. 22, 2003.

Yehuda, Rachel, PhD. Professor of Psychiatry, Mount Sinai School of Medicine. Dec. 29, 2003.

3. OUR CULTURE OF WORRY

Greenberg, Jeff, Andy Martens, Eva Jonas, Donna Eisenstadt, Thomas Pyszczynski, and Sheldon Solomon. "Psychological Defense in Anticipation of Anxiety: Eliminating the Potential for Anxiety Eliminates the Effect of Mortality Salience on Worldview Defense." *Psychological Science* 14, no. 5 (Sept. 2003): 516.

Pyszczynski, Thomas A., Sheldon Solomon, and Jeff Greenberg. *In the Wake of 9/11: The Psychology of Terror.* Washington, D.C.: American Psychological Association, 2002.

Siegel, Marc. "Fear Created by the Unknown." *Los Angeles Times Health,* Jan. 26, 2004.

Solomon, Sheldon, Jeff Greenberg, and Tom Pyszczynski. "Reminders of Death Increase the Need for Psychological Security and Therefore the Appeal of Leaders Who Emphasize the Greatness of the Nation and a Heroic Victory over Evil." *Psychological Science* 15, no. 12 (Dec. 2004).

Whelan, Elizabeth M. *Toxic Terror: The Truth behind the Cancer Scares.* Amherst, Mass.: Prometheus Books, 1993.

4. PLAYING POLITICS WITH FEAR

Ajami, Fouad. "A Tigris Chronicle." *Wall Street Journal,* Dec. 18, 2003.

Anderson, Curt. "Al Qaeda Said Almost Ready to Attack U.S." *Associated Press,* May 26, 2004.

Barber, Benjamin. *Fear's Empire: War, Terrorism, and Democracy.* New York: W.W. Norton, 2003.

Blomquist, Brian. "Death Jet Plot." *New York Post,* Jan. 3, 2004.

Bobbitt, Philip. "Being Clear about Present Dangers." *New York Times,* Aug. 11, 2004.

Brooks, Renana. "A Nation of Victims." *Nation,* June 30, 2003.

Bumiller, Elisabeth. "Bush Makes Danger His Campaign Theme." *New York Times,* Jan. 25, 2004.

Bush, George W. Interview by Tim Russert, *Meet the Press,* NBC, Feb. 8, 2004.

Connor, Tracy. "How Al Qaeda Eyed Its Target." *New York Daily News,* Aug. 9, 2004.

Cooper, Joel. "What's Inside the Voter's Mind?" *Newsday,* Oct. 31, 2004.

Corey, Robin. *Fear: The History of a Political Idea.* New York: Oxford University Press, 2004.

Corn, David. *The Lies of George W. Bush: Mastering the Politics of Deception.* New York: Crown, 2003.

Diehl, Jackson. "Dubious Threat, Expensive Defense." *Washington Post,* Apr. 26, 2004.

Easterbrook, Gregg. "In an Age of Terror, Safety Is Relative." *New York Times,* June 27, 2004.

Glassner, Barry. *The Culture of Fear: Why Americans Are Afraid of All the Wrong Things.* New York: Basic Books, 1999.

Harwood, John. "Theme of Fear Plays Key Role in Election and May Favor Bush." *Wall Street Journal,* Sept. 1, 2004.

Hind, Rick, and David Halperin. "Lots of Chemicals, Little Reaction." *New York Times,* Sept. 22, 2004.

Ignatieff, Michael. *The Lesser Evil: Political Ethics in an Age of Terror.* Princeton, N.J.: Princeton University Press, 2004.

Jehl, Douglas, and David Johnston. "Reports That Led to Terror Alert Were Years Old, Officials Say." *New York Times,* Aug. 3, 2004.

———. "Terror Detainee Is Seen as Leader in Plot by Qaeda." *New York Times,* Aug. 6, 2004.

Jehl, Douglas, and Richard W. Stevenson. "New Qaeda Activity Is Said to Be Major Factor in Alert." *New York Times,* Aug. 4, 2004.

Johnston, David. "Fears of Attack at Conventions Drive New Plans." *New York Times,* July 5, 2004.

Kennedy, Robert F., Jr. "The Junk Science of George W. Bush." *Nation,* Feb. 19, 2004.

Krauthammer, Charles. "The Case for Fearmongering." *Time,* Oct. 18, 2004.

Krugman, Paul. "To Tell the Truth." *New York Times,* May 28, 2004.

Landau, Mark J., Sheldon Solomon, and Jeff Greenberg. "Deliver Us from Evil: The Effects of Mortality Salience and Reminders of 9/11 on Support for President George W. Bush." *Personality and Social Psychology Bulletin* 30, no. 9 (2004): 1136–50.

Landro, Laura. "Disaster Medicine Becomes a Specialty." *Wall Street Journal,* Aug. 12, 2004.

Lichtblau, Eric. "U.S. Warns of High Risk of Qaeda Attack." *New York Times,* Aug. 2, 2004.

Meek, James Gordon. "6 Flights Nixed by Terror Fears." *New York Daily News,* Dec. 25, 2003.

New York Times. "The Face of Scare Politics" (editorial). Dec. 11, 2003.

———. "A Real Nuclear Danger" (editorial). May 28, 2004.

———. "The Terror Alerts" (editorial). Aug. 5, 2004.

Nunberg, Geoffrey. "The -Ism Schism: How Much Wallop Can a Simple Word Pack?" *New York Times,* July 11, 2004.

Pan, Michael, Amanda Terkel, Robert Boorstin, P. J. Crowley, and Nigel Holmes. "Op-Chart: Safety Second." *New York Times,* Aug. 8, 2004.

Purnick, Joyce. "Rationing Fear and Assessing Vulnerability." *New York Times,* Aug. 2, 2004.

Rashbaum, William K., and Judith Miller. "New York Police Take Broad Steps in Facing Terror." *New York Times,* Feb. 15, 2004.

Reich, Robert. "A Failure of Intelligence." *American Prospect,* Aug. 2004.

Rich, Frank. "Operation Iraqi Infoganda." *New York Times,* Mar. 28, 2004.

———. "The Best Goebbels of All?" *New York Times,* June 27, 2004.

———. "3 Hours, 4 Nights, 1 Fear." *New York Times,* July 25, 2004.

Robin, Corey. "When Fear Is a Joint Venture." *Washington Post,* Oct. 24, 2004.

Rothstein, Edward. "Is Fear Itself the Enemy? Or Perhaps the Lack of It?" *New York Times,* Feb. 14, 2004.

Shenon, Philip. "Sweeping Overhaul of Intelligence." *New York Times,* July 23, 2004.

Stevenson, Richard W., and Adam Nagourney. "Bush's Campaign Emphasizes Role of Leader in War." *New York Times,* Mar. 17, 2004.

Swarns, Rachel. "2 More Flights Are Called Off after Warnings." *New York Times,* Jan. 1, 2004.

USA Today. "Has Iraq War Made U.S. Safer? That's Questionable" (editorial). July 16, 2004.

5. DISASTERS: REAL OR IMAGINED

Bertrand, Donald, Warren Woodberry, and Dave Goldiner. "Isa-Belted!" *New York Daily News,* Sept. 19, 2003.

Bode, Nicole, and Tracy Connor. "Rolling! Back on Track, City's Buzzing Again—With Minor Hitches." *New York Daily News,* Aug. 17, 2003.

Dao, James, Jennifer Lee, and David Halbinger. "Storm Leaves Nearly Two Dozen Dead and Millions without Power." *New York Times,* Sept. 20, 2003.

Gottlieb, Martin. "In Calm Blackout, Views of Remade City." *New York Times,* Aug. 16, 2003.

Kennedy, Randy, and Eric Lipton. "Subways Run, Planes Fly, as Bloomberg Shifts Focus to Communication Lapses." *New York Times,* Aug. 17, 2003.

Mahler, Jonathan. "The New York That's Visible in the Dark." *New York Times,* Aug. 17, 2003.

Peterson, Iver. "Isabel's Fury Winds Down after All of the Talking Up." *New York Times,* Sept. 20, 2003.

Seifman, David, Brad Hamilton, and Adam Miller. "Heroes Stunned by a Radio Daze." *New York Post,* Aug. 17, 2003.

6. FINDING THINGS TO WORRY ABOUT

Allan, Stuart. *Media, Risk, and Science.* Berkshire, UK: Open University Press, 2002.

Cohl, H. Aaron. *Are We Scaring Ourselves to Death? How Pessimism, Paranoia, and a Misguided Media Are Leading Us toward Disaster.* New York: St. Martin's Press, 1997.

De Becker, Gavin. *Fear Less: Real Truth about Risk, Safety, and Security in a Time of Terrorism.* New York: Little Brown, 2002.

———. *The Gift of Fear.* New York: Little Brown, 1997.

Easterbrook, Gregg. "The Smart Way to Be Scared." *New York Times,* Feb. 16, 2003.

Furedi, Frank. *Culture of Fear: Risk-Taking and the Morality of Low Expectations.* New York: Continuum, 2002.

Longeman, Jere. *Among the Heroes: United Flight 93 and the Passengers and Crew Who Fought Back.* New York: HarperCollins, 2002.

Morgan, M. Granger, Baruch Fischhoff, Ann Bostrom, and Cynthia J. Atman. *Risk Communication: A Mental Models Approach.* New York: Cambridge University Press, 2002.

Peters, Ralph. "Not So Innocent, Media's Devastating Impact." *New York Post,* Oct. 8, 2003.

Ropeik, David, and George Gray. *Risk: A Practical Guide for Deciding What's Really Safe and What's Really Dangerous in the World around You.* New York: Houghton Mifflin, 2002.

Ropeik, David, and Nigel Holmes. "Never Bitten, Twice Shy: The Real Dangers of Summer." *New York Times,* Aug. 9, 2003.

Schneier, Bruce. *Beyond Fear.* New York: Copernicus, 2003.

Siegel, Marc. "Diary of a 9/11 Doctor." *Doctors Who Volunteer,* Diversion Issue. Apr. 15, 2002.

———. "I'm Sorry, Your Illness Is Coded for Only 15 Minutes." *Washington Post*, Sept. 14, 2003.

Slovic, Paul. *The Perception of Risk*. London: Earthscan, 2000.

Sunstein, Cass. *Risk and Reason: Safety, Law, and the Environment*. New York: Cambridge University Press, 2002.

Thompson, Paul. "The Two Ziad Jarrahs." The Center for Cooperative Research, www.cooperativeresearch.org/essay.jsp?article=essayjarrah (accessed Aug. 24, 2002).

Tulloch, John, and Deborah Lupton. *Risk and Everyday Life*. Thousand Oaks, Calif.: Sage Publications, 2003.

Wright, Scott M., David E. Kern, Ken Kolodner, Donna M. Howard, and Frederick L. Brancati. "Attributes of Excellent Attending-Physician Role Models." *New England Journal of Medicine* 339, no. 27 (Dec. 31, 1998): 1986–93.

7. PROFITING FROM FEAR

Abramson, John. "Information Is the Best Medicine." *New York Times*, Sept. 18, 2004.

Allen, Jane. "Aspirin, Pain Relievers Can Be a Risky Mix." *Los Angeles Times*, July 6, 2004.

Avorn, Jerry. *Powerful Medicines: The Benefits, Risks, and Costs of Prescription Medicine*. New York: Knopf, 2004.

Barfield Berry, Deborah. "The New Deal on Medicare." *Newsday*, Nov. 25, 2003.

Brodie, Mollyann. "Understanding the Effects of Direct-to-Consumer Prescription Drug Advertising." Henry J. Kaiser Family Foundation, Nov. 2001.

Chan, Andrew T., Edward L. Giovannucci, Eva S. Schernhammer, Graham A. Colditz, David J. Hunter, Walter C. Willett, and Charles S. Fuchs. "A Prospective Study of Aspirin Use and the Risk for Colorectal Adenoma." *Annals of Internal Medicine* 140, no. 3 (Feb. 3, 2004): 157–66.

Cox, Emily R., Mark Frisse, Andrew Behm, and Kathleen A. Fairman. "Over-the-Counter Pain Reliever and Aspirin Use within a Sample of Long-Term Cyclooxygenase 2 Users." *Archives of Internal Medicine* 164, no. 11 (June, 2004): 1243–46.

Duenwald, Mary. "Choosing a Pain Remedy Carefully." *New York Times*, July 6, 2004.

DTC Perspectives Magazine. "DTC Perspectives." RX Insight, Inc., 2002 Conference Series. Jan. 17, 2002.

Freudenheim, Milt. "Difficult Path for Competition in Medicare Bill." *New York Times*, Nov. 28, 2003.

Goode, Erica. "Antidepressants Lift Clouds, But Lose 'Miracle Drug' Label." *New York Times*, June 30, 2002.

Grady, Denise. "Aspirin Seen as Preventing Breast Tumors." *New York Times*, May 26, 2004.

Hayden, Michael, Michael Pignone, Christopher Phillips, and Cynthia Mulrow. "Aspirin for the Primary Prevention of Cardiovascular Events: A Summary of the Evidence for the U.S. Preventive Services Task Force." *Annals of Internal Medicine* 136, no. 2 (Jan. 2002): 157–60.

Iglehart, John K. "Prescription-Drug Coverage for Medicare Beneficiaries." *New England Journal of Medicine* 349, no.10 (Sept. 4, 2003): 923–26.

IMS Health. Drug company reported prices and profits, www.imshealth.com (accessed Jan. 28, 2005).

Kolata, Gina, and Melody Peterson. "Hormone Replacement Study a Shock to the Medical System." *New York Times,* July 10, 2002.

Leake, Jonathan, and Andrew Porter. "Burgers Are as Addictive as Drugs." *London Times,* July 13, 2003.

Lieberman, Adam J., and Simona C. Kwon, MPH. *Facts versus Fears: A Review of the 20 Greatest Unfounded Health Scares of Recent Times,* 4th ed. New York: American Council on Science and Health, 2004.

Lueck, Sarah. "The New Medicare: How It Works." *Wall Street Journal,* Nov. 25, 2003.

Mathews, Anna Wilde, and Christopher Windham. "FDA Findings Bolster Prozac Use by Teens." *Wall Street Journal,* Aug. 25, 2004.

McGinley, Laurie, and Sarah Lueck. "Behind Drug-Benefit Debate: How to Mix Medicare, Markets." *Wall Street Journal,* Nov. 17, 2003.

Mello, Michelle M., Meredith Rosenthal, and Peter J. Neumann. "Direct-to-Consumer Advertising and Shared Liability for Pharmaceutical Manufacturers." *Journal of the American Medical Association* 289, no. 4 (Jan. 22, 2003): 477–81.

Miller, Adam. "N.Y. Rx Price Shock." *New York Post,* Oct. 15, 2003.

New York Times. "Holding Down Drug Prices" (editorial). Nov. 28, 2003.

———. "Of Smoking Bans and Heart Attacks" (editorial). Apr. 27, 2004.

Olivier, Suzannah. "Pill for All Ills?" *London Times,* Mar. 29, 2004.

Ostrove, Nancy M. "Statement of Nancy M. Ostrove, Ph.D., Deputy Director, Division of Drug Marketing, Advertising and Communications Center for Drug Evaluation and Research, Food and Drug Administration Department of Health and Human Services, before the Subcommittee on Consumer Affairs, Foreign Commerce, and Tourism, Senate Committee on Commerce, Science, and Transportation, July 24, 2001." U.S. Food and Drug Administration, www.fda.gov/ola/2001/drugpromo0724.html (accessed Nov. 7, 2004).

Parker-Pope, Tara. "Controversial Study Reignites Debate over Autism and Childhood Vaccines." *Wall Street Journal,* Sept. 7, 2004.

Pear, Robert. "New Medicare Plan for Drug Benefits Prohibits Insurance." *New York Times,* Dec. 7, 2003.

Pollack, Andrew. "For Some, Aspirin May Not Help Hearts." *New York Times,* July 20, 2004.

Prevention Magazine. "Consumer Reaction to DTC Advertising of Prescription Medicines." Dec. 2002.

Rosenthal, Meredith B., Ernst R. Berndt, Julie M. Donohue, Richard G. Frank, and Arnold M. Epstein. "Promotion of Prescription Drugs to Consumers." *New England Journal of Medicine* 346, no. 7 (Feb. 14, 2002): 498–505.

Schaefer, Sara, and Laurie McGinley. "Census Sees a Surge in Americans without Insurance." *Wall Street Journal,* Sept. 30, 2003.

Siegel, Marc. "Profits of Fear." *Nation,* Oct. 2001.

———. "The Drug Ad Wars." *Nation,* June 17, 2002.

————. "This Doesn't Have to Be the Price We Pay." *Washington Post,* June 22, 2003.

————. "Why Reforms Won't Help Harry." *Los Angeles Times Health,* Dec. 15, 2003.

Stossel, John. "The Anti-Junk Scientists." *New York Post,* Dec. 4, 2003.

Terry, Mary Beth, Marlie D. Gammon, et al. "Association of Frequency and Duration of Aspirin Use and Hormone Receptor Status with Breast Cancer Risk." *Journal of the American Medical Association* 291, no. 20 (May 26, 2004): 2433–40.

Toedtman, James. "Medicare Bill Profits Some." *Newsday,* Nov. 25, 2003.

U.S. Food and Drug Administration. "Assessment of Physician and Patient Attitudes Toward Direct-to-Consumer Promotion of Prescription Drugs." *Federal Register* 66, no. 157 (Aug. 14, 2001): 42664–65.

U.S. Food and Drug Administration, Department of Health and Human Services. "Agency Information Collection Activities: Proposed Collections; Comment Request; Extra Label Drug Use in Animals." www.fda.gov/ohrms/dockets/98fr/oc9950.pdf (accessed Aug. 27, 2004).

Vernon, John A. "Drug Research and Price Controls." *Regulation* (Winter 2002–2003): 22–25.

Whelan, Elizabeth M. "Salmon Scare Smells Fishy." *New York Post,* Aug. 29, 2003.

Wilkes, Michael S., Robert A. Bell, and Richard L. Kravitz. "Direct-to-Consumer Prescription Drug Advertising: Trends, Impact, and Implications." *Health Affairs* 19, no. 2 (2000): 111.

8. ANTHRAX

Alibek, Ken. *Biohazard: The Chilling True Story of the Largest Covert Biological Weapons Program in the World—Told from Inside by the Man Who Ran It.* New York: Dell Publishing, 2000.

Altman, Lawrence K. "Anthrax Missteps Offer Guide to Fight Next Bioterror Battle." *New York Times,* Jan. 6, 2002.

American Council on Science and Health. "Anthrax: What You Need to Know." www.acsh.org/publications/pubID.268/pub_detail.asp (accessed Oct. 1, 2003).

Bumiller, Elisabeth. "Public Health or Public Relations." *New York Times,* Oct. 21, 2001.

Centers for Disease Control and Prevention, Division of Bacterial and Mycotic Diseases. "Anthrax: Frequently Asked Questions." www.cdc.gov/ncidod/dbmd/diseaseinfo/anthrax_g.htm (accessed Oct. 2001).

Centers for Disease Control and Prevention, Emergency Preparedness and Response. "National Pharmaceutical Stockpile." www.cdc.gov (accessed Dec. 18, 2002).

Centers for Disease Control and Prevention, Health Advisory. "Updated Information about How to Recognize and Handle a Suspicious Package or Envelope." www.cdc.gov (accessed Oct. 31, 2001).

Centers for Disease Control and Prevention, Office of Communications. "Recognition of Illness Associated with the Intentional Release of a Biological Agent." *Morbidity and Mortality Weekly Report* 50, no. 41 (Oct. 19, 2001): 893–97.

Cieslak, Theodore J., and Edward M. Eitzen. "Clinical and Epidemiologic Principles of Anthrax." *Emerging Infectious Diseases* 5, no. 4 (July 1999): 552–55.

Committee on Research Standards and Practices to Prevent the Destructive Application of Biotechnology, Development, Security, and Cooperation, National Research Council. *Biotechnology Research in an Age of Terrorism.* Washington, D.C.: The National Academies Press, 2004.

Dao, James, and Judith Miller. "Pentagon Shifts Anthrax Vaccine to Civilian Uses." *New York Times,* June 28, 2002.

Gerber, Michael S. "Anthrax Delay Blamed on Lack of Ties." *The Hill,* Apr. 18, 2002.

Hensley, Scott. "Antibiotic Purchases Jump in New York." *Wall Street Journal,* Oct. 9, 2001.

Inglesby, Thomas V., Tara O'Toole, et. al. "Anthrax as a Biological Weapon, 2002: Updated Recommendations for Management." *Journal of the American Medical Association* 287, no. 17 (May 1, 2002): 2236–52.

Jernigan, D. B., P. L. Raghunathan, B. P. Bell, et al., "Investigation of Bioterrorism-Related Anthrax, United States: 2001; Epidemiological Findings." *Emerging Infectious Diseases* 8, no. 10 (Oct. 2002): 1019–28.

Joellenbeck, Lois M., Lee L. Zwanziger, Jane S. Durch, and Brian L. Strom, eds. "The Anthrax Vaccine: Is It Safe? Does It Work?" Committee to Assess the Safety and Efficacy of the Anthrax Vaccine, Medical Follow-Up Agency, Institute of Medicine, *National Academy of Sciences,* March 2002.

Kortepeter, Mark G., and Gerald W. Parker. "Potential Biological Weapons Threats." *Emerging Infectious Diseases* 5, no. 4 (July–Aug. 1999): 523–27.

Kristof, Nicholas D. "Anthrax? The F.B.I. Yawns." *New York Times,* July 2, 2002.

Lipton, Eric, and Kirk Johnson. "Tracking Bioterror's Tangled Course." *New York Times,* Dec. 26, 2001.

Mandell, Gerald L., John E. Bennett, and Raphael Dolin. *Mandell, Douglas, and Bennett's Principles and Practice of Infectious Diseases,* 5th ed. London: Churchill Livingstone, 2000.

Martinez, Barbara, and Gardiner Harris. "Anxious Patients Plead with Doctors for Antibiotics; Some Physicians Refuse Requests for Anthrax-Treating Drug, While Many Others Give In." *Wall Street Journal,* Oct. 2001.

Pittman, Phillip, et al. "Anthrax Vaccine: Immunogenicity and Safety of a Dose-Reduction, Route-Change Comparison Study in Humans." *Vaccine* 20, no. 9–10 (Jan. 31, 2002): 1412–20.

Rosen, Jeffrey. "Naked Terror." *New York Times Magazine,* Jan. 14, 2004.

Rotz, Lisa D., Ali S. Khan, et al. "Public Health Assessment of Potential Biological Terrorism Agents." *Emerging Infectious Diseases* 8, no. 2 (Feb. 2002).

Schoofs, Mark, and Gary Fields. "Poor Anthrax Information Led FBI to Restart from Scratch." *Wall Street Journal,* Mar. 25, 2002.

Siegel, Marc. "Cipro, A Doctor's Tale." *New York Times,* Oct. 21, 2001.

———. "Antibiotics Don't Cure Fear." *Los Angeles Times,* Oct. 31, 2001.

———. "Anthrax Fumble." *Nation,* Mar. 18, 2002.

———. "A Recipe for Even More Bureaucracy, Bioterror Safety Net May Be Full of Holes." *Chicago Tribune,* June 11, 2002.

Van Natta, Don, Jr., Don Johnston, and David Johnston. "F.B.I. Alert Warns of Threat Tied to July 4th." *New York Times,* June 30, 2002.

Vergano, Dan, and Steve Sternberg. "Anthrax Slip-Ups Raise Fears about Planned Biolabs." *USA Today,* Oct. 14, 2004.

Interviews

Cohen, Mitchell, MD. Director of Bacterial Disease, Centers for Disease Control and Prevention. Jan. 13, 2002.

Smith, Perry, MD. Chief Epidemiologist, New York State. Oct. 12, 2001.

9. INSECTS, POX, AND LETHAL GAS

Altman, Lawrence K. "West Nile and Its Lessons for Doctors." *New York Times, Doctor's World,* Aug. 11, 2002.

———. "Experts Expect Rapid Rise in West Nile Virus Cases." *New York Times,* Aug. 16, 2002.

———. "Linking West Nile and Transplants May Take Weeks." *New York Times,* Sept. 2, 2002.

———. "Smallpox Inoculation Urged for Employees of Hospitals." *New York Times,* Oct. 16, 2002.

———. "Close Monitoring Is Planned for Smallpox Vaccinations." *New York Times,* Oct. 17, 2002.

Associated Press. "States Respond to CDC's Prediction of 1,000 West Nile Cases." Aug. 16, 2002.

———. "West Nile Link in Transplant Probed." Sept. 2, 2002.

Barry, John. "Misplaced Fear of a Viral Epidemic." *New York Times,* Aug. 10, 2002.

Branigin, William, and Joby Warrick. "Deadly Nerve Agent Sarin Is Found in Roadside Bomb." *Washington Post,* May 18, 2004.

Breman, Joel G., and D. A. Henderson. "Current Concepts: Diagnosis and Management of Smallpox." *New England Journal of Medicine* 346, no. 17 (Apr. 25, 2002): 1300–1308.

Broad, William J. "U.S. to Vaccinate 500,000 Workers against Smallpox." *New York Times,* July 7, 2002.

———. "Study Favors Different Tack on Smallpox." *New York Times,* July 9, 2002.

———. "Bioterror Researchers Build a More Lethal Mousepox." *New York Times,* Oct. 31, 2002.

Broad, William J., Stephen Engelberg, and James Glanz. "Assessing Risks, Chemical, Biological, Even Nuclear." *New York Times,* Nov. 1, 2001.

Centers for Disease Control and Prevention. "Smallpox Fact Sheet." www.cdc.gov (accessed Dec. 2002).

Centers for Disease Control and Prevention, Emergency Preparedness and Response. "Potassium Iodide (KI)." www.bt.cdc.gov/radiation/ki.asp (accessed Sept. 2002).

Centers for Disease Control and Prevention, National Center for Environmental Health. "Radiation Studies: Casualty Management after a Deliberate Release of Radioactive Material." www.bt.cdc.gov/radiation/casualtiesradioactive. asp (accessed Sept. 2002).

Centers for Disease Control and Prevention, National Institute for Occupational Safety and Health. "Guidance for Filtration and Air-Cleaning Systems to Protect Building Environments from Airborne Chemical, Biological, or Radiological Attacks." www.cdc.gov/niosh/docs/2003-136/pdfs/2003-136.pdf, no. 2003–2136 (accessed Apr. 2003).

Chicago Tribune. "Fighting Fear and West Nile" (editorial). Apr. 13, 2002.

Dunston, Ashlee, Gilbert L. Ross, MD, and Elizabeth Whelan, ScD, MPH, eds. *New Yorker's Guide to Terrorism Preparedness and Response: Chemical, Biological, Radiological, and Nuclear.* New York: American Council on Science and Health, 2003.

Engler, R. J. M., J. Kenner, and D. Y. Leung. "Smallpox Vaccination: Risk Considerations for Patients with Atopic Dermatitis." *Journal of Allergy and Clinical Immunology* 110, no. 3 (Sept. 2002): 357–65.

Fauci, Anthony S. "Editorial: Smallpox Vaccination Policy—The Need for Dialogue." *New England Journal of Medicine* 346, no. 17 (Apr. 25, 2002): 1319–20.

Frelinger J. A., and M. L. Garba. "Responses to Smallpox Vaccine." *New England Journal of Medicine* 347, no. 9 (2002): 689–90.

Fritz, S. B., A. M. Singer, V. B. Revan, and J. R. Baker Jr. "Bioterrorism: Relevance to Allergy and Immunology in Clinical Practice." *Journal of Allergology and Clinical Immunology* 109, no. 2 (Feb. 2002): 214–28.

Gettleman, Jeffrey. "Hospitals Refuse Smallpox Program." *New York Times,* Dec. 19, 2002.

Glass, Thomas A., and Monica Schoch-Spana. "Bioterrorism and the People: How to Vaccinate a City against Panic." *Clinical Infectious Diseases* 34, no. 2 (2002): 217–223A.

Henderson, Donald A., Thomas V. Inglesby, et al. "Smallpox as a Biological Weapon: Medical and Public Health Management." *Journal of the American Medical Association* 281, no. 22 (June 9, 1999): 2127–37.

Johnson, Reed. "An Elevated Risk of a Panic Attack and a Wisecrack." *Los Angeles Times,* Feb. 19, 2003.

Kaplan, Edward H., David L. Kraft, and Lawrence M. Wein. "Smallpox Vaccination Strategies." *Proceedings of the National Academy of Sciences,* July 2002.

Lee, Ernest C., MD, MPH. "Clinical Manifestations of Sarin Nerve Gas Exposure." *Journal of the American Medical Association* 290, no. 5 (Aug. 6, 2003): 659–62.

Manning, Anita. "Smallpox Vaccination Plan Ceased." *USA Today,* Oct. 15, 2003.

Mayo Clinic Staff. "Biological, Chemical Weapons: Arm Yourself with Information." Mayo Foundation for Medical Education and Research, www.mayo clinic.com/invoke.cfm?objectid=832829DC-9081-4506-BB736DDDD8192FBF (accessed July 3, 2002).

National Law Enforcement and Technology Center. "What Every Public Safety Officer Should Know about Radiation and Radioactive Materials: A Resource

Guide." *Tech Beat,* www.nlectc.org/techbeat/summer2003/RadiationSumm03. pdf (accessed summer 2003).

New York City Department of Health and Mental Hygiene, Office of Communications Press Release. "New York City Department of Health and Mental Hygiene Will Begin Voluntary Smallpox Vaccination Program in Jan. 2003 to Establish Strategic Reserve of Health and Public Health Response Teams." www.nyc.gov/ html/doh/html/public/press02/pr1101213.html (accessed Dec. 13, 2002).

New York Times. "The West Nile Epidemic" (editorial). Aug. 25, 2002.

Plotkin, Stanley A., Walter A. Orenstein, and Paul A. Offit. "A Short History of Vaccination," in *Vaccines,* 4th ed. Philadelphia: WB Saunders Company, 2003.

Reuters. "U.S. Probes West Nile Infection Via Donated Organs." Sept. 2, 2002.

Rosenthal, Steven R., Michael Merchlinsky, Cynthia Kleppinge, and Karen L. Goldenthal. "Developing New Smallpox Vaccines." *Journal of Emerging Infectious Diseases* 7, no. 6 (Nov.–Dec. 2001).

Siegel, Marc. "Greatest Risk of Smallpox Is Fear." *Los Angeles Times,* Oct. 31, 2002.

———. "False Comfort from the Smallpox Vaccine." *New York Times,* Dec. 14, 2002.

———. "Reality Check." *American Prospect Online,* Feb. 21, 2003.

———. "Fear and Its Discontents." *Nation,* May 19, 2003.

Sorenson, John H., and Barbara M. Vogt. "Will Duct Tape and Plastic Really Work?" *Oak Ridge National Laboratory,* Aug. 2001.

U.S. Department of Health and Human Services, Agency for Toxic Substances and Disease Registry. "Managing Hazardous Materials Incidents." www.atsdr. cdc.gov/mhmi-v1-p.pdf, vols. I and III, version 2001 (accessed Aug.15, 2004).

U.S. Food and Drug Administration, Center for Drug Evaluation and Research. "Guidance: Potassium Iodide as a Thyroid Blocking Agent in Radiation Emergencies." www.fda.gov/cder/guidance/4825fnl.htm (accessed Dec. 2001).

U.S. National Library of Medicine, Specialized Information Services, National Institutes of Health, Department of Health and Human Services. "Chemical Warfare Agents." www.sis.nlm.nih.gov/Tox/ChemWar.html (accessed Feb. 15, 2005).

Waldholz, Michael. "When a Sense of Control Vanishes." *Wall Street Journal,* Dec. 2002.

World Health Organization. *Public Health Response to Biological and Chemical Weapons: WHO Guidance,* 2nd ed. 2001.

———. *Preparedness for the Deliberate Use of Biological Agents: A Rational Approach to the Unthinkable.* May 2002.

Interviews

Zavasky, Dani-Margot, MD. New York City Police Department Deputy Medical Director for Counterterrorism. American Council on Science and Health press conference, Sept. 15, 2003.

10. SARS

Altman, Lawrence K. "Step by Step, Scientists Track Mystery Ailment." *New York Times,* Apr. 1, 2003.

———. "What Is the Next Plague?" *New York Times,* Nov. 11, 2003.

———. "New SARS Reports, New Questions on Tracking." *New York Times,* Jan. 2, 2004.

Associated Press. "CDC: SARS Fears Could Swamp Emergency Rooms This Winter." Oct. 2003.

BBC. "China Guards against SARS." Oct. 13, 2003.

Bradsher, Keith. "From Tourism to High Finance, Mysterious Illness Spreads Havoc." *New York Times,* Apr. 2, 2003.

———. "Illness Takes a Toll on Hotels in Asia." *New York Times,* Apr. 4, 2003.

Callan, Sara. "Sorry, Fear of Illness Isn't Covered—Travel Insurance Can Help If You're Too Sick to Go, Not If You're Too Scared." *Wall Street Journal,* Apr. 3, 2003.

CDC Health Update. "Preliminary Clinical Description of Severe Acute Respiratory Syndrome." Mar. 22, 2003.

Chase, Marilyn. "Epidemics Take Variety of Courses, History Offers Some Clues to How the SARS Outbreak May Grow—or Dissipate." *Wall Street Journal,* Apr. 4, 2003.

Fritsch, Peter, Matt Pottinger, and Leslie Chang. "Divergent Asian Responses Show Difficulties in Dealing with SARS." *Wall Street Journal,* Apr. 7, 2003.

Gerberding, Julie Louise. "Faster . . . But Fast Enough? Responding to the Epidemic of Severe Acute Respiratory Syndrome." *New England Journal of Medicine,* Apr. 2, 2003.

Grady, Denise. "SARS Is New and It Kills, But How Dangerous Is It?" *New York Times,* Apr. 6, 2003.

———. "Fear Reigns as Dangerous Mystery Illness Spreads in Asia and Beyond." *New York Times,* Apr. 7, 2003.

Harmon, Amy. "Public Confronts New Virus on Laymen's Terms." *New York Times,* Apr. 6, 2003.

"Health Experts Go to the Source of SARS Virus—Team Is in Southern China as Cases Multiply in Asia; Toronto Extends Quarantine." *Wall Street Journal,* Apr. 4, 2003.

Lieber, Ron, and Scott Neuman. "Airlines Step Up Effort to Prevent SARS." *Wall Street Journal,* Apr. 3, 2003.

McNeil, Donald G., Jr., and Lawrence K. Altman. "China Admits to Having More of Mystery Illness." *New York Times,* Apr. 3, 2003.

New York Times. "Preparing for SARS [Return]" (editorial). Oct. 26, 2003.

Normile, D. "Second Lab Accident Fuels Fears about SARS." *Science* 303 (June 2, 2004): 26.

Parker-Pope, Tara. "Reality Check: Asian Mystery Disease Is Scary Mostly Because It's New." *Wall Street Journal,* Apr. 2, 2003.

Pottinger, Matt, Betsy McKay, and Elena Cherney. "Treating a Medical Mystery." *Wall Street Journal,* Apr. 3, 2003.

Siegel, Marc. "Hysteria Spreads Faster Than SARS." *Boston Globe,* Apr. 5, 2003.

————. "A Virus of Fear." *New York Times,* May 4, 2003.

Svoboda, Tomislav, et al. "Public Health Measures to Control the Spread of the Severe Acute Respiratory Syndrome during the Outbreak in Toronto." *New England Journal of Medicine* 350, no. 3 (June 3, 2004): 2352–61.

Weinstein, Robert A. "Planning for Epidemics—The Lessons of SARS." *New England Journal of Medicine* 350, no. 3 (June 3, 2004): 2332–34.

Wonacott, Peter, Betsy McKay, and David P. Hamilton. "Fear of SARS Rises as Cases—and Rumors—Spread." *Wall Street Journal,* Apr. 2, 2003.

Wong, Edward. "Stop-and-Go Traffic on a Global Scale." *New York Times,* Apr. 6, 2003.

11. FLU

Altman, Lawrence K. "Despite Lacking Latest Virus, Flu Vaccine Is Thought to Work." *New York Times,* Nov. 18, 2003.

Associated Press. "Beating the Flu: A Spray or a Shot?" Sept. 23, 2003.

————. "Hospitals Restrict Visitors to Prevent Infection." Dec. 12, 2003.

Barry, John M. *The Great Influenza: The Epic Story of the Deadliest Plague In History.* New York: Viking Books, 2004.

BBC. "Cure for Killer Flu Discovered." Oct. 20, 2003.

Centers for Disease Control Morbidity and Mortality Weekly Report. "Prevention and Control of Influenza: Recommendations of the Advisory Committee on Immunization Practices." No. RR-4 (1999): 48.

Centers for Disease Control and Prevention. "Key Facts about the Flu: How to Prevent the Flu and What to Do When You Get Sick." www.cdc.gov/flu/pdf/keyfacts.pdf (accessed Oct. 6, 2004).

————. "Weekly Influenza Activity Estimates, Week Ending Nov. 29, 2003." www.cdc.gov/flu/weekly/usmap.htm (accessed Nov. 29, 2003).

Clover R. D., T. Abell, L. A. Becker, et al. "Family Functioning and Stress as Predictors of Influenza B Infection." *Journal of Family Practice* 28 (1989): 535–39.

Cox, N. J., and K. Subbarao. "Influenza." *Lancet* 354 (1999): 1277–82.

Kenworthy, Tom. "Even Though Flu Season 'Is Going Gangbusters,' It Could End Quickly Too." *USA Today,* Dec. 10, 2003.

Lui, K.-J., and A. P. Kendal. "Impact of Influenza Epidemics on Mortality in the United States from Oct. 1972 to May 1985." *American Journal of Public Health* 77 (1987): 712–16.

Manning, Anita. "Universal Flu Shots Considered." *USA Today,* Feb. 24, 2004.

National Institutes of Health, Office of Communications and Public Liaison, National Institute of Allergy and Infectious Diseases, Flu Drugs. www.niaid.nih.gov/factsheets/flu.htm (accessed June 17, 2003).

Pauling, Linus. *Vitamin C, the Common Cold, and the Flu.* San Francisco: W. H. Freeman & Company, 1976.

Pearson, Helen. "Diluted Flu Vaccine Works Well." *Nature Online,* www.nature.com/news/2004/041101/pf/041101-13_pf.html (accessed Nov. 4, 2004).

Schmid, M. L., G. Kudesia, S. Wake, and R. C. Read. "Prospective Comparative Study of Culture Specimens and Methods in Diagnosing Influenza in Adults." *British Medical Journal* 316 (1998): 275.

Siegel, Marc. "Ho-Hum Killer Creates Real Risk." *USA Today,* Oct. 16, 2003.

Simonsen, L., L. B. Schonberger, D. F. Stroup, N. H. Arden, and N. J. Cox. "The Impact of Influenza on Mortality in the USA," in *Options for the Control of Influenza III,* ed. L. E. Brown, A. W. Hampson, and R. G. Webster. Amsterdam: Elsevier Publishing Co., 1996.

Tuller, David. "Promoting Flu Shots for All." *New York Times,* Oct. 14, 2003.

Winquist, Andrea G., Keija Fukuda, Carolyn B. Bridges, and Nancy J. Cox. "Neuraminidase Inhibitors for Treatment of Influenza A and B Infections." Centers for Disease Control, Division of Viral and Rickettsial Diseases, National Center for Infectious Disease. Dec. 17, 1999 / 48(RR14): 1–9.

World Health Organization. Communicable Disease Surveillance and Response, WHO Global Influenza Surveillance Network. www.who.int/csr/disease/influenza/influenzanetwork/en/ (accessed Oct. 6, 2004).

———. Flunet activity map showing "hot areas" in Chile and Australia, (8/24/03-9/27/03). www.phac-aspc.gc.ca/fluwatch/03-04/w36_03 (accessed Dec. 14, 2003).

Yale New Haven Health. "Complementary Medicine: Information about Complementary and Alternative Medical Therapies to Influenza." www.yalenewhavenhealth.org/library/healthguide/en-us/Cam/topic.asp?hwid=hn-1398005 (accessed Jan. 15, 2004).

Zambon, M. "Laboratory Diagnosis of Influenza," in *Textbook of Influenza,* ed. K. G. Nicholson, R. G. Webster, and A. J. Hay. Oxford: Blackwell Science, 1998.

12. COWS, BIRDS, AND HUMANS

Altman, Lawrence K. "Avian Flu Said to Be Resistant to a Main Flu-Fighting Drug." *New York Times,* Jan. 25, 2004.

———. "As Bird Flu Spreads, Global Health Weaknesses Are Exposed." *New York Times,* Feb. 3, 2004.

———. "Experts Urge Bird Vaccination against Flu." *New York Times,* Feb. 6, 2004.

———. "U.S. Issues Its First Plan for Responding to a Flu Pandemic." *New York Times,* Aug. 26, 2004.

American Lung Association. "Flu." www.lungusa.org (accessed Oct. 23, 2004).

Associated Press. "Bird Flu Surfaces in Delaware." Feb. 6, 2004.

Barry, John. "History Offers Lessons on Flu's Threats." *USA Today,* Feb. 10, 2004.

BBC. "1918 Killer Flu Secrets Revealed." Feb. 5, 2004.

Bradsher, Keith, and Lawrence K. Altman. "Thais Infected with Bird Flu; Virus Spreads." *New York Times,* Jan. 24, 2004.

Brown, David. "This Year's Potential Pandemic, HHS Calls for Plan to Counter Threat of Flu." *Washington Post,* Aug. 25, 2004.

Bundy, Jennifer. "Thousands Line Up for Desperate Shot at Flu Vaccine." *Associated Press,* Oct. 16, 2004.

Carter, Sylvia. "What Can We Eat? Not So Fishy Alternatives for Ones Wary of Recent Food Scares." *Newsday,* Jan. 11, 2004.

Centers for Disease Control and Prevention. "Information on Influenza Anti-Viral Drugs." *Morbidity and Mortality Weekly Report,* www.cdc.gov/mmwr (accessed Oct. 31, 2004).

Crispin, Shawn, Margot Cohen, and Timothy Mapes. "Bird-Flu Outbreak Revives Concerns Stirred by SARS." *Wall Street Journal,* Jan. 28, 2004.

Davis, Matthew. "The Failure to Deal with the Flu." *Los Angeles Times,* Oct. 8, 2004.

Grady, Denise. "U.S. Issues Safety Rules to Protect Food against Mad Cow Disease." *New York Times,* Dec. 31, 2003.

———. "Before Shortage of Flu Vaccine, Many Warnings." *New York Times,* Oct. 17, 2004.

Haney, Daniel Q. "Experts: Bird Flu Could Become Epidemic." *Associated Press,* Jan. 24, 2004.

Heikkinen, Terho, Aimo Salmi, and Olli Ruuskanen. "Comparative Study of Nasopharyngeal Aspirate and Nasal Swab Specimens for Detection of Influenza." *British Medical Journal* 322, no. 7279 (Jan. 20, 2001): 138.

Maier, Thomas. "Flu Vaccine: Two Pictures of Health." *Newsday,* Oct. 24, 2004.

Manning, Anita. "Demand for Flu Shots Takes Off." *USA Today,* Oct. 8, 2004.

Matsumoto, K. "Anti-Influenza Drugs and the Standard of Use." *Nippon Rinsho* 58, no. 11 (Nov. 2000): 2283–87.

McFadden, Robert D. "Frustration and Fear Reign over Flu Shots." *New York Times,* Oct. 16, 2004.

McNeil, Donald G. "Mad Cow Case Leads Government to Consider Greater Meat Testing." *New York Times,* Dec. 26, 2003.

New York Times. "Preparing for the Bird Flu" (editorial). Dec. 17, 2003.

———. "The Spread of Avian Influenza" (editorial). Jan. 30, 2004.

———. "An Influenza Vaccine Debacle" (editorial). Oct. 20, 2004.

Parker-Pope, Tara. "Do You Really Need to Get a Flu Shot?" *Wall Street Journal,* Oct. 26, 2004.

Regaldo, Antonio. "Scientists Rush to Create Vaccine for Bird Flu—Just in Case." *Wall Street Journal,* Jan. 28, 2004.

Ross, Emma. "WHO: Unsafe Handling Raises Bird Flu Risk." *Associated Press,* Mar. 3, 2004.

Schlosser, Eric. "The Cow Jumped over the U.S.D.A." *New York Times,* Jan. 2, 2003.

Siegel, Marc. "Vaccine Poker." *Nation,* Oct. 14, 2004.

———. "A Tough Choice: Who Gets the Shot." *Los Angeles Times,* Oct. 25, 2004.

———. "Flu Tips." *Family Circle,* Nov. 30, 2004.

Singer, Peter, and Karen Dawn. "When Slaughter Makes Sense." *Newsday,* Feb. 8, 2004.

Talan, Jamie. "Mad Cow Scare, Fears Confirmed, More Questions Than Answers." *Newsday,* Dec. 26, 2003.

Wald, Matthew L., and Eric Lichtblau. "U.S. Is Examining a Mad Cow Case, First in Country." *New York Times,* Dec. 24, 2003.

233

———. "U.S. Scours Files to Trace the Source of Mad Cow Case." *New York Times,* Dec. 24, 2003.

Whelan, Elizabeth. "Mad Cow Kerfuffle." *New York Sun,* Dec. 26, 2003.

Wysocki, Bernard, Jr., and Betsy McKay. "Flu-Vaccine Shortage Signals U.S. Vulnerability to Pandemic." *Wall Street Journal,* Oct. 8, 2004.

13. THE FEAR PROPHETS

Rational Christianity: Christian Apologetics. "Is Christian Morality Based on Fear?" www.rationalchristianity.net/fear_morality.html (accessed Feb. 10, 2005).

Scherman, Nosson. *The Chumash: The Stone Edition.* New York: Mesorah Publications, 1993.

Schuller, Robert H., ed. *Possibility Thinkers Bible: The New King James Version: Positive Verses for Possibility Thinking Highlighted in Blue.* Nashville: Thomas Nelson, Inc., 1996.

14. IS THERE A CURE FOR FEAR?

Barsky, Ahern. "Therapy for Hypochondriasis: A Randomized Controlled Trial." *Journal of the American Medical Association* 291, no. 12 (2004): 1464.

Bremner, J. D. *Does Stress Damage the Brain? Understanding Trauma-Related Disorders from a Neurological Perspective.* New York: W.W. Norton & Co., 2002.

Descartes, René. *The Passions of the Soul: An English Translation of Les Passions De L'Ame.* Trans. Stephen Voss. Indianapolis: Hackett Publishing Company, 1990.

Duenwald, Mary. "A New Era in Treating Imaginary Ills." *New York Times,* Mar. 30, 2004.

Fowles, Jinnet B., Allan C. Kind, et al. "Patients' Interest in Reading Their Medical Record, Relation with Clinical and Sociodemographic Characteristics and Patients' Approach to Health Care." *Archives of Internal Medicine* 164 (Apr. 12, 2004): 793–800.

Groopman, Jerome. *The Anatomy of Hope: How People Prevail in the Face of Illness.* New York: Random House, 2003.

Honig, Robin Marantz. "The Quest to Forget." *New York Times Magazine,* Apr. 4, 2004.

Hoptman, Laura. *Yayoi Kusama.* New York: Phaidon Press, 2000.

Jeffers, Susan. *Feel the Fear and Do It Anyway.* New York: Harcourt, 1987.

———. *Feel the Fear . . . and Beyond: Master the Techniques for Doing It Anyway.* New York: Ballantine Books: 1998.

Kass, Leon. *Beyond Therapy: Biotechnology and the Pursuit of Happiness.* New York: Regan Books, 2003.

Kipnis, Jonathon, Hagit Cohen, Michal Cordan, et al. "T Cell Deficiency Leads to Cognitive Dysfunction, Implications for Therapeutic Vaccination for Schizophrenia and Other Psychiatric Conditions." *Proceedings of the National Academy of Sciences,* May 2004.

Lee, William M. "Aches, Pains, and Warning Labels." *New York Times,* Mar. 17, 2004.

Mason, Daniel. *The Piano Tuner: A Novel.* New York: Knopf, 2002.

McNeil, Donald G., Jr. "Plan to Battle AIDS Worldwide Is Falling Short." *New York Times,* Mar. 27, 2004.

Miller, Judith. "City and F.B.I. Reach Agreement on Bioterror Investigations." *New York Times,* Nov. 21, 2004.

Mitchell, Luke. "A Run on Terror." *Harper's Magazine,* Mar. 2004.

Nuland, Sherwin. *How We Die: Reflections on Life's Final Chapter.* New York: Knopf, 1994.

Parker-Pope, Tara. "News You Can Lose: The Health Risks of Watching the War." *Wall Street Journal,* Mar. 25, 2003.

Pitman, R. K., K. M. Sanders, R. M. Zusman, et al. "Pilot Study of Secondary Prevention of Posttraumatic Stress Disorder with Propranolol." *Biological Psychiatry* 51 (Jan. 15, 2002): 189–92

Rashbaum, William K. "Roles in Disaster Cause Rift in City." *New York Times,* Apr. 3, 2004.

Reuters. "U.S. Summer Travel Picks Up." May 28, 2004.

Sapadin, Linda. *Master Your Fears: How to Triumph over Your Worries and Get On with Your Life.* Hoboken, N.J.: John Wiley & Sons, Inc., 2004.

Siegel, Marc. "He Found His Own Path Back to Good Health." *Los Angeles Times Health,* June 28, 2004.

———. "How Terror Fears Make You Sick." *USA Today,* Oct. 14, 2004.

Slater, Lauren. "The Cruelest Cure." *New York Times Magazine,* Nov. 2, 2003.

U.S. Department of Homeland Security, Office for Domestic Preparedness Grants. "2004 Counterterrorism Grants State Allocation." www.dhs.gov/dhspublic/interweb/assetlibrary/Grants-ODP-04.pdf (accessed Apr. 1, 2004).

Zuger, Abigail. "Doctors, Too, Have Fears, They Just Go Underground." *New York Times,* Mar. 30, 2004.

Interviews

Leon Pachter, MD. Chief, Division of General Surgery, NYU Medical Center. Mar. 23, 2004.

AFTERWORD

Pullman, Philip. "Why I Don't Believe in Ghosts." *New York Times,* Oct. 31, 2003.

Siegel, Marc. "MASH—NYC." *New York Post,* Sept. 16, 2001.

INDEX

Withdrawn

Z 12/05
Z 5/06

**Indianapolis
Marion County
Public Library**

Renew by Phone
269-5222

Renew on the Web
www.imcpl.org

For general Library information
please call 269-1700.